Venice Biennale 2006

10th International Architecture Exhibition

Biennale Venedig 2006 10. Internationale Architekturausstellung

Cities, Architecture and Society

Modes of Densification and Dissolving Boundaries

Formen der Verdichtung und Entgrenzung

Convertible City

Inhalt

contents

Preface Vorwort

Der Bundesminister für Verkehr, Bau und Stadtentwicklung: Wolfgang Tiefensee

The Federal Minister for Transport, Building and Urban Affairs: Wolfgang Tiefensee

The International Architecture Exhibition Venice Biennale is the most important global forum for international exchange about architecture and its importance for the development of our cities. Germany regularly uses its own contribution as an opportunity to participate in the international discourse, and to make use of the German pavilion to make a statement about German architecture and building culture.

The theme of this year's Biennale has been well chosen: "Cities, architecture and society". This identifies the two most important elements we are dealing with in the context of cities. Firstly our material surroundings, the planned and built space. Then people living together, social cohesion, the economy, urban society in all its facets.

The two are inseparable. Our role as politicians, and that of the architects and town planners, is to think about both at the same time. Society cannot be planned. Urban development always means dealing with change; with movement. The real situation is never the one that has just been analysed. But that is where the opportunity lies as well. Change is a characteristic of cities.

Cities are centres of economic, scientific and cultural development, innovation, growth, employment and social conciliation. Economic and demographic changes have a particular impact here, where problems and opportunities of modern society are concentrated. So urban development in Germany is a national matter as well. The federal government supports the individual states and local authorities with investment and with planning laws that are among the most modern in Europe.

Die Architektur-Biennale ist das weltweit wichtigste Forum für den internationalen Austausch über Architektur und deren Bedeutung für die Entwicklung unserer Städte. Deutschland nutzt regelmäßig mit einem eigenen Beitrag die Chance, sich am internationalen Diskurs zu beteiligen und mit dem deutschen Pavillon ein Statement über die deutsche Architektur und Baukultur einzubringen.

Das diesjährige Thema der Biennale ist gut gewählt: „Cities, architecture and society". Das benennt die beiden wichtigsten Elemente, mit denen wir beim Thema Stadt umgehen. Das materiale Umfeld, der geplante und bebaute Raum auf der einen Seite. Das Zusammenleben der Menschen, der soziale Zusammenhalt, die Wirtschaft, die städtische Gesellschaft in all ihren Facetten auf der anderen Seite.

Beides ist nicht zu trennen. Unsere Aufgabe, die der Politik und die der Architekten, der Stadtplaner ist es, beides zusammen zu denken. Gesellschaft lässt sich nicht planen. Stadtentwicklung ist immer ein Umgang mit Veränderungen, mit Bewegung. Die Situation stellt sich nie so dar, wie man sie eben noch analysiert hat. Aber darin liegt auch die Chance. Die Veränderung ist der Stadt zu eigen.

Städte sind Zentren der wirtschaftlichen, wissenschaftlichen und kulturellen Entwicklung. In ihnen vollziehen sich in besonderem Maße Innovation, Wachstum, Beschäftigung und sozialer Ausgleich. Hier wirkt sich der wirtschaftliche und demografische Wandel besonders aus, hier konzentrieren sich Probleme und Chancen der modernen Gesellschaft. Stadtentwicklung ist in Deutschland daher auch eine nationale Aufgabe. Der Bund unterstützt die Länder und Kommunen mit Investitionen und mit einem Planungsrecht, das zu dem modernsten Europas gehört.

Diese Rahmenbedingungen müssen mit kreativen Konzepten ausgefüllt werden. Das ist wesentlich die Verantwortung der privaten und öffentlichen Bauherren, der Investoren und natürlich der Planer.

Die Kultur einer Stadt, und damit auch die Baukultur, die Architektur, kann einen wichtigen Beitrag leisten, um die Herausforderungen erfolgreich zu bewältigen, die sich aus dem demografischen und dem wirtschaftlichen Wandel, aus Segregation und Migration ergeben.

This general framework has to be filled in with creative concepts. Doing that is essentially the responsibility of private and public building clients, developers and, of course, the planners.

The culture of a city and therefore its building culture, its architecture, can make an important contribution to tackling the challenges arising from demographic and economic change, from segregation and migration. Our model is internal development and the sustainable European city. I am convinced that this European city model – historically aware, environmentally friendly, varied, featuring attractive public spaces – also retains its relevance within the global change process, and that it has a future. To exploit this potential we need a shift of perception within architecture, to pay more attention to conversion and changes of use, stimulating changes of design in existing urban structures, and a creative approach in terms of design and implications to existing buildings.

We went through a selection process with a distinguished jury and received a large number of suggestions and applications. I am delighted that we have a team for the general commissariat, Grüntuch Ernst Architekten, that is architecturally distinguished, innovative, creative and successful. The selection committee was in favour of this concept because it addresses an internal development that husbands resources carefully, does not promote densification to the extent of overdevelopment, achieves high outward urban effect with small architectural interventions, supports joint thinking by architects and engineers – and also lays these qualities open to concrete experience, in addition to the individual projects, through an interesting conversion of the pavilion building that points the way forward.

The federal government sees its involvement in the Venice Biennale as a building block in its building culture quality offensive. This also includes the Federal Building Culture Foundation, for which legislation is currently being enacted, and which we want to set up by early 2007. It is intended to support the building culture network nationally and internationally. In this respect it will complement the German Biennale appearance in future.

I am certain that the German pavilion will further enhance the attention paid to and the understanding of the role and importance of architecture in our society.

Unser Leitbild ist die Innenentwicklung, die nachhaltige europäische Stadt. Ich bin davon überzeugt, dass das Modell der europäischen Stadt – geschichtsbewusst, umweltschonend, vielgestaltig, mit attraktiven öffentlichen Räumen – auch im globalen Veränderungsprozess seine Relevanz behält und zukunftsfähig ist. Um dieses Potenzial zu nutzen, bedarf es auch eines Wahrnehmungswandels innerhalb der Architektur, einer größeren Zuwendung mit Blick auf Umbau- und Umnutzungsaufgaben, stimulierender Umgestaltungen in bestehenden urbanen Strukturen, einer gestalterischen und inhaltlichen Aufwertung innerhalb des bereits Bestehenden.

Wir haben ein Auswahlverfahren mit einer renommierten Jury durchgeführt und eine Vielzahl an Vorschlägen und Bewerbungen erhalten. Ich freue mich, dass wir mit Gruentuch Ernst Architekten ein Team für das Generalkommissariat gewonnen haben, das architektonisch renommiert, innovativ, kreativ und erfolgreich ist. Die Auswahlkommission hat dieses Konzept favorisiert, weil es sich der ressourcenschonenden Innenentwicklung zuwendet, bauliche Verdichtung nicht auf Kosten einer Zersiedelung propagiert, mit geringen architektonischen Eingriffen hohe urbane Außenwirkung erzielt, gemeinsames Denken von Architekten und Ingenieuren unterstützt – und diese Qualitäten auch konkret, neben den Einzelprojekten, durch einen interessanten Umbau des Pavillongebäudes mit Signalwirkung erfahrbar macht.

Die Bundesregierung sieht ihre Mitwirkung an der Biennale Venedig als Baustein ihrer Qualitätsoffensive für Baukultur. Dazu gehört auch die Bundesstiftung Baukultur, für die derzeit das Gesetzgebungsverfahren läuft, und die wir bis Anfang 2007 errichten wollen. Sie soll das Netzwerk der Baukultur national und international unterstützen. Insofern ergänzt sie in Zukunft den deutschen Biennale-Auftritt.

Ich bin mir sicher, dass der deutsche Pavillon die Aufmerksamkeit und das Verständnis für die Rolle und Bedeutung der Architektur in unserer Gesellschaft weiter erhöhen wird.

Armand Gruentuch, Almut Ernst

Convertible City

Formen der Verdichtung und Entgrenzung

Modes of densification and dissolving boundaries

The 10th International Venice Architecture Biennale 2006, "Cities. Architecture and Society", directed by Richard Burdett, highlights changes taking place in urban life in the early 21st century. Over half the world's population live in cities. Urban life is being shaped more than ever by the varied interaction between economic, social, geographical, political, cultural and creative transformation processes.

The theme of the German contribution takes us into the heart of Germany's big cities, to places where the oldest traces of the past are combining with the newest thrusts into the future. The centrifugal force that has forced families and businesses into the outskirts for decades is weakening. The city centre, viewed for a long time as being noisy, unattractive and dangerous, is once more esteemed by people of all ages and lifestyles.

The European city is still largely determined by history and tradition, and is thus different from the new Asian or Latin-American metropolises that are growing at such a frantic pace. This is a wonderful quality, yet we don't want to turn it into a museum, we want to develop it further,

Die 10. Internationale Architektur-Biennale Venedig 2006 „Cities, Architecture and Society" thematisiert unter der Leitung von Richard Burdett die Veränderungen urbanen Lebens zu Beginn des 21. Jahrhunderts. Mehr als die Hälfte der Weltbevölkerung lebt heute in Städten. Mehr denn je wird städtisches Leben von vielfältigen Überlagerungen ökonomischer, sozialer, geografischer, politischer, kultureller und gestalterischer Transformationsprozesse geprägt.

Das Thema des deutschen Beitrages führt in die Kernbereiche deutscher Großstädte, zu Orten, an denen sich die ältesten Spuren aus der Vergangenheit mit den neuesten Spuren in die Zukunft überlagern. Die Zentrifugalkraft, die jahrzehntelang Familien und Unternehmen an den Stadtrand drängte, wird schwächer. Die Innenstadt, die lange Zeit nur als laut, unattraktiv und gefährlich angesehen wurde, erlebt über alle Altersschichten und Lebensstile hinweg neue Wertschätzung.

Die Europäische Stadt ist noch immer in ihrer Gestalt wesentlich durch Tradition und Historie bestimmt und somit anders als die rasant wachsenden neuen Metropolen im asiatischen oder lateinamerikanischen Raum. Das ist eine wunderbare Qualität, aber es geht nicht um die Musealisierung der Europäischen Stadt, sondern um ihre Weiterentwicklung, um Kontinuität und den Eigensinn einer jeden Epoche, d.h um um das Weiterbauen an der Stadt.

to ensure its continuity whilst highlighting the particular significance of each epoch. What we want is to continue building the city. German architects and urban developers are particularly challenged by restructuring industrial society, current demographic change and an increasingly pluralistic society.

The city must be restablilised and regenerated to mirror its lively and complex society. Demographic developments and social change produce concepts for new ways of living. Older people are moving back into the cities, and thirty- and forty-year-olds no longer migrate to the outskirts as a matter of course. The classical nuclear family is being replaced by lifestyle concepts for single people, lone parents, communes or multiple generations living together. Cities are faced with the task of integrating immigrants and activating the potential to enrich our society culturally. The change from an industrial to a service and information society opens up new possibilities for using the existing infrastructure of cities, their buildings, streets and supply facilities, better and more sustainably.

As architects, we have been concerned with reviving cities for some time now. We have come to realise that it increasingly generates more kinds of work for us by making us look at existing situations more carefully and addressing urban quality more imaginatively. Many German cities are in a state of upheaval. Hamburg, Duisburg, Düsseldorf and Cologne are reclaiming the urban periphery of their former port areas for the city. Berlin is repairing its historical centre and making it more dense. Frankfurt is opening up urban space in its cramped inner-city areas by increasing vertical density and transforming derelict industrial sites. Restructuring rail transport is opening up large areas for new city life and work in Munich and Stuttgart. Tübingen and Freiburg, for example, have new urban quarters where once there was a sprawl of barracks.

As architects we are being asked for highly individual approaches to various locations and functions within all this rapid change. Conversions and buildings on gap sites are often early pioneers for reprogramming urban locations. New worlds of life and work mean

Die Umstrukturierung der Industriegesellschaft, der aktuelle demografische Wandel und eine zunehmend pluralistische Gesellschaft stellen in Deutschland besondere Herausforderungen an Architektur und Städtebau. Die Stadt als Spiegel einer Gesellschaft lebendiger Vielschichtigkeit muss neu stabilisiert und generiert werden. Die demografische Entwicklung und der Wandel der Gesellschaft bringen neue Lebensentwürfe hervor. Ältere Menschen ziehen zurück in die Stadt, die Dreißig- und Vierzigjährigen wandern nicht mehr automatisch an den Stadtrand. An die Stelle der klassischen Kleinfamilie treten Single-, allein Erziehende-, Wohngemeinschafts- oder Mehrgenerationen-Lebensentwürfe. In den Städten stellt sich die Aufgabe der Integration von Zuwanderern in unsere Gesellschaft, die auch eine kulturelle Bereicherung anbieten. Der Umbau von einer Industrie- zu einer Dienstleistungs- und Informationsgesellschaft eröffnet neue Möglichkeiten, die vorhandenen Infrastrukturen der Städte, ihre Gebäude, Straßen und Versorgungseinrichtungen besser und nachhaltiger zu nutzen.

Die Revitalisierung der Städte beschäftigt uns als Architekten schon seit längerer Zeit. Wir stellen fest, dass dabei immer häufiger Aufgaben auf uns zukommen, die Architekten einen kreativeren Umgang mit Bestandssituationen und eine innovativere Auseinandersetzung mit Urbanität abfordern. Im Umbruch befinden sich viele deutsche Städte. Hamburg, Duisburg, Köln und Düsseldorf erobern den Stadtrand ihrer früheren Hafenareale wieder für die Stadt zurück. Berlin repariert und verdichtet sein historisches Zentrum. Frankfurt erweitert den Stadtraum seiner engen Innenstadt durch vertikale Verdichtung und die Transformation früherer Gewerbegelände. Umstrukturierungen des Bahnverkehrs eröffnen München und Stuttgart große Gebiete für neues städtisches Leben und Arbeiten. Wo sich ehemals Kasernen erstreckten, entstehen nicht nur in Tübingen und Freiburg neue Stadtquartiere.

Höchst individuelle Lösungsansätze für verschiedene Orte und Funktionen im Umbruch werden uns als Architekten abverlangt. Konversionen und Lückengebäude sind oft die ersten Pioniere für das Reprogrammierung städtischer Orte. Neue Lebens- und Arbeitswelten verlangen nach einer Neuinterpretation von Lebensqualität und stehen für ein neues Lebensgefühl, für eine neue Lust an der Stadt. Die erlebte und gefühlte Stadt wird zu einem Thema, das sich aus ganz persönlichen Erfahrungen entwickelt, wie etwa dem Wunsch Büro und Familie in der Innenstadt zu verbinden. Andererseits erreichen Events und temporäre Gebäude in der Stadt eine immer größere Aufmerksamkeit und wecken das öffentliche Interesse für eine Stadt weit über den Kreis ihrer Stadtbewohner hinaus. Gerade während der Fußball-Weltmeisterschaft haben wir erleben können, wie rasch sich Städte verwandeln und positive Energien aktivieren konnten.

Mit dem diesjährigen Thema der Biennale „Cities, Architecture and Society" stellt sich uns auch die Frage nach der gesellschaftspolitischen Rolle der Architekten: Welchen Beitrag können Architekten zum Stadtumbau leisten? Welche Transformationsprozesse

ökonomischer, sozialer, politischer, kultureller oder gestalterischer Art werden nicht zuletzt auch von Architekten mit vorangetrieben? Welche interdisziplinären Konzepte, Vernetzungen und Aktivitäten sind für eine lebendige Stadt erforderlich? Wie leben und erleben wir die verdichtete Innenstadt der Großstädte?

13

Der Wandel der Städte ist vielschichtig, Architekten müssen Stellung beziehen. Dies legte es nahe, den deutschen Beitrag für die 10.Architekturbiennale auf stimulierende Projekte der Transformation bestehender stadträumlicher Situationen zu fokussieren, auf Projekte, deren Dynamik und Kreativität städtisches Leben bereichern. Die Transformation im urbanen Umfeld erfordert auch einen sich innerhalb der Architektur vollziehenden Wahrnehmungswandel. Die Ausstellung will die Neubewertung des noch vielen Architekten wenig attraktiv erscheinenden Aufgabenfeldes des Umbaus und der Umnutzung fördern. Die Thematisierung dieser Aufgaben soll aber nicht nur Resonanz in der Fachwelt, sondern auch im breiten öffentlichen Bewusstsein finden.

that the quality of life has to be reinterpreted; they also represent a new sense of life and of relishing the city. The city as lived in and felt is becoming a theme that develops from entirely personal experiences, like for example the desire to combine office and family home in the city centre. Events and temporary buildings in cities are also attracting more and more attention, and arousing an urban public interest that extends way beyond the circle of people who live there. The Football World Cup 2006 has shown us how quickly cities can change and activate positive energies. The theme of this year's Biennale, "Cities, Architecture and Societies", also asks questions about architects' socio-political role: What can architects contribute to converting cities? What economic, social, political, culture or design-related transformation processes can architects ultimately also help to drive forward? Which interdisciplinary concepts, networks and activities does a living city need? How do we live in and experience the denser metropolitan centres?

Die spannungsreiche Verwandlung von Architektur und Stadtgefüge sowie die nachhaltige Nutzung vorhandener Potenziale für neue urbane Wohn- und Arbeitswelten wird „Convertible City" anhand beispielhafter Projekte aufzeigen. Grundlage sind programmatische Thesen:

Convertible City ist Ausdruck der Kontinuität und der Wandlungskraft urbanen Raumes
Convertible City ist Appell für den Erhalt der Vielseitigkeit städtischen Lebens
Convertible City ist Aufforderung zur nachhaltigen Nutzung der Kernstädte
Convertible City ist Alternative zur Zersiedlung der Naturräume
Convertible City ist Auflösung von Grenzen im Lebensraum Stadt
Convertible City ist Aufruf zur kreativen Aneignung der städtischen Räume
Convertible City ist Ausdruck eines positiven Lebensgefühls in der Stadt
Convertible City ist Anregung und Stimulation für neue Lebensentwürfe

Change in cities is a complex matter, architects have to take up a position. Thus our decision to focus the German Biennale contribution on stimulating projects for transforming existing urban situations; on projects whose dynamics and creativity enrich urban life. Transformation in urban contexts also requires transformation within architecture. This exhibition intends to promote a reassessment of challanges relating to conversion and change of use, which many architects still tend not to find very attractive. Addressing this field should not only elicit a response in the specialist world, but also in the consciousness of a wider public.

"Convertible City" documents exciting changes in architecture and urban structure and how existing potential can be sustainably exploited for new urban worlds of living and working. It is based on the following key ideas:

Convertible City is an expression of the continuity and transformative power of urban space
Convertible City is a call for maintaining the diversity of city life
Convertible City is a demand for the sustainable use of core cities
Convertible City is an alternative to urban sprawl encroaching on natural areas
Convertible City is the dissolution of boundaries in the urban habitat
Convertible City is a call for creative appropriation of metropolitan areas
Convertible City is the expression of a positive attitude to urban life
Convertible City is an inspiration and stimulation for new concepts of living

14

Über Wochen und Monate hinweg fand eine breite interdisziplinäre Diskussion statt; Projekte wurden erwogen, verworfen und erneut geprüft. Mit einem ganzheitlichen Ansatz wie beim Planen und Bauen näherten wir uns allen Projekten, Akteuren und Stadträumen. Viele Gespräche und Besuche vor Ort halfen das umfangreiche Material zu sichten, abzuwägen und den Kreis der für das Thema geeigneten Projekte zu präzisieren. Dabei verstanden wir unsere Tätigkeit als Kuratoren als ein Experiment und offenen Prozess.

So präsentiert „Convertible City" weniger allgemeingültige Lösungen als vielmehr ein breites Spektrum von Projekten, die sich in ihrem Selbstverständnis, in der Interaktion ihrer Akteure und Wirkungen den Anforderungen einer sich verändernden Gesellschaft und Kulturlandschaft stellen: Projekte der Umnutzung, des gesellschaftlichen Wandels und der Reprogrammierung städtischen Raumes, die den Erwartungen an eine reale Architektur des Alltags standhalten können. Dazu präsentiert die Ausstellung realisierte sowie nicht realisierte Arbeiten bekannter und weniger bekannter Architekten, Stadtplaner, Landschaftsarchitekten und Künstler. Durch flexibles Denken und Konzepte der Nachhaltigkeit zeigen diese Projekte neue Chancen der Architektur und des Stadtraumes auf. Sie geben den Ausstellungsbesuchern einen Einblick in die große Vielfalt kreativer Transformationen im urbanen Raum Deutschlands. Die 36 ausgewählten Projekte thematisieren exemplarisch verschiedene Formen der Umwandlung und Verdichtung zeitgenössischen Stadtraums:

Manche Projekte zeigen die Möglichkeiten architektonischer Anlagerung an bereits vorhandene Bauten. Durch Überlagerung, Verschiebung und Durchdringung werden bestehende Gebäudestrukturen erweitert, neu verbunden und definiert. Andere Projekte demonstrieren einen spielerischen und spontanen Umgang mit der Wahrnehmung und Nutzung städtischen Raumes. Dabei handelt es sich sowohl um mediale Bespielungen urbaner Oberflächen als auch um Aktivierungen stadtnaher Leerflächen zu urban vernetzten Räumen. Einige Projekte zeigen die Möglichkeiten der Auflösung und Neudefinition der Nutzungsformen vorhandener Bauten. Dazu zählt auch die Neuentdeckung architektonischer und städtebaulicher „Erblasten", etwa wie ungeliebte Bauten und Räume der Nachkriegszeit, die mit neuen Funktionen und Wahrnehmungs-Angeboten für die Stadt zurückgewonnen werden können.

Convertible City is the result of a broad interdisciplinary discussion that took place over weeks and months; one where projects were researched, assessed, rejected or re-evalued. We approached all the projects, players and urban spaces in a manner similar to the one we adopt for planning and building A number of conversations and visits helped us to view the wide range of material, weigh it up and define the circle of projects suitable for our theme. We viewed our curatorial work as an experiment and an open process.

"Convertible City" does not present generally valid solutions. Instead it offers a broad spectrum of projects that meet the requirements of a changing society and cultural landscape in their self-perception, in their protagonists' interaction and the impact they make. They are projects for altered use, social change and reprogramming urban space that can meet the expectations placed on real everyday architecture. The exhibition also presents work (both realised and unrealised) by well-known and less well-known architects, town planners, landscape architects and artists. These projects identify new opportunities for architecture and urban space through flexible thinking and sustainability concepts. They give exhibition visitors an insight into the great variety of creative transformation in Germany's urban space. The 36 selected projects offer examples of various forms of transformation and increased density for contemporary urban space. Some projects demonstrate the possibilities of architectural addition onto existing buildings: superimposition, shifting and penetration make it possible to extend existing building structures, and combine and define them in new ways. Other projects show the ways in which urban space is perceived, used and handled playfully and spontaneously. This involves media use of urban surfaces as well as activating empty areas near the city as spaces networked into the urban structure. Some projects show possibilities for breaking down and redefining use forms for existing buildings. This also includes rediscovering architectural and urban "inherited problems", finding out how unpopular buildings, for example, and post-war spaces can be won back for the city with new functions and use potentials.

On entering the German pavilion visitors experience a scene of urban vitality and architectural variety. Here we have a city, lively but cramped, staged as a place of communication and contrasts. In contrast with the liveliness of the main hall, the side wings with their calmer atmosphere invite visitors to concentrate on the projects. Another surprising additional feature comes in the form of the "Convertible Boxes". Objects filled by the architects that fold open to extend beyond the projects. They are designed by each participant individually and address the given task in both a creative and very personal way.

For the first time the pavilion thrusts out and extends its space by means of an additional staircase structure leading from the main hall to roof level. An added altana – a typically Venetian architectural element – opens up the opportunity to fully experience of the German pavilion's elevated position by creating a viewing platform and meeting place for visitors. These temporary additions redefine the German pavilion as a transitory space and activate the hitherto unused roof area as an unexpected place for communication, offering some surprising perspectives. Thus the German Pavilion is no longer merely a casing for the exhibits, but can be explored for the duration of the Biennale as an exhibit in its own right, showing an overlapping structure that includes both past and present. It will also be a venue for several accompanying events during the Biennale inviting visitors to discuss the many open questions posed by the contemporary city and its architecture.

We have also applied this principle of converting structures that already exist to our own publication, this issue of the German architecture magazine "archplus", which we have edited and designed for the "Convertible City" issue. Alongside the projects, we conceived a collection of thematic essays and interdisciplinary contributions for this rather different kind of exhibition catalogue that puts forward various points of view about the phenomenon of urban life. To this end, we invited futurologists, film-makers, choreographers and many others to pass on their views and positions relating to the city. Just as the city is a laboratory for different forms of life, so "Convertible City" reflects upon a variety of perceptions and interpretations expressed in the form of the exhibition, the catalogue and the transformation of the German Pavilion.

Beim Betreten des Deutschen Pavillons erlebt der Besucher einen Schauplatz städtischer Vitalität und architektonischer Vielfalt. Hier findet sich Stadt in lebendiger Enge als Ort der Kommunikation und Kontraste inszeniert. Im Kontrast zur Belebtheit der Haupthalle laden die Seitenflügel zur konzentrierten Beschäftigung mit den Projekten ein. Eine überraschende Erweiterung sind auch die „Convertible Boxes". Die aufklappbaren, über die Projekte hinausweisenden Objekte der Architekten, die von jedem Teilnehmer individuell gestaltet wurden reagieren ebenso kreativ wie eigensinnig auf die gestellte Aufgabe.

Erstmals durchstößt und erweitert der Pavillon seinen Raum mit dem gestalterischen Element eines von der Haupthalle zur Dachebene führenden Treppenkörpers. Mit einer aufgesetzten „Altana" – einem typisch venezianischen Architekturelement – wird die erhöhte Lage des deutschen Pavillons erfahrbar und den Besuchern eine Aussichtsplattform und ein Treffpunkt geboten. Die temporären Ergänzungen definieren den Deutschen Pavillon als transistorischen Raum neu und aktivieren die bislang nicht genutzte Dachfläche als einen unerwarteten Ort der Kommunikation mit überraschenden Perspektiven. Der Deutsche Pavillon dient nicht mehr allein als Hülle für Exponate, sondern kann nun für die Dauer der Biennale als Exponat einer strukturellen Überlagerung von Vergangenheit und Gegenwart entdeckt werden. So wird er auch Ort mehrerer Begleitveranstaltungen, die zur Diskussion über die vielen offenen Fragen der zeitgenössischen Stadt und Architektur einladen.

Das Prinzip der Konversion bereits existierender Strukturen haben wir auch auf die Publikation übertragen, auf die existierende Architekturzeitschrift „archplus", deren Redaktion und Gestaltung wir für die Ausgabe „Convertible City" übernahmen. Neben den Projekten konzipierten wir für diese andere Art eines Ausstellungskatalogs thematische Essays und interdisziplinäre Beiträge mit unterschiedlichen Perspektiven zum Phänomen städtischen Lebens. Dazu haben wir u.a. Zukunftsforscher, Filmemacher, Choreografen eingeladen, um ihren Blick und ihre Position zur Stadt einzubringen. Wie die Stadt ein Laboratorium für unterschiedliche Lebensformen ist, so ist „Convertible City" das Bild vielfältiger Wahrnehmungen und Interpretationen umgesetzt in der Ausstellung, dem Katalog und durch die Verwandlung des deutschen Pavillons.

CONVERTIBLE BOX >>
All participants were asked to produce
individual designs for the contents
of a white acrylic box (24 x 39 x 14 cm)
as part of the exhibition in the
German Pavilion.

CONVERTIBLE BOX >>
Alle Teilnehmer hatten die Aufgabe,
eine weiße Plexiglaskiste
(24 x 39 x 14 cm) als Teil der
Ausstellung im Deutschen Pavillon
individuell zu gestalten.

Modes of **Densification** and Dissolving **Boundaries**

Formen der Verdichtung und Entgrenzung

**Die Möglichkeiten
architektonischer
Transformationen**
Vom Charme des Alten in den
neuen Konstellationen der
zeitgenössischen Stadt

Possibilities of Architectural Transformation

The charm of the old within the new constellations of the contemporary city

Today factory floors are being turned into playgrounds for the New Economy, tower-blocks are becoming exclusive residential addresses, barracks change into colleges and prisons into archives. There seems to be no limit to the current interest in old buildings, nor to the possibilities of transforming them, functionally and architecturally. Old buildings have always been put to new uses and converted, but the present scale and speed of urban building stock adaptation represents a new challenge. Modernism defined itself mainly by drawing a clear line between itself and the historical city, and threw its weight behind radical re-invention, but our contemporary architecture seems increasingly compelled to define itself in relation to what already exists. Change of use and conversion are not to be understood as just peripheral fields, but as central themes in a rapidly changing global society.

Architectural and urban development congresses may cite the argument of resource-friendly sustainability for the increasing significance of changed use for old buildings, but growing interest in conversion hardly originates there. On the contrary, it is a profound change in image value that makes architects, politicians and building entrepreneurs prefer conversion to demolishing old buildings. We have started to reassess the value of the past, and increasingly relativise everything new, and this means adopting new positions.

Our current relationship with the built heritage, with space and object, expresses a need for compensation. We need to make up for ultra-rapid changes in the reality of our lives by adopting slowing-down strategies. "The more quickly the future becomes new and alien for us in a modern way, the more continuity and history we have to take with us – like teddy-bears – into that future .." says the German philosopher Odo Marquard on this subject in his essay "Kleine Anthropologie der Zeit".(2) He adds that today's world heightens both the tempo of innovation and the need to "cultivate slowness". "More [is] forgotten and thrown away than ever before; but today more is remembered and stored away respectfully than ever before: the age of the waste disposal dumps is also the age of veneration dumps." Or, "The modern tendency to 'take away magic' is – in a specifically modern way – compensated for by the great substitute conferment of magic on the aesthetic. Globalisations and universalisations are compensated for by regionalisation, localisation and individualisation."(3)

The French monument theoretician Françoise Chouay explained the consequences that this civilization process would have on the way we respond to and handle cities in her 1996 book "L'Allégorie du Patrimoine",(4) which was very critical about the increasing significance of images:

Claus Käpplinger

Heute verwandeln sich Fabriketagen zu Spielwiesen der New Economy, Silos zu exklusiven Wohnadressen, Kasernen zu Hochschulen oder Gefängnisse zu Archiven. Schier unbegrenzt scheint das Interesse der Gegenwart für alte Bauten zu sein, schier unbegrenzt auch die Möglichkeiten ihrer funktionalen und architektonischen Transformation. Immer schon wurden alte Bauten umgenutzt und umgebaut, doch das Ausmaß und die Geschwindigkeit heutiger Veränderungen an der Stadtsubstanz stellen eine neue Herausforderung dar. Definierte sich die Moderne zumeist in scharfer Abgrenzung zur historischen Stadt und setzte auf radikale Neuerfindung, so sieht sich heute zeitgenössische Architektur immer mehr gefordert sich in Relation zum Existierenden zu definieren, Umnutzung und Umbau nicht als Randbereiche, sondern als zentrale Themen einer sich rasch wandelnden Weltgesellschaft zu begreifen.

Architektur- und Städtebaukongresse mögen das Argument ressourcenschonender Nachhaltigkeit für die zunehmende Bedeutung von Umnutzungen alter Gebäude anführen, dennoch hat das wachsende Interesse am Umbau wohl kaum darin seinen Ursprung. Vielmehr ist es ein tiefgreifender Wertbilderwandel, der Architekten, Politiker und Bauherren veranlasst immer häufiger den Umbau einem Abriss von Gebäuden vorzuziehen. Eine neue Wertschätzung für das Vergangene und eine zunehmende Relativierung alles Neuen ist eingetreten, die nach neuen Kriterien verlangt.

Unser gegenwärtiges Verhältnis zum baulichen Erbe, zu Raum und Objekt ist vor allem Ausdruck eines Kompensationsbedürfnisses, die rasan-

"... in our eyes photography is the kind of monument that corresponds most closely with the individualism of our day. Photography is a monument to privacy (...) As well as this, photography contributes to semanticising the kind of monument that functions as a signal. These signals increasingly reach contemporary society via their image and by disseminating such images in the press, on television and in the cinema. They only provide signs if these signs have become either image or a meaningless replica in which their symbolic value is concentrated, which is thus separated from their practical value. The new "communication" techniques mean that every building can become a monument, regardless of its own designation."

HISTORY AS MATERIAL

A new trinity, individualisation, privatisation and auratisation, now shapes our relationship with the built heritage. More and more frequently the value of a building derives not from its former function or social significance but from its possibilities for individual auratisation and socio-cultural recoding. It is only this that can explain the global success of Thomas Ruff and Thomas Struth etc., pupils of the Düsseldorf documentary photographers Bernd and Hilla Becher, who devoted themselves first of all to places where something had disappeared. They capture buildings laconically head-on, detached from their former functions, from any activity. But something that looks like documentation at first often says little about the reality of the buildings, auratises the last traces of human use and iconifies them as objects in a place of indefinable scattered light, without depth and free of social connotations.

Any kind of building can acquire significance today if it is no longer interrogated about its value as a historical artefact but is used above all as a symbolically charged projection screen for the self or for a specific group. New acquisition possibilities come crowding in. Ironically, these came into being only through the process of removing hierarchy and history from all buildings in the Modernist period. The fact is that liberated from the burden of historical knowledge and its fixed codes, which used to separate the sphere of architecture clearly from that of everyday building, codes that irrevocably ascribed every typology to a clearly defined social stratum and task, every building today can be interpreted and transformed by anybody as raw material that is available and changeable at will.

Certainly building is more frequently cited in the Western industrial countries as the core of cultural identity when legitimising urban and architectural interventions, but recourse to the history and culture of a place often turns out to be nothing but a marketing instrument. History has become a very soft location factor, freely open to interpretation, a factor that can be highly significant economically on the level of attracting tourists. The victims of this development are often the social milieus and historical background of the newly re-valued properties and quarters, often intended not for a local audience, but for the nomads of the new service society.

ten Veränderungen unserer Lebensrealität mit Strategien der Verlangsamung zu kompensieren. „Je schneller die Zukunft für uns das Neue – das Fremde – wird, desto mehr Kontinuität und Vergangenheit müssen wir – teddybärgleich – in die Zukunft mitnehmen", führt dazu der deutsche Philosoph Odo Marquard in seinem Aufsatz „Kleine Anthropologie der Zeit"(2) aus. Die heutige Welt steigere sowohl das Innovationstempo als auch den Bedarf nach „Langsamkeitspflege". Es werde „zwar mehr vergessen und weggeworfen als je zuvor; aber es wird auch heute mehr erinnert und respektvoll aufbewahrt als je zuvor: Das Zeitalter der Entsorgungsdeponien ist zugleich das Zeitalter der Verehrungsdeponien." Oder „die neuzeitliche „Entzauberung" wird – spezifisch modern – kompensiert durch die große Ersatzverzauberung des Ästhetischen. Globalisierungen und Universalisierungen werden kompensiert durch Regionalisierungen, Lokalisierungen und Individualisierungen."(3)

Welche Folgen dieser zivilisatorische Prozess für unsere Rezeption und unseren Umgang mit der Stadt und ihren Gebäuden hat, führte 1996 die französische Denkmaltheoretikerin Françoise Choay in ihrem Buch „L´Allégorie du Patrimoine"(4) aus, die sehr kritisch die wachsende Bedeutung von Bildern kommentierte: „[...] in unseren Augen ist die Fotografie die Art von Denkmal, die dem Individualismus unserer Zeit am ehesten entspricht. Die Fotografie ist das Denkmal der Privatheit [...]. Darüber hinaus trägt die Fotografie zu einer Semantisierung jener Form des Denkmals bei, welches als Signal fungiert. Diese Signale erreichen die Gesellschaft der Gegenwart immer mehr über ihr Bild und über die Verbreitung dieser Bilder in der Presse, im Fernsehen und im Kino. Zeichen geben sie nur noch, wenn diese Zeichen zum Bild oder zu einer bedeutungslosen Replik geworden sind, in denen sich ihr symbolischer Wert konzentriert, der somit von ihrem Gebrauchswert getrennt ist. Durch die neuen „Kommunikations"-Techniken kann jedes Bauwerk unabhängig von seiner eigentlichen Bestimmung zum Denkmal werden."

GESCHICHTE ALS MATERIAL

Eine neue Trinität, nämlich die von Individualisierung, Privatisierung und Auratisierung prägt heute unser Verhältnis zum baulichen Erbe. Immer häufiger macht sich der Wert eines Gebäudes nicht an seiner früheren Funktion oder gesellschaftlichen Bedeutung, sondern an seinen Möglichkeiten zur individuellen Auratisierung und soziokulturellen Neukodierung fest. Nur so etwa lässt sich im Bereich der Hochkultur der globale Erfolg der Schüler der Düsseldorfer Dokumentarfotografen Bernd und Hilla Becher erklären, von Thomas Ruff, Thomas Struth etc., die sich zuerst vor allem Orten eines Verschwindens widmeten. Lakonisch frontal, losgelöst von ihren früheren Funktionen, von jeder Aktivität werden die Gebäu-

from left to right / von links nach rechts: Imitation – "Huhnsgasse", Cologne, Raderschall Architekten, Cologne >> Camouflage – "Alter Hof", Munich, Peter Kulka, Cologne/Dresden >> Maniera Povera – "Alte Pinakothek", 1952-57, Munich, Hans Döllgast, Munich >> Emphatic Adaptation – "Ostfriesland", Riemann Architekten, Lübeck

THE SEARCH FOR NEW IDENTITY PATTERNS

Contemporary society obviously has a profound longing for images, for image quotations and identity patterns that can be grasped rapidly. They are useful to many people as a very effective compensation resource in the face of the increasing pace of change in the present and also given the often by no means conflict-free meeting of different identities within the cultural pluralism of the new "Global Village". It is not just the architectural popularists, the neotraditionalists and neoclassicists of "New Urbanism", who have recognised this, so too has any architecture that tries explicitly to identify itself clearly as contemporary against a whole range of retro-movements.

If architectural popularism more frequently dominates the urban periphery, contemporary architecture now expresses itself more and more in many Western countries via the previously taboo tasks of changed uses and conversion for old building stock, not least buildings formerly associated with industry and work. Their large, abundant volumes with low rents, the sheer availability of space with a special aura of emptiness, make them absolutely cry out to be filled with new spatial concepts and mixed uses.

It is no coincidence that their potential clients are often companies and actors in the "time" industry, who now evince the greatest interest in old buildings and contemporary interventions. "Time" stands for the new service branches of telecommunications, the internet and the media. Their protagonists have found their true location in the "loft" with its very tactile spatial experiences, that compensates them for their work in a virtual globalised world. Ultimately what they want, these young experts who are vied for so hotly, is a wide range of events and quarters that offer not only intensive communication, but also buildings with an unmistakable aura.

Conventional offices and flats are taboo for them, but there is considerable demand for buildings that combine ambience with flexibility: old commercial buildings, harbour warehouses, buildings associated with energy or industry. So in Europe this branch of the economy, which itself does not have a history or an architecture of its own, is conducting an almost manic search for places with borrowed identities whose past clearly extends back before the information age. Their buildings should be authentic and seem as physical and "hand-made" as possible.

This means that architects have to learn new skills. As the property market plans in ever decreasing cycles, and more and more old buildings become available as a result of economic developments,

de von ihnen festgehalten. Was zuerst den Anschein von Dokumentation weckt, sagt jedoch oft wenig über die Wirklichkeit der Bauten aus, auratisiert die letzten Spuren menschlichen Gebrauchs und ikonisiert sie als Objekte in einem tiefenlosen, sozialfreien Raum undefinierbaren Streulichts.

Jede Art von Gebäude kann heute Bedeutung erlangen, wenn nun nicht mehr dessen Wert als historisches Artefakt hinterfragt wird, sondern es vor allem als symbolisch-aufgeladene Projektionsfläche des eigenen Selbst bzw. einer spezifischen Gruppe genutzt wird. Neue Möglichkeiten der Aneignung drängen sich auf, die sich ironischerweise erst durch den Prozess der Enthierarchisierung und Enthistorisierung aller Bauaufgaben während der Epoche der Moderne ergeben haben. Denn befreit von der Last historischen Wissens und dessen festen Codes, die früher die Sphäre der Architektur klar von der des Alltagsbauens trennten und die jede Typologie unüberwindbar einer klar definierten Gesellschaftsschicht und Aufgabe zuschrieben, kann heute jedes Gebäude von jedem als beliebig verfüg- und veränderbares Rohmaterial interpretiert und transformiert werden.

Geschichte wird zwar wieder häufiger in den westlichen Industrieländern als Kern der kulturellen Identität zur Legitimation städtebaulicher und architektonischer Interventionen zitiert, doch erweist sich der Rekurs auf Historie und Kultur des Ortes oft nur als ein Marketing-Instrument. Geschichte ist zu einem sehr weichen wie frei interpretierbaren Standortfaktor geworden, der nicht zuletzt auf der Ebene der touristischen Attraktion beachtliche ökonomische Bedeutung gewinnen kann. Opfer der Entwicklung sind oft die sozialen Milieus und der historische Hintergrund der neu aufgewerteten Objekte und Quartiere, die zumeist nicht mehr für lokale Adressaten, sondern für die Nomaden der neuen Dienstleistungsgesellschaft bestimmt sind.

DIE SUCHE NACH NEUEN IDENTITÄTSMUSTERN

Groß ist offenbar das Verlangen der zeitgenössischen Gesellschaft nach Bildern, nach Bildzitaten und rasch erfassbaren Identitätsmustern. Angesichts der zunehmenden Veränderungsgeschwindigkeit der Gegenwart sowie dem häufig gar nicht so nicht konfliktfreien Aufeinandertreffen unterschiedlicher Identitäten im kulturellen Pluralismus des neuen „Global Village" dienen sie vielen als sehr effektive Kompensationsmittel. Nicht nur das Lager des architektonischen Popularismus, die Neotraditionalisten und Neoklassizisten des „New Urbanism" haben dies erkannt, sondern auch die Architektur, die sich explizit als zeitgenössische von diversen Retro-Bewegungen abzugrenzen versucht.

Dominiert der architektonische Popularismus immer häufiger die Ränder der Städte, so verwirklicht sich in vielen westlichen Ländern zeitgenössische Architektur nun immer mehr mit den früher verpönten Aufgaben der Umnutzung und des Umbaus alter Bausubstanz, nicht zuletzt früherer Bauten der Industrie und Arbeit. Ihre großen, überschüssigen Volumina, die pure Verfügbarkeit von Raum mit einer besonderen Aura der Leere versprechen, drängen sich geradezu auf, mit neuen Raumkonzepten und Nutzungsmischungen gefüllt zu werden.

Nicht von ungefähr sind ihre Adressaten oftmals die Unternehmen und Akteure der „Time"-Branche, die heute das größte Interesse für alte Bauten und zeitgenössische Interventionen zeigen. „Time" steht für die neue

architects increasingly become programme developers rather than designers. Change of use more and more often means developing hybrid use structures whose building programmes are now more often initially defined and sharpened by the architects, rather than the developers. Complex links between old and new are required and, much more often than is the case with new buildings, this offers architects a chance to create an integrated design including the interior.

CONCEPTUAL TRANSFORMATION STRATEGIES

When converting or extending buildings, architects can now have recourse to a number of strategies that follow the principle of either fusing or differentiating old and new. Beyond the older, essentially conservative strategies of Imitation, Camouflage or Emphatic Variation, which all stem from a more or less unbroken continuity between old and new, strategies involving a categorical separation of old and new have been increasingly important for about a decade. The new complexity of ever more hybrid spatial programmes is increasingly confronted with strategies of old and new standing side by side, playing in particular with the difference between inside and outside. Here the historical building is often not the remarkable feature: the remarkable feature is the result of the process, precisely because the existing building was not particularly original before.

Today architects like Andreas Papadakis and Quinlan Terry go down the path of Imitation, trying to continue the old seamlessly in form, material and typology, and usually inclining towards neoclassicism. The possibilities offered by Camouflage, the art of concealment, are creatively more diverse. Here completely new buildings can be found behind preserved façades, but amazing new building skins can be wrapped around an old building, making it seem visually ambiguous, as in Peter Kulka's Lorenzistock in Munich. The architects of Emphatic Adaptation do not strive to be faithful to detail, but to continue old architecture sensually, though the danger of trivialization often lurks here. For them, form and the urban development configuration are usually sacrosanct. But typology and material can be freely interpreted and become charged with sensuality, as in the case of Spoerri's Mediterranean holiday facilities or Helmut Reimann's "New Way" in northern East Friesland.

Maniera Povera and Modification have now almost disappeared. They were very popular Modernist strategies that based themselves conceptually on the historical stock. The Maniera Povera was very popular in post-war German Modernism, deliberately reconstructing partially destroyed buildings with poorer, often barer material quality and construction. Döllgast's "Alte Pinakothek" in Munich can be

Dienstleistungssparte der Telekommunikation, des Internet und der Medien. Im „Loft" haben ihre Akteure ihren genuinen Ort sehr haptischer Raumerfahrungen entdeckt, der ihnen als Kompensation für ihre Arbeit an einer virtuellen globalisierten Welt dient. Schließlich verlangen sie, die heiß umworbenen jungen Fachkräfte, nach vielfältigen Ereignissen, nicht nur nach Quartieren intensiver Kommunikation, sondern auch nach Gebäuden unverwechselbarer Aura.

Verpönt ist der konventionelle Büro- und Wohnungsbau, stark nachgefragt sind alle Bauten, die Ambiente mit Flexibilität verbinden wie alte Gewerbebauten, Hafenspeicher, Energie- oder Industriegebäude. So verlangt die Branche, die selbst über noch keine eigene Geschichte und Architektur verfügt und deren Mitarbeiter selten älter als 40 Jahre sind, in Europa geradezu manisch nach Orten geborgter Identitäten, deren Vergangenheit deutlich vor das Informationszeitalter zurückreicht. Authentisch sollen ihre Gebäude sein und möglichst physisch wie „handmade" erscheinen.

Dies fordert den Architekten neue Kompetenzen ab. Da der Immobilienmarkt in immer kürzeren Zyklen plant und alte Bauten immer mehr durch die wirtschaftlichen Entwicklungen zur Disposition stehen, werden die Architekten zunehmend von Gestaltern zu Programmentwicklern. Umnutzung bedeutet immer häufiger, hybride Nutzungsstrukturen zu entwickeln, deren Raumprogramme immer seltener von den Bauherren, sondern erst von den Architekten definiert und präzisiert werden. Komplexe Verbindungen zwischen Alt und Neu werden abverlangt, die den Architekten viel häufiger als bei Neubauten die Chance einer integralen Gestaltung bis hin zum Interieur eröffnen.

KONZEPTIONELLE STRATEGIEN DER TRANSFORMATION

Zum Umbau oder zur Erweiterung von Gebäuden können heute Architekten auf eine Vielzahl konzeptioneller Strategien zurückgreifen, die entweder dem Prinzip der Verschmelzung oder der Differenz von Alt und Neu folgen. Jenseits der älteren, eher konservativen Strategien der Imitation, Camouflage oder Emphatischen Variation, die alle von einer mehr oder minder ungebrochenen Kontinuität zwischen Alt und Neu ausgehen, haben seit einem Jahrzehnt die Strategien eines kategorialen Separierens von Alt und Neu an Bedeutung gewonnen. Der neuen Komplexität immer hybriderer Raumprogramme stehen so zunehmend Strategien eines klaren Nebeneinanders von Alt und Neu gegenüber, die besonders mit der Differenz zwischen Innen und Außen spielen. Dabei ist immer häufiger nicht das historische Gebäude bemerkenswert, sondern erst das Ergebnis, gerade weil der Bestand zuvor nicht besonders originell war.

Dem Weg der Imitation folgen heute Architekten wie Andreas Papadakis oder Quinlan Terry, die in Form, Material und Typologie das Alte völlig bruchlos fortzusetzen versuchen und die zumeist dem Klassizismus zuneigen. Gestalterisch vielfältiger sind die Möglichkeiten der Camouflage, der Kunst der Tarnung. Hierbei kann es sich um völlig neue Gebäude hinter erhaltenen Fassaden, aber auch um verblüffende, neue Gebäude-

from left to right / von links nach rechts: **Modification – "Remise", Berlin-Kreuzberg, Augustin Frank, Berlin** >> Modification – "Plattenbau", Dresden, Knerer & lang, Dresden >> Bricolage – "Programmkino Ost", Dresden, code unique, Dresden >> "Stadtarchiv", Halle, Kister Scheithauer Gross, Cologne/Dessau >> Camouflage – "Linienstraße", Berlin, Jürgen Mayer H., Berlin >> Bricolage – "Amtsgericht Bad Liebenwerda", Chestnutt_Niess, Berlin

21

given as just one example. There everything new blends in with the old or complements it with a contrast, but in an absolutely non confrontational way. Today the Swiss architect Miroslav Sil is almost the only one still pursuing this strategy. Modification, the typological adaptation of what is already there, as practised in post-war Italian architecture by Franco Albini, Giancarlo de Carlo and also Luigi Snozzi, is almost as rare now too. Aiming at a close symbiosis of old and new both structurally and morphologically, it seems to attract scarcely any attention today outside Ticino or Grisons.

Bricolage is another device for addressing old building stock. This also attempts to treat old and new as a unit, or makes the old look recognisably different from the new by transforming type and material quality sensually, and cultivating contrasts. Scarpism is a variation on Bricolage. This was an architecture style named after Carlo Scarpia, who worked with demonstrative caesuras, layers and details, so that the new could be made to stand out in a dialogue from the background of the old and thus open up new spatial experiences. This conceptual strategy was widely used in the eighties and early nineties.

The polarizing strategy of Assemblage was also very highly thought of in this period. This was a design concept that drew on aesthetic principles quite independently of the existing stock; it is usually subsumed within the concept of deconstructivism. Old connections were deliberately destroyed to create new links or rather spatial and physical polarisations, questioning conventions, usually ironically. Here the old is just raw material, acquiring significance only through the architectural interventions. Enrique Mirailles, COOP Himmelblau and Eric Moss proved themselves to be masters of this approach.

An idea that is still relatively young is Morphological Transformation, which is just as disinterested in the material quality and typology of the old building stock. It aims at fusing what is found into a new and larger form, following aesthetic principles usually derived from biology or computer-generated design. The existing building is morphed, reshaped and enlarged, in order to create a new, decidedly non-Euclidian solid. So the approach goes beyond the morphology of the traditional city, its geometries of grid, axialism or radialism, so that the results can be implanted into the city as dynamic

häute handeln, die sich um ein altes Haus legen und es visuell mehrdeutig erscheinen lassen – wie etwa im Falle von Peter Kulkas Lorenzistock in München. Keine detailgetreue, sondern eine sensuelle Fortsetzung alter Architektur streben hingegen die Architekten der Emphatischen Adaption an, was jedoch oft die Gefahr einer Trivialisierung birgt. Die Form und städtebauliche Figur ist ihnen zumeist sakrosankt, Typologie und Material jedoch frei interpretierbar und sensuell aufladbar, wie etwa bei Spoerris mediterranen Ferienanlagen oder Helmut Riemanns „Neuem Weg" im ostfriesischen Norden.

Nahezu verschwunden sind Maniera Povera und Modifikation, sehr beliebte Strategien der Moderne, die konzeptionell vom historischen Bestand ihren Ausgang nahmen. Sehr beliebt war die Maniera Povera in der deutschen Nachkriegsmoderne, die teilweise zerstörte Gebäude bewusst mit einer ärmeren, oft nackteren Materialität und Konstruktion wiederherstellte. Als Beispiel sei nur die „Alte Pinakothek" von Döllgast in München genannt. Strukturell klar erkennbar lagert sich dort alles Neue in das Alte ein oder ergänzt es kontrastreich, aber keineswegs konfrontativ. Heute folgt dieser Strategie fast nur noch der Schweizer Miroslav Sík. Die Modifikation, die explizit konstruktive oder typologische Adaption des Vorgefundenen wie sie die italienische Nachkriegsarchitektur, Franco Albini, Giancarlo de Carlo, aber auch Luigi Snozzi pflegten, ist heute ebenso selten geworden. Strukturell und morphologisch auf eine enge Symbiose von Alt und Neu zielend scheint sie heute jenseits des Tessins oder Graubündens kaum mehr Interesse zu finden.

Eine andere Auseinandersetzung mit dem Altbestand stellt die Bricolage dar, die Alt und Neu ebenfalls als eine Einheit zu thematisieren versucht, aber das Alte durch eine sensuelle Transformation von Typus und Materialität in erkennbare Differenz zum Neuen setzt und Kontraste kultiviert. Eine Variante der Bricolage stellt der Scarpismus dar, jene Architektur in der Nachfolge von Carlo Scarpa, der mit demonstrativen Zäsuren, Fugen, Schichten und Details arbeitete, um dialogisch das Neue vom Hintergrund des Alten abzuheben und dadurch neue Raumerlebnisse zu eröffnen. In den Achtzigern und frühen Neunzigern fand diese konzeptionelle Strategie weite Verbreitung.

In diesem Zeitraum fand die polarisierende Strategie der Assemblage große Beachtung – ein Entwurfskonzept, das sich auf ästhetische Prinzipien ganz unabhängig vom Bestand beruft und zumeist unter den Begriff Dekonstruktivismus subsumiert wird. Alte Zusammenhänge werden bewusst gesprengt, um neue Verbindungen oder doch eher räumlich-körperliche Polarisierungen hervorzubringen, die Konventionen zumeist ironisch in Frage zu stellen. Das Alte ist hier nur Rohmaterial, das erst durch die architektonischen Eingriffe an Bedeutung gewinnt. Enrique Miralles, COOP Himmelblau und Eric Moss erwiesen sich als Meister dieser Strategie.

Noch relativ jung ist die Morphologische Transformation, die an der Materialität und Typologie des Altbestands ebenso wenig interessiert ist. Sie zielt auf eine Verschmelzung des Vorgefundenen in eine neue, größere Form ab, die ästhetischen Prinzipien folgt, die zumeist der Biologie oder dem computergenerierten Entwerfen entlehnt sind. Das vorhandene Ge-

"...the real is not impossible;
it is simply more
and more artificial..."

„Das Reale ist nicht unmöglich,
in ihm ist und wird vielmehr alles möglich."

Gilles Deleuze / Félix Guattari, Anti-Ödipus (1)

23

catalysts intended to lead to oscillating urban structures. Here the aim is usually, as the music theoretician Diedrich Diedrichsen said of morphing, "to produce something that is already known, but brought about surprisingly. Not something entirely new that is introduced comprehensibly". (5)

Implantation, with its variants, particularly popular today, of Introversion and Parasitical Implants, is largely neutral to the typology, material quality or the form of the existing stock. Sections of buildings and spaces are embedded in what is already there autonomously, with an explicit logic of their own, or docked on to it. Its interventions are subversive and illusive, aiming at staging a different reality within the real. So it is in a way closely related to contemporary sampling: alien and local material is combined and disrespectfully mounted into the code of what it already there.

Introversion backs atmosphere above all, with deliberate surprise effects making their impact after viewers have entered the building. It usually follows the building-in-a-building principle, a clear division of old and new in the interior, as for example in the case of the "Hans Eisler Music College" in the Royal Stables in Berlin by Anderhalten Architekten. But younger architects like the Graft group pursue more strongly combined concepts of introversion and morphing that completely neutralize the old stock in the interior, as for example in the "Ku'damm Dental Practice Berlin".

Parasitical Implants represent the exact opposites of Introversion. They first appeared in the late eighties, and spread very rapidly. They position themselves extrovertly on the old building as host body in the form of parasitical components. They usually make their nests in the airy heights, and use their host's infrastructure, but no dialogue with the old stock is really intended. On the contrary, they see themselves as temporarily limited interventions, as well calculated interruptions

bäude wird gemorpht, überformt und vergrößert, um einen neuen, dezidiert nicht euklidischen Körper entstehen zu lassen. Jenseits der Morphologie der traditionellen Stadt, ihren Geometrien der Raster, Axialität oder Radialität versuchen sich so ihre Ergebnisse als dynamische Katalysatoren in die Stadt zu implantieren, die zu oszilierenderen Stadtstrukturen führen sollen. Dabei geht es zumeist, wie der Musiktheoretiker Diedrich Diederichsen zum Morphing ausführte, „um das überraschend herbeigeführte immer schon Gewusste. Nicht um das nachvollziehbar hergeleitete ganz Neue." (5)

Weitgehend neutral gegenüber Typologie, Materialität oder Form des Vorhandenen ist die Implantation mit ihren heute besonders beliebten Varianten der Introversion und der Parasitären Implantate. Körper und Räume werden autonom mit explizit eigener Logik in das Existierende eingelagert oder angedockt. Subversiv und illusionistisch sind ihre Zugriffe, die auf eine Inszenierung einer anderen Wirklichkeit innerhalb des Realen zielen. Eng verwandt mit dem zeitgenössischen Sampling wird dazu fremdes und eigenes Material kombiniert und respektlos in den Code des Vorgefundenen einmontiert.

Auf Atmosphären und gezielte Überraschungseffekte nach Betreten des Gebäudes setzt vor allem die Introversion. Zumeist folgt sie dem „Haus-im-Haus"-Prinzip, einer klaren Trennung von Alt und Neu im Innern, wie etwa bei der „Hanns Eisler-Musikhochschule" im Berliner Marstall von „Anderhalten Architekten". Doch jüngere Architekten wie die Gruppe „Graft" verfolgen stärker kombinierte Konzepte der Introversion und des Morphings, die den Altbestand im Innern völlig neutralisieren, wie etwa bei der „Zahnarztpraxis Ku'damm Berlin".

Den Antipoden zur Introversion stellen die Parasitären Implantate dar, die erst Ende der Achtziger Jahre auftauchten und rasche Verbreitung fanden. Extrovertiert positionieren sie sich als parasitäre Ergänzungen am Wirtskörper des Alten. Sie nisten sich zumeist in luftiger Höhe ein und bedienen sich der Infrastruktur ihres Wirtes, ein Dialog mit dem Alten ist jedoch nicht wirklich beabsichtigt. Vielmehr verstehen sie sich als temporär begrenzte Eingriffe, als wohl kalkulierte Störungen und Katalysatoren, die zu einer erweiterten Stadtwahrnehmung beitragen sollen, wie

from left to right / von links nach rechts: **Assemblage – "Kulturfabrik"** Hamburg, dinsefeestzurl Architekten, Hamburg >> **Morphologic Transformation – "Universitätsbibliothek Freiburg"**, Degelo Architekten, Basel >> **Implantation – "Kindergarten Traumbaum"**, Berlin, die Baupiloten, Berlin >> **"Hanns-Eisler-Musikhochschule"**, Berlin, Anderhalten Architekten, Berlin >> **Introversion – "KU64"**, Berlin, GRAFT Architekten, Berlin/Los Angeles/Beijing >> **Building-in-a-Building Principle – "Industrie- und Handelskammer"**, Carsten Roth Architekt, Hamburg

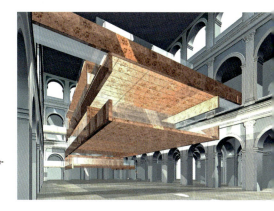

and catalysts intended to contribute to extended perception of the city, like for example Stefan Ebert's "Rucksack House". This is a similar strategy to introversion, which relies on clearly limited interventions, as it no longer seems worth striving for or possible to take creative responsibility for the whole building, never mind the city.

Diametrically opposed to the Parasitical Implants is the new strategy of the Swiss Box. This completely and irreversibly empties out the existing stock, reducing it to the essential core of its structure and construction. The Swiss Box aims to create a new whole in the form of a flexible housing, radically refusing any sense of theatrical staging. Architecture should be no more than a structural framework, a physical and minimalist casing for contemplation and interaction. The "Yellow House" in Films by Valerio Olgiati or the "Palais de Tokyo" in Paris by Lacaton & Vassal were pioneers of the Swiss Box strategy.

URBAN QUALITY AS A CHALLENGE

Many of the strategies mentioned rarely appear in a pure form in architectural reality, and several strategies are often mixed in conversion work. And yet it is scarcely possible to overlook a tendency towards strategies of categorically separating old and new in contemporary architecture. The reason for this may be the dwindling architectural attractiveness of many old buildings available today, but also tighter building budgets and many architects' preference for limited yet clearly recognisable interventions into the old stock that express contemporary architecture in a more uncompromising way.

In a similar way to contemporary architectural photography, the surrounding area is often used only as a visual background: creative aspirations end at the building site boundary. Shifting conversion work from public to private clients must be in part responsible for the fact that public space is disintegrating into segregated, pseudo-public territories. But this increase should require more responsibility from architects. Not least in order to do justice to their new role as programme developers for many re-use projects, where increasingly hybrid spatial programmes demand social interlinking and compensation for the private through new forms of the public.

Studies of the German-speaking countries predict that over 60% of building activity will take place in existing stock. (6) The generation of '60s and '70s buildings that are now available represent new challenges with their serial structures and mono-functional spaces, In particular the transformation of office space that is no longer marketable into attractive homes, which has been successful on a considerable scale in Paris since 1994 thanks to a dedicated funding programme.

etwa das Rucksack-Haus von Stefan Eberstadt. Ähnlich der Introversion handelt es sich um eine Strategie, die auf klar begrenzte Eingriffe setzt, da eine gestalterische Verantwortung für das ganze Gebäude oder gar die Stadt nicht mehr erstrebenswert bzw. möglich erscheint.

Diametral steht den Parasitären Implantaten die völlig neue Strategie der Swiss Box gegenüber, die radikal das Vorhandene irreversibel leer räumt und es auf den wesentlichen Kern seiner Struktur und Konstruktion reduziert. Auf ein neues Ganzes als flexibles Gehäuse zielt die Swiss Box. Radikal verweigert sie sich der Inszenierung. Architektur soll nicht mehr als ein struktureller Rahmen, ein physisch-minimalistisches Gehäuse für Kontemplation und Interaktion sein. Das „Gelbe Haus" in Flims von Valerio Olgiati oder das „Palais de Tokyo" in Paris von Lacaton & Vassal waren Pioniere der Strategie der Swiss Box.

DAS STÄDTISCHE ALS HERAUSFORDERUNG

Viele der genannten Strategien treten in der architektonischen Wirklichkeit selten in Reinform auf, oftmals mischen sich bei Umbauten mehrere Strategien. Dennoch ist die Tendenz zu Strategien eines kategorialen Separierens von Alt und Neu in der zeitgenössischen Architektur unübersehbar. Grund dafür mag die schwindende architektonische Attraktivität vieler heute zur Disposition stehender Altbauten sein, aber auch geringere Baubudgets und die Präferenz vieler Architekten für begrenzte, dafür jedoch klar erkennbare Eingriffe in den Altbestand sein, die zeitgenössische Architektur kompromissloser zum Ausdruck bringen.

Ähnlich wie in der zeitgenössischen Architekturfotografie wird häufig das Umfeld nur als visueller Hintergrund genutzt, endet heute der Gestaltungsanspruch an der Baugrenze. Die Verlagerung des Umbaugeschehens vom öffentlichen zum privaten Auftraggeber dürfte für die Auflösung des öffentlichen Raums in segregierte, pseudo-öffentliche Territorien nicht ganz unverantwortlich sein. Doch deren Zunahme sollte den Architekten mehr Verantwortung abverlangen – nicht zuletzt um ihrer neuen Rolle als Programmentwickler vieler Umnutzungs-Projekte gerecht zu werden, deren immer hybridere Raumprogramme nach sozialer Vernetzung verlangen, nach Kompensationen des Privaten durch neue Formen des Öffentlichen.

Untersuchungen im deutschsprachigen Raum prognostizieren, dass in naher Zukunft mehr als 60 Prozent aller Bautätigkeit im Bestand stattfinden werden. (6) Die Generation von Bauten der 60er und 70er Jahre, die heute zur Disposition stehen, stellen mit ihren seriellen Strukturen und monofunktionalen Räumen neue Herausforderungen dar – nicht zuletzt die Herausforderung, nun nicht mehr vermarktbaren Büroraum in attraktive

from left to right / von links nach rechts: Parasites – "Metastructures", Frankfurt, Stefan Ochs, Darmstadt >> Swiss Box – "Das gelbe Haus", Flims, Valerio Olgiati, Chur >> Provisional – "Luitpold Lounge", Munich, M. Link Architekt, Munich >> Ephemer – "Der Berg", Palast der Republik, Berlin, raumlabor, Berlin

The question of what conversion strategies architects prefer is now one of individual inclinations and styles. We have to work against the tendency to turn our inner cities into museums, and to feel permitted to continue working creatively on our cities: Georg Dehio, the father of German monument preservation, warned as early as 1905 that "the damage done by overenthusiastic affection for restoration is greater than anything that could have happened by simply letting things go".

Young architects in particular increasingly resist the tendency to create a museum by using surprising new forms of spatial intervention, and they also resist the mere economic revaluation of cities by a very small number of players. Working somewhere between art and the everyday world, they make use of performance elements, happenings, ready-made or environments (One example is a mobile gangway and lounge that the architect M. Link sent wandering through central Munich). They deliberately rely on temporary interactions, on the ephemeral and the fleeting, the provisional and the makeshift, in order to break up and question our urban acquisition conventions and lay them open to renegotiation.(7)

Campaigns by groups like raumlabor, complizen, urbikon, L21 and strandbox open up new and unexpected scope for action. Ephemeral events, like the "Berg+Gasthof Bergkristall" by the raumlabor group in and around the Berlin "Palast der Republik", create thoughtful playing fields for a new urban society that has to be shaped, made up of patchwork families and identities, from the new finance-ocracy, which defines itself as explicitly urban, and the service nobility, all of whom demand new symbols and territories with a wealth of significance. Here they can experiment freely and learn new rules for social participation.

Their strength and their weakness is their temporary state: this refuses to be pinned down and made permanent, and poses more questions than it provides answers. Their actions thrive on their departure from convention and are transitional phenomena. They sensitise us to suppressed conflicts with relish and revealing the fracture points in our cities and societies in a surprising way.

The message from the young urban activists is that we all have to readdress the question of the reality we will live, and want to live. Especially as reality defines itself through signs and events in an increasingly visual world, and thus is perceived more and more artificially and individually. Or as the architectural theorist Martin Steinmann put it: "In reality signs are ambiguous, interpreting them represents a choice that cannot be deemed true, just probable".(8)

Revised version of the article / Revidierte Fassung des Artikels: "Interpretatie van meerduidige symbolen", in: De Architect/The Hague, Dec 2005

Wohnungen zu verwandeln, was in Paris seit 1994 dank eines eigenen Förderprogramms schon in größerem Umfang gelang.

Welche Strategien des Umbaus nun Architekten präferieren, ist heute eine Frage der individuellen Neigung und des Stils. Allein der Musealisierung unserer Innenstädte muss gegengearbeitet werden und an den Städten kreativ weitergebaut werden dürfen – warnte doch schon 1905 Georg Dehio, der Ahnherr der deutschen Denkmalpflege, dass „der durch übereifrige Liebe zum Restaurationswesen angerichtete Schaden (...) für die Denkmäler größer [sei], als er je durch einfaches Gehenlassen hätte werden können".

Gerade jüngere Architekten wehren sich immer mehr mit überraschend neuen Formen räumlicher Interventionen gegen Musealisierung wie auch gegen eine rein ökonomische Verwertung der Städte durch wenige Akteure. Zwischen Kunst und Alltag bedienen sie sich Elementen der Performance, des Happenings, Ready-Made oder Environments – wie etwa einer mobilen Gangway und Lounge, die der Architekt Markus Link durch Münchens Innenstadt wandern ließ. Sie setzen bewusst auf temporäre Interaktionen, auf das Ephemere, das Flüchtige, und das Provisorische, das Behelfsmäßige, um unsere Konventionen der Stadtaneignung aufzubrechen, zu hinterfragen und neu verhandeln zu lassen.(7)

Gruppen wie „raumlabor", „complizen", „urbikon", „L21", „strandbox" eröffnen mit ihren Aktionen neue, unerwartete Handlungsräume. Ephemere Ereignisse wie der „Berg+Gasthof Bergkristall" im und um den Berliner „Palast der Republik" von der Gruppe „raumlabor" schaffen hintersinnige Spielfelder für eine neu zu formierende Stadtgesellschaft der Patchwork-Familien und -Identitäten, des neuen, sich explizit urban definierenden Prekariats und der Dienstleistungsnoblesse, die alle nach neuen, mehrdeutbaren Symbolen und Territorien verlangen und die hier zwanglos neue Regeln gesellschaftlicher Teilhabe erproben und erlernen können.

Ihre Stärke wie Schwäche ist das Provisorium, das sich einer Festlegung und Permanenz entzieht, das mehr Fragen eröffnet als Antworten bietet. Ihre Aktionen leben von ihrer Differenz zu den Konventionen, sind Phänomene des Übergangs, die uns lustvoll und stets verblüffend für verdrängte Konflikte sensibilisieren und die Bruchstellen unserer Städte und Gesellschaften offenlegen.

In welcher Realität wir leben werden und wollen, so die Botschaft der jungen Stadtaktivisten, ist von uns allen neu zu beantworten. Zumal Realität, die sich in einer Welt zunehmender Visualität über Zeichen und Ereignisse definiert, immer künstlicher und individueller empfunden wird. Oder wie es der Schweizer Architekturtheoretiker Martin Steinmann für die Architektur ausdrückte: „In Wirklichkeit sind Zeichen mehrdeutig, ihre Deutung stellt eine Wahl dar, die nicht wahr sein kann, nur wahrscheinlich."(8)

1) Gilles Deleuze/ Félix Guattari: Anti-Ödipus, Minneapolis 1983, p. 34   2) Odo Marquard: "Kleine Anthropologie der Zeit" in: Individuum und Gewaltenteilung - Philosophische Studien, Ditzingen 2004, pp. 9-12   3) ditto, from the essay "Skepsis als Philosophie der Endlichkeit", p. 18   4) Françoise Choay: L´Allégorie du Patrimoine, Paris 1992, p. 19   5) Diedrich Diedrichsen: "Montage/Sampling/Morphing. Zur Trias von Ästhetik/Technik/Politik", in: http://www.medienkunstnetz.de/themen/bild-ton-relationen/montage_sampling_morphing   6) Wüstenrot-Stiftung (ed.): Umnutzungen im Bestand. Neue Zwecke für alte Gebäude, Stuttgart/Zurich 2000   7) Antje Havemann / Margit Schild: "Der Nylonstrumpf als temporäre Aktion – oder: Was können Provisorien?", in: dérive 21/Jan. 2006   8) Martin Steinmann: "Wirklichkeit als Geschichte", in: Martin Steinmann: Forme forte. Schriften 1972-2002, Basel 2003, pp. 143-152

1) Gilles Deleuze / Félix Guattari: Anti-Ödipus, Minneapolis 1983, S. 34; deutsch: Gilles Deleuze / Felix Guattari: Anti-Ödipus, Frankfurt am Main 1977, S. 37   2) Odo Marquard: „Kleine Anthropologie der Zeit", in: Individuum und Gewaltenteilung, Philosophische Studien, Ditzingen 2004, S. 9-12   3) dito, aus dem Aufsatz „Skepsis als Philosophie der Endlichkeit", S. 18   4) Françoise Choay: Das architektonische Erbe. Eine Allegorie, Braunschweig-Wiesbaden 1997, S. 19. Erstausgabe „L´Allégorie du Patrimoine", Paris 1992   5) Diedrich Diedrichsen: „Montage/Sampling/Morphing. Zur Trias von Ästhetik/Technik/Politik", in: http://www.medienkunstnetz.de/themen/bild-ton-relationen/montage_sampling_morphing   6) Wüstenrot-Stiftung (hrsg.), Umnutzungen im Bestand. Neue Zwecke für alte Gebäude, Stuttgart/Zürich 2000   7) Antje Havemann, Margit Schild: „Der Nylonstrumpf als temporäre Aktion – oder: Was können Provisorien?", in: dérive 21/Jan. 2006   8) Martin Steinmann: „Wirklichkeit als Geschichte", in: Martin Steinmann: Forme forte. Schriften 1972-2002, Basel 2003, S. 143-152

26

Panoramic Curve

Kontextualismus im zeitgenössischen Gewand

Contextualism in contemporary clothing

Project: Kemper Trautmann Haus | Location: Hamburg | Architects: André Poitiers , Hamburg

28

Parasite Perspective

Neue Blicke auf die Stadt

New views on the city

Project: Rucksack House   **Location:** Leipzig; Cologne; Essen | **Artist:** Stefan Eberstadt, Munich

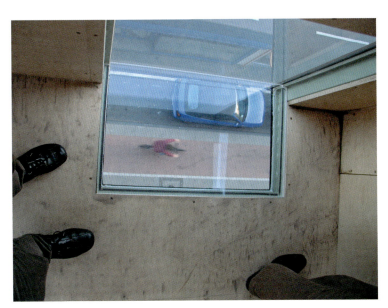

"Why should a
building end precisely
where the walls are?"

„Warum sollte ein Gebäude genau da
enden, wo seine Wände sind?"

Other Economies for Another Architecture

Saskia Sassen in conversation with Armand Gruentuch, Almut Ernst and Anh-Linh Ngo

Andere Ökonomien für eine andere Architektur
Saskia Sassen im Gespräch mit Armand Gruentuch, Almut Ernst und Anh-Linh Ngo

Saskia Sassen is presently working on informalisation patterns in highly developed global cities. Sassen mainly considers the spatial and economic segmentations that she observes from the point of view of creative sectors and migrant players. She is the sociologist responsible for the central essay at the 10th Venice Architecture Biennale and teaches at both the University of Chicago and the London School of Economics.

In your research you are dealing with the effect informal economies have on the spatio-economic segmentation of global cities. You describe these micro economies as imposing themselves on and transforming existing economic structures via informal processes. In architectural terms, similar processes have been observed in Germany in recent years. Now that professional status alone often fails to offer a tenable supporting framework for young and small architecture offices, many are actively and creatively respond to perpetually evolving circumstances by occupying and reinventing existing urban spaces.

Do you see any connections between the political and economic developments you describe, and this informal transformation and conversion of a dominant urban context within the sphere of architecture in Germany today?

Saskia Sassen beschäftigt sich derzeit mit Mustern von Informalisierung in hoch entwickelten globalen Städten. Die von ihr untersuchten räumlich-ökonomischen innerstädtischen Segmentierungen betrachtet Sassen vornehmlich in der Perspektive von Kreativsektoren und migrantischen Akteuren. Die Soziologin ist für den zentralen Essay der 10. Architektur Biennale Venedig verantwortlich und lehrt an der University of Chicago als auch an der London School of Economics.

In Ihrer Forschung beschäftigen Sie sich unter anderem mit den Auswirkungen informeller Ökonomien auf die räumlich-ökonomische Segmentierung globaler Städte. Diese Mikroökonomien zwingen sich den existierenden ökonomischen Strukturen mittels informel-

Today's cities contain conditions that unsettle older ideas and experiences of the city and of public space in particular. How can architecture, especially older architectures of permanence escape this unsettlement? The kind of conditions I am thinking of are the scale at which the urban experience plays out today; the overwhelming presence of massive and dense infrastructures and the irresistible utility logics that organise many of the investments in today's cities. This takes me to three arguments for a practice that can work with and off these conditions:

One is best captured in an image that came to my mind years ago when I was asked to have a dialogue with Norman Foster in – of all places

ler Prozesse auf und verwandeln sie. Bezogen auf die Architektur lassen sich in den letzten Jahren in Deutschland vergleichbare Prozesse beobachten. Da der professionelle Status allein zunehmend weniger in der Lage ist, jungen und kleinen Architekturbüros eine tragfähige Arbeitsgrundlage zu bieten, reagieren viele von ihnen aktiv und schöpferisch auf die sich ständig entwickelnden Rahmenbedingungen, indem sie vorhandene städtische Räume besetzen und umwandeln.

Gibt es einen Zusammenhang zwischen den von Ihnen beschriebenen politischen und ökonomischen Entwicklungen und der hier kurz skizzierten Praxis der informellen Transformation und Konversion eines vorherrschenden urbanen Kontextes?

Die heutigen Städte weisen Bedingungen auf, die ältere Ideen und Erfahrungen der Stadt und vor allem des öffentlichen Raums erschüttern. Wie kann die Architektur, besonders eine auf Permanenz angelegte, dieser Erschütterung entkommen? Die Bedingungen, an die ich dabei denke, sind der Maßstab, in dem sich die städtische Erfahrung heutzutage abspielt, die überwältigende Präsenz gewaltiger Infrastrukturen sowie das verlockende Nützlichkeitsdenken, das den Investitionsfluss lenkt.
Dies führt mich zu drei Argumenten für eine Praxis, die mit und ausgehend von diesen Bedingungen arbeiten kann.

Eines dieser Argumente lässt sich am besten mit einem Bild veranschaulichen, das mir vor Jahren in den Sinn kam, als ich, ausgerechnet in einem Dorf in den Schweizer Alpen, ein Gespräch mit Norman Foster

– a village in the Swiss Alps. The image was architecture as "inhabited infrastructure". In the case of his buildings I was coming from a particular angle: the engineering, the aim of environmental dimensions embedded in the architecture. In the context of the larger issue I raise above, it is more a question of making architecture under inhospitable conditions. Architectural practice needs to engage unforthcoming spaces. Much of today's massive urban infrastructure should become a puzzle: detecting the possible architectures that can ride these infrastructures.

A second type of practice arises out of the fact that these large cities contain a diversity of under-used spaces, often characterised more by memory than current meaning. These spaces lie outside today's organising utility-driven logics and spatial frames. Yet they are part of the interiority of the city. Jumping at these spaces to maximise real estate development would be a mistake, a loss. The practices I can think of is one that keeps destabilising the meaning of such spaces, so that they never becomes a mere under-used space but is a continuous provocation. That takes making, it does not happen by itself. It takes a particular type of practice not centred in architecture of permanence. The recent explosion in urban interventions is an example. For instance the simultaneous projects in Brussels, Barcelona, London and others (see www.generalizedempowerment.org) or, in a very different part of the world, Buenos Aires, the works by Rally Conurbano (www.rallyconurbano.com.ar) and Kermés Urbana, which seek to produce public space by reactivating such forgotten or abandoned urban spaces (www.m7red.com.ar), or the work of Transgressive Architecture (www.transgressivearchitecture.org) which is genuinely subversive and often gets them into trouble with the forces of social order, as they are called. Somehow these types of interventions make me think of barefoot architects, along the lines of China's barefoot doctors.

A third type of practice is the one you allude to in your question. I think it is critical. It takes a making that oscillates or navigates between formal systems and interventions that might be formal in some aspects but also come with a creative vigour that often cannot be accommodated formally by the systems within which it has to function.

How does this oscillation between informal action and formal systems affect this form of practice? Many of these projects claim – often in a very naive way – to change the conditions or to provoke a shift of perspective. Do architects really have any sustainable impact on the formal system they have to work in?

The ways in which this oscillating between formal and informal practices affects architectural practice will vary. Sometimes the effect will be evanescent, contingent, interstitial – all those compelling words…and, hopefully, also compelling practices. At other times the effect may well be to shift the boundaries of the meaning of architecture.

In my own research, focused on political, social, economic and technical issues, I find interesting parallels to your problematic of an architecture that oscillates between the formal and the informal. One critical aspect is the time frame: for informal practices to have a lasting effect takes much more time than the building of a building. For instance, if we take a sufficiently long historical period, we can see that in the West some of the best formal rights we have as citizens have been achieved through the practices of the excluded and through their informal political claim-making.

führen sollte: Architektur als „bewohnte Infrastruktur". Dieses Bild war geprägt von der besonderen Rolle der Technik in Fosters Architektur sowie von dessen Anliegen, Umweltfragen in die Architektur einzubetten. Im Kontext des umfassenderen Themas, das ich eingangs skizziert habe, verweist diese Metapher jedoch eher auf die unausweichliche Aufgabe der Architektur, sich auf die unwirtlichen Räume der gewaltigen städtischen Infrastruktur einzulassen, um sie mit allen denkbaren Lösungen nutzbar zu machen.

Eine zweite Art der Praxis ergibt sich daraus, dass diese großen Städte eine Vielzahl von untergenutzten Räumen aufweisen, die häufig eher durch Erinnerung charakterisiert werden als durch ihre aktuelle Bedeutung. Diese Räume liegen außerhalb der Nützlichkeitslogik und der räumlichen Vorgaben heutiger Verwertungsbedingungen. Trotzdem sind sie Teil der mentalen Verfasstheit der Stadt. Sich auf diese Räume zu stürzen, um der Immobilienwirtschaft weitere Felder zu erschließen, wäre ein Fehler, ein Verlust. Man sollte die Bedeutung solcher Räume unablässig destabilisieren, sodass sie nicht nur als untergenutzte Räume gelten, sondern eine ständige Provokation darstellen. Dies setzt ein aktives Engagement voraus, das wenig mit der Architektur der Permanenz zu tun hat. Die jüngste Explosion von urbanen Eingriffen ist ein Beispiel dafür – etwa die gleichzeitigen Projekte in Brüssel, Barcelona, London und anderen Städten (vgl. www.generalizedempowerment.org) oder die Arbeiten Rally Conurbano (http://www.rally-conurbano.com.ar) und Kermés Urbana für einen völlig anderen Teil der Welt, Buenos Aires. Sie erschaffen öffentliche Räume, indem sie vergessene oder verlassene städtische Räume reaktivieren (www.m7red.com.ar/). Ein weiteres Beispiel wäre die Arbeit von Transgressive Architecture (www.transgressivearchitecture.org), die wirklich subversiv ist und häufig zu Konflikten mit den so genannten Kräften der sozialen Ordnung führt. Irgendwie lässt mich diese Art von Interventionen jedoch an barfüßige Architekten denken, in einer Linie mit Chinas barfüßigen Ärzten.

Eine dritte Art der Praxis, auf die Sie in Ihrer Frage anspielen, ist eine kritische. Sie erfordert ein Handeln, das zwischen formalen Systemen und Eingriffen oszilliert oder navigiert, die in mancher Hinsicht formal sein mögen, die aber gleichzeitig eine unbändige schöpferische Kraft besitzen, die oftmals nicht formal von den Systemen erfasst werden kann, innerhalb derer sie funktionieren muss.

Wie wirkt sich dieses Oszillieren zwischen informellem Handeln und formalen Systemen auf die Praxis aus? Viele dieser Projekte erheben den Anspruch – häufig auf eine ziemlich naive Weise –, die Bedingungen zu verändern oder einen neuen Blickwinkel zu provozieren. Haben Architekten wirklich irgendeinen nachhaltigen Einfluss auf das formale System, in dem sie arbeiten müssen?

Dieses Oszillieren zwischen formalen und informellen Praktiken wird sich auf verschiedene Weise auf die architektonische Praxis auswirken. Manchmal wird die Wirkung ephemer, kontingent und interstitiell sein – all diese bezwingenden Begriffe … und hoffentlich ebenso bezwingenden Praktiken. Manchmal wird die Wirkung wohl auch darin bestehen, dass die Bedeutungsgrenzen der Architektur verschoben werden.

This type of historic dynamic may well have a parallel in the history of architectural practice. I can imagine a dynamic where informal practices, or the notions of those excluded from the profession, have in the long run become part of the formal practices of architecture; the formal notions of the profession and the formal range of materials considered appropriate. Is not much, and perhaps all, experimental and innovative architecture part of such shifts? In my new book I speak of "novel assemblages" of territory, authority, and rights – bits of each that were hitherto ensconced in the national, get dislodged and become part of novel cross-border assemblages. I can't help but think that conceptually we could do a similar analysis for architecture.

This notion of "novel assemblages" could indeed be a good starting point for a form of analysis that describes the changes we observe in architecture and planning these days: changes in alliances of participants, planning methods, urban behaviours etc. The positive connotations of "novel assemblages" and the historic dynamic you have mentioned both hint at ways of using the informalisation processes of advanced capitalism for an informal architectural practice in order to establish a new kind of informal architectural claim-making.

But one should not hide the fact that these informal practices are often associated with a lot of self-exploitation by the new urban precariat, or the "excluded" as you call them in historical terms.

I totally agree. One point that needs to be made is that the informal often comes at a cost to its practitioners. Most recognised are the informal economic systems – whether they be immigrant informal economies or the new types of creative professional informal economies we see emerging

in many complex global cities today, like Berlin for example. In my book I explore the question of informality in the political realm. Here too the informal carries costs. It is often the excluded who make informal politics and by the time their political claims are formalised they are often long dead. But it does raise the importance of the distinction between power and politics: the excluded may not have power but they can make politics, and it is this making of the political that I emphasise.

Bei meinen Untersuchungen, die sich auf politische, soziale, ökonomische und technische Fragestellungen konzentrieren, entdecke ich interessante Parallelen zu Ihrer Problematik einer zwischen dem Formalen und dem Informellen oszillierenden Architektur. Ein kritischer Aspekt ist der Zeitrahmen: Sollen informelle Praktiken eine dauerhafte Wirkung haben, so beansprucht dies wesentlich mehr Zeit als das Bauen eines Gebäudes. Über einen ausreichend langen historischen Zeitraum betrachtet, sind beispielsweise einige der besten formalen Rechte, die wir als Bürger der westlichen Welt heute genießen, erreicht worden durch das Handeln der von der Macht Ausgeschlossenen und durch deren informelles Erheben politischer Forderungen bzw. deren Claim-Making, wie es in der Soziologie so schön heißt.

Diese Art von historischer Dynamik hat womöglich eine Parallele in der Geschichte der architektonischen Praxis. Ich kann mir vorstellen, dass durch solch eine Dynamik langfristig informelle Praktiken oder auch die Vorstellungen der von der Profession Ausgeschlossenen zu einem Teil der formalen Architekturpraxis geworden sind. Basiert nicht die meiste und vielleicht sogar alle experimentelle, innovative Architektur auf solchen Veränderungen? In meinem jüngst erschienenen Buch spreche ich von „neuartigen Assemblagen" von Territorium, Autorität und Rechten – Teile dieser Konzepte, die bisher im Nationalen aufgegangen sind, werden nun herausgelöst und zu neuen grenzüberschreitenden Assemblagen zusammengefügt. Ich bin fest davon überzeugt, dass wir konzeptuell eine ähnliche Analyse für die Architektur erstellen könnten.

Dieses Konzept von „neuartigen Assemblagen" könnte tatsächlich ein guter Ausgangspunkt für eine Analyse sein, die die aktuellen Veränderungen in Architektur und Planung beschreiben hilft – Veränderungen in den Allianzen von Akteuren, Planungsmethoden, urbanen Verhaltensweisen usw. Die positive Konnotation des Konzepts und die von Ihnen angedeutete historische Dynamik verweisen nämlich darauf, wie man die Informalisierungsprozesse des fortgeschrittenen Kapitalismus als Chancen für eine mögliche informelle Architekturpraxis nutzen kann, um eine neue Art des informellen architektonischen Claim-Making durchzusetzen.

Man darf aber auch nicht verschweigen, dass diese informellen Praktiken häufig verbunden sind mit einer erheblichen Selbstausbeutung des neuen städtischen Prekariats, oder der Ausgeschlossenen, wie Sie sie in historischer Terminologie nennen.

Richtig, ich habe immer darauf hingewiesen, dass das Informelle häufig auf Kosten derjenigen erfolgt, die es praktizieren. Am bekanntesten ist die informelle Ökonomie – ob es sich dabei um die informellen Ökonomien von Einwanderern handelt oder um die neuen Arten von kreativen, professionellen informellen Ökonomien, wie sie heute in Berlin und in vielen anderen globalen Städten entstehen. In meinem neuen Buch befasse ich mich mit der Frage des Informellen im politischen Bereich. Auch hier ist das Informelle mit Kosten verbunden. Es sind häufig die Ausgeschlossenen, die informelle Politik machen, und zu der Zeit, wo ihre Forderungen schließlich anerkannt werden, sind diese Menschen oft schon lange tot. Aber dies unterstreicht die Wichtigkeit der Unterscheidung zwischen Macht und Politik: Die Ausgeschlossenen mögen keine Macht haben, aber sie können Politik machen, und es ist dieses Machen des Politischen, das ich betone.

Location: Berlin | **Architects:** raumlabor_berlin, Peanutz Architekten, HAU

Project: Dolmusch X-press

Taxi from Turkey

Informelle Transportsysteme mit sozialer Interaktion

Informal transport systems with social interaction

A House Moves Home

Project: www.lebe-deine-stadt.de   **Location:** Germany | **Architects:** MESS, Kaiserslautern

Optische Begleitmusik für ein Online-Magazin

Optical soundtrack for an online magazine

34

Over the Top

Wo der unmittelbare Sinn aufhört und der Unterschied beginnt

Where literal meaning ends and difference begins

Project: Over the Top | Location: Cologne | Architects: b&k+brandlhuber&co + marc frohn, Cologne

36

Project: Floating Grounds   Location: Berlin | **Architects:** HSH Hoyer Schindele Hirschmüller & Art+Com, Berlin

Reactive Alleyways

Wohnbrücke mit bewegten Oberflächen

Bridge homes with moving surfaces

Project: Town House O – 10 | Location: Berlin | **Architects:** David Chipperfield Architects, Berlin

37

Vertical
Bungalow

Simulation von Geschichte durch die
Verdichtung künstlich generierter Baulücken

**Simulating history by densifying
artificially generated gap sites**

Dressing Up

Neue Kleiderordnung für die Einsatzzentrale

A new uniform for the station house

Project: Police and Fire Station   **Location:** Berlin | **Architects:** Sauerbruch Hutton, Berlin

40

Project: SPOTS Light and Media Facade | **Location:** Berlin | **Architects:** realities:united, Berlin

Subcutanious Communication

Das Spiel mit dem leuchtenden Leerstand

Vacant space in a new light

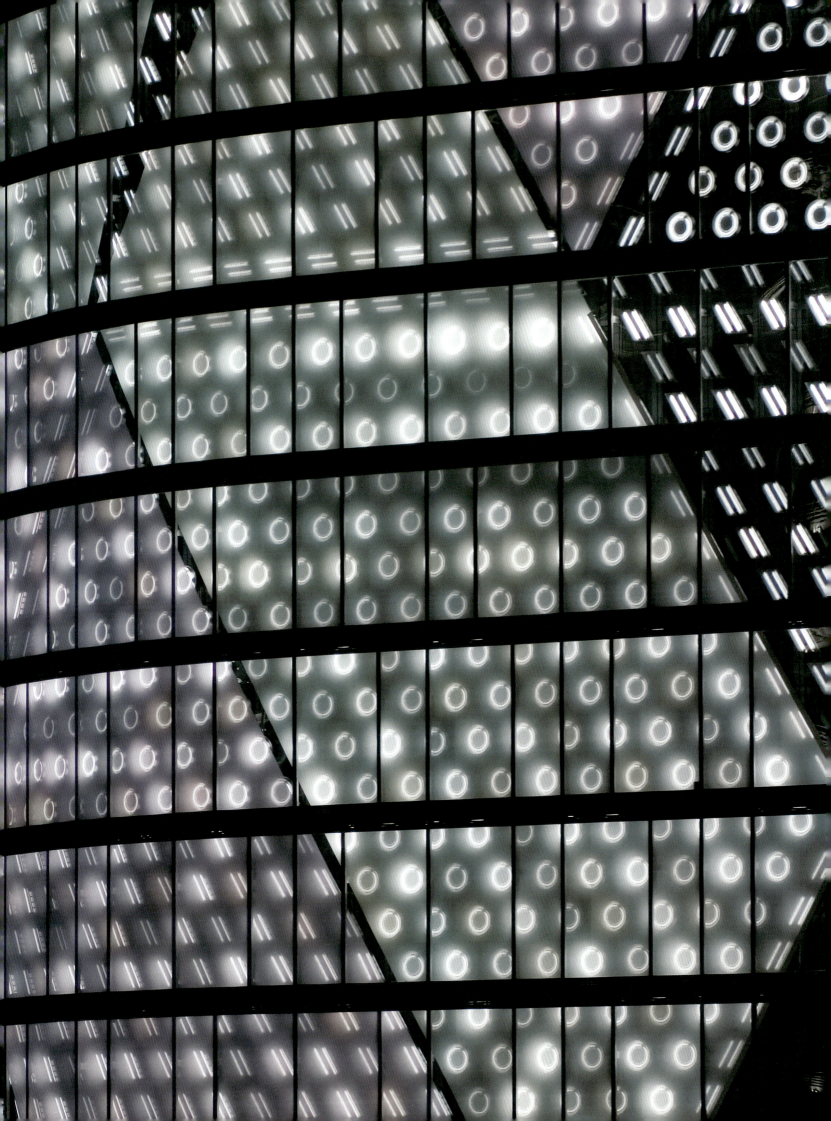

Medial Surfaces

Mediatecture as an integral part of architecture and a measure to create identity within the urban environment

Mediale Oberflächen
Mediatektur als integraler Bestandteil
von Architektur und Identität
stiftende Maßnahme im urbanen Raum

The face of the world's metropolises is changing as the use of media façades becomes more widespread, bringing the presence of new technology in our everyday lives to a new level. From Berlin to Seoul via New York and Tokyo, artists, architects and investors appear to be increasingly absorbed with this new way of thinking about buildings. The trend is becoming apparent as more and more large-scale architectural media surfaces go up in cities around the globe, attracting attention and creating a new and contemporary dimension and a distinctive character to buildings.

The concept of the 'media façade' is defined by the fusion of an architectural entity with new technology that can communicate moving images and sound with the surrounding area. In architecture, the façade has traditionally been understood as a medium of expression and often conveys not only the aesthetic taste of the contractor or architect, but also essential functions of the building itself.

RELEVANT DESIGN PRINCIPLES

The word 'façade' can be traced back to the Latin facies for 'face'. A person's face is more than just a visual surface; it is an integral part of the body. Using this metaphor we can derive relevant design principles for the 'media façade': it too should be an integral element of the architecture, and not, as often the case, simply masking or concealing the building.

Our face is an active medium of expression and it changes according to the nature of communication. In keeping with the metaphor, this means that the expression and narration of the media façade must correspond to the use and the architecture of a building, and should under no circumstances be merely a theatrical act, or a role contradicting the building's contents.

Joachim Sauter, Susanne Jaschko

Die Omnipräsenz neuer Technologien in unserem Alltag hat mit den Medienfassaden, die in zunehmendem Maße in den Metropolen der Welt die Stadtbilder neu prägen, eine neue Stufe erreicht. Ob in Berlin, Seoul, New York, Tokio – das gleichermaßen große Interesse von Gestaltern und Auftraggebern an dieser neuen Ausdrucksmöglichkeit von Gebäuden manifestiert sich vielerorts in großen, medialen Architekturoberflächen, welche den Blick unwiderstehlich auf sich lenken und den jeweiligen Bauten eine völlig neue raum-zeitliche Dimension und einen unverwechselbaren Charakter geben wollen.

Der Begriff der Medienfassade meint die Synthese von architektonischem Körper und neuen Technologien, die eine Kommunikation bewegter Bilder und Klänge in den umgebenden Raum hinein ermöglichen. Traditionell wird die Fassade in der Architektur als Ausdrucksmedium verstanden und vermittelt, über das ästhetische Empfinden des Auftraggebers hinaus, oft auch dem Gebäude innewohnende Funktionen.

RELEVANTE GESTALTUNGSPRINZIPIEN

Der Begriff Fassade lässt sich etymologisch auf das lateinische Wort facies für Gesicht zurückführen. Das Gesicht des Menschen ist mehr als nur eine visuelle Oberfläche; es ist ein integraler Teil des Körpers. Daraus leiten sich relevante Gestaltungskriterien für die Medienfassade ab: Sie sollte integraler Bestandteil der Architektur sein und nicht, wie häufig zu sehen, das Gebäude maskieren oder überdecken.

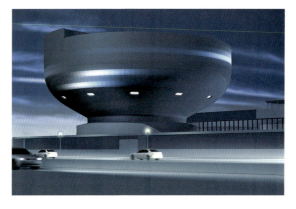

(fig 1)

One of the first media façades was Toyo Ito's Tower of Winds (1986). Ito built a 21 metre high ventilation tower for an underground shopping centre. The supporting frame is encased in a perforated aluminium cylinder. Between the cylinder and the girder, Ito mounted a range of illuminations. While the aluminium plates reflect the sunlight during the day, making the tower appear opaque, the framework is clearly visible from the back and at dusk the lights between the tower and the aluminium cladding react to the movement of air in the vault and render an internal process in real time visible.

Eine der ersten Medienfassaden war Toyo Itos Tower of Winds aus dem Jahre 1986. Der 21 Meter hohe Belüftungsturm eines unterirdischen Einkaufszentrums in Yokohama besteht aus einem ovalen Zylinder aus perforiertem Aluminium. Abhängig von der Lichtsituation erscheint der Turm in der Reflexion entweder als solider Baukörper oder im Gegenlicht als durchscheinendes Bauwerk. Zwischen Tragwerk und Aluminiummantel wurden verschiedene ansteuerbare Leuchtmittel angebracht, die mit Beginn der Dämmerung auf die Luftbewegungen im Schacht reagieren und so innere Prozesse in Echtzeit nach außen sichtbar machen.

Blinkenlights, Haus des Lehrers, Berlin 2001-02, Chaos Computer Club

DIFFERENT STATES AND OPERATING MODES

As a changeable membrane, the media façade has the potential to act as an agent between the outside and the inside. This can be done in a number of different ways.

In an 'auto-active' state the media façade has a mono-directional effect on its environment, as it is not affected by internal or external processes. Moving images, for example, are simply 'played' on the façade. A good example is the recently constructed media façade on Chanel's flagship store in Tokyo, which projects short animations in the corporate colours of black and white, portraying the company's well-known aesthetics.

In a 'reactive state', on the other hand, the façade responds to the internal or external environment, staging a two-way interaction between inside and outside. Integrated sensors recognise alterations in the vicinity and shape the visual contents of the façade. A wide range of factors has been used in the context of reactive media façades, such as local traffic. The façade of Taipei's city hall for example, realized by ART+COM, reacts to passing pedestrians.

Das Gesicht dient dem Menschen als dynamisches Ausdrucksmedium, das sich seiner jeweiligen Kommunikationssituation und seinem inneren Zustand anzupassen vermag. Übertragen auf die Medienfassade bedeutet dies, dass sie in ihrem Ausdruck und in ihrer Narration der Nutzung und Architektur entsprechen und keinesfalls eine „schauspielerische", dem Inhalt des Gebäudes widersprechende Rolle übernehmen sollte.

ZUSTÄNDE UND WIRKUNGSWEISEN

Als veränderliche Membran zwischen Innen und Außen besitzt die Medienfassade das Potenzial, zwischen diesen beiden Bereichen zu vermitteln. Dies kann auf unterschiedliche Weisen geschehen.

In einem autoaktiven Zustand wirkt die Medienfassade monodirektional auf ihre Umgebung, ohne dass sie durch innere oder äußere Prozesse gesteuert wird. Inhalte werden auf der Fassade abgespielt. So zeigt die erst kürzlich in Tokio entstandene Medienfassade des Flagship-Store von Chanel vorproduzierte, kurze Animationen in den typischen Chanel-Farben Schwarz und Weiß und vermittelt die Ästhetik, für die die Modefirma weltberühmt ist.

The BMW Trias 'media façade axis' in Munich, Germany: Integrating a media façade into Karl Schwanzer's 1973 landmark BMW museum (known as the 'Bowl') was a planned measure intended to regain an equilibrium with Coop Himmelblau's adjacent glowing glass structure of the BMW World. A media façade was developed for Schwanzer's building to subtly accentuate the structure at night: Passing vehicles are caught by a system of cameras, which trigger animations on the surface of the façade (fig1).

Konzept für eine mediale „Fassadenachse" BMW Trias, München: Mit der Integration einer Medienfassade in die 1973 von Karl Schwanzer entworfene „Schüssel" des BMW Museums, die bisher als Ikone im Stadtraum fungierte, soll ein visuelles Gleichgewicht zu der von Coop Himmelblau als gläserner, nachts leuchtender Baukörper entworfenen BMW Welt hergestellt werden. Das Konzept sah vor, dass vorbeifahrende Fahrzeuge, die von einem Kamerasystem erkannt werden, Animationen auf der Fassade auslösen (abb1).

The light system of the façade consists of individual phosphorus tubes covered by diffusion foil and perforated metal sheeting (fig2).

Das Lichtsystem der Fassade besteht aus einer Schicht einzeln ansteuerbarer Leuchtstoffröhren, einer darüberliegenden Diffusorfolie und einer Lochblechverkleidung (abb2).

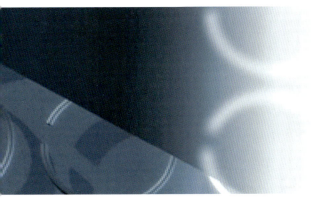

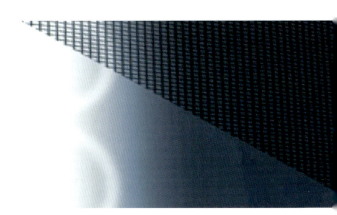

(fig2)

The unrealised façade concept for Berlin's new Hauptbahnhof (central station) envisaged a visual reference of trains entering and leaving the station. Golan Levin's temporary concept for the façade of the Linz Ars Electronica Center (Austria) was based on the movement of vehicles. Christian Möller created one of the first weather-based systems with the façade on the Zeil-Galerie in Frankfurt (Germany).

By going a step further and integrating interfaces into an interactive system, people can enter into a dialogue with the media façade. Controlling façades with anything from mobile phones and microphones to video gateways is technically possible, but has all too often only been realised in temporary installations. Taking advantage of the integrated interfaces, the surroundings can be influenced as the façade becomes a performance medium.

Even when not in a reactive but in an interactive state, the media façade enters a dynamic and reciprocal dialogue with its environment, which is, from an architectural perspective, a very interesting, albeit potentially problematic, attribute. This type of media façade can provide a completely new urban experience, determine a location's identity and even offer, by way of interaction, a personalised control over the façade's appearance.

The formative role of the individual can be taken further still if the façade is designed as a public platform. In this case, the contents can be generated by virtually anyone. The temporary projection by the Chaos Computer Club at the Bibliothèque National in Paris for example, allowed any Internet user to produce and play short animations on the façade. Rafael Lozano-Hemmer's project for the Spots façade developed by realities:united at Berlin's Potsdamer Platz, offered visitors the chance to enter questions into a local terminal that would then run along the façade. When there was no interaction, when, that is, there were no visitors, the system went into an auto-active state.

TEMPORARY AND PERMANENT

The Spots façade is typical of many projects of a temporary nature in that it is not strictly speaking a media façade, since it was added to the architecture as an afterthought. Usually, the link between architecture and façade is incoherent in these cases: the building is typically used only as a 'public screen'.

However, an awareness about the possibilities of permanent media façades for both buildings and the cityscape as a whole is beginning to emerge. The competence required to design such façades skilfully is growing, along with the developing technology, economic feasibility and sustainability. Naturally, these permanent media façades involve substantially more responsibility on the part of both designer and contractor than the temporary projects. The

In einem reaktiven Zustand reagiert die Fassade auf ihr inneres oder äußeres Umfeld. Integrierte Sensoren erkennen hierbei Veränderungen der Umgebung. Die so gewonnenen Daten beeinflussen die zumeist visuellen Inhalte der Fassade. Verschiedenste Faktoren wurden bereits im Kontext von reaktiven Medienfassaden einbezogen, beispielsweise der lokale Verkehr. Die Fassade des Rathauses in Taipeh, die von ART+COM entwickelt wird, reagiert auf vorübergehende Passanten; das Fassadenkonzept für den neuen Berliner Hauptbahnhof sah eine visuelle Referenz ein- und durchfahrender Züge vor; Golan Levins temporär realisiertes Konzept für die Fassade des Ars Electronica Center in Linz basierte auf der Bewegung von Fahrzeugen. Mit der Fassade der Zeil-Galerie in Frankfurt schuf Christian Möller eines der ersten Systeme, die auf das Wetter reagieren.

Ist die Fassade durch die Integration von Interfaces als interaktives System gestaltet, kann der Mensch mit der Fassade als einem performativen Medium interagieren, um auf den ihn umgebenden Raum einzuwirken. Die Ansteuerung von Fassaden z.B. mittels Mobiltelefonen, Mikrofonen oder Videoschnittstellen ist heute technisch machbar, wird bislang jedoch häufig nur temporär realisiert.

Sowohl im reaktiven als auch im interaktiven Zustand tritt die Medienfassade in einen dynamischen Dialog mit ihrer Umgebung. Diese Medienfassaden ermöglichen ein neuartiges, unmittelbares und Identität stiftendes Erlebnis von Stadtraum und in der Interaktion sogar die personalisierte Kontrolle über die Erscheinungsformen der Fassade.

Diese gestaltende Rolle des Einzelnen kann außerdem noch erweitert werden, indem die Fassade als öffentliche Plattform konzipiert wird. Bei einer derartigen Gestaltung können Inhalte theoretisch von jedem kreiert werden. Die temporäre Bespielung der Bibliothèque Nationale in Paris durch den Chaos Computer Club ermöglichte jedem Internetbenutzer die Produktion und das Abspielen von kurzen Animationen auf der Fassade. Rafael Lozano-Hemmers Projekt für die von realities:united realisierte Spots Fassade am Potsdamer Platz in Berlin gab den Besuchern die Möglichkeit, Fragen über ein lokales Terminal einzugeben, die dann über die Fassade liefen. Gab es keine Interaktion, fiel die Fassade in einen autoaktiven Zustand.

TEMPORÄR UND PERMANENT

Wie die Spots Fassade sind viele früher und heute realisierten Projekte nur temporärer Natur, also im engen Sinne keine Medienfassaden, da sie meist nachträglich in die Architektur eingebracht werden. In diesen temporären Projekten tritt eine stimmige Beziehung zwischen Gebäude und den durch die Fassade vermittelten Inhalte meist in den Hintergrund. Das Gebäude wird hierbei meist als „public screen" genutzt.

Jedoch wächst zunehmend die Kompetenz und die ökonomische Machbarkeit permanenter Medienfassaden sowie das Bewusstsein für die Möglichkeiten, die sie für den Stadtraum und das Gebäude bieten.

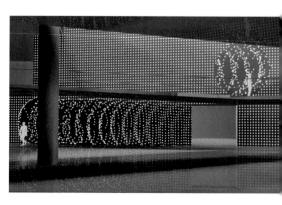

(fig3) (fig4)

integrated system should not only be functional over a long period of time, but the whole concept must be incorporated into the cityscape with particular attention to detail.

Architectural training, however, increasingly involves working with new media and so perhaps in future, the architect will come to be responsible for the overall planning and design of integrative media façades. What is meant here by 'integrative' is not only the need to effectively integrate the media with the building's architecture, but, more importantly, to integrate its two-way dialogue with the other buildings, the surrounding area and its users, within the context of an increasingly medial city.

Regrettably, today's technical opportunities often tempt contractors, designers and architects into ineffective and unimaginative projects. Architectural exteriors are often made into permanent spectacles using nothing more than colourful lights. What is important for the successful integration of media façades with a building is that the whole system, the contents as well as the long-term effect on the surrounding area are all carefully considered. When this occurs, when, that is, the design is successful, then buildings with a media façade can improve the cityscape aesthetically without over-accentuating it, and contribute to a special, personalised identity for the location.

Natürlich tragen Gestalter und Bauherr bei der Realisierung von permanenten Medienfassaden eine wesentlich größere Verantwortung als bei der Verwirklichung temporärer Projekte, sodass das Konzept mit besonderer Umsicht an den städtischen Raum angepasst werden sollte.

Zunehmend beschäftigen sich Architekten in ihrer Ausbildung mit neuen Medien, sodass in Zukunft voraussichtlich die Gestaltung integrativer medialer Fassaden im Kontext des Gesamtentwurfs ganz in ihrer Verantwortung liegt. Integrativ meint hierbei nicht nur die bereits angesprochene Bedingung der adäquaten Integration der Medien in die Gebäudearchitektur, sondern auch deren Wechselwirkung mit anderen Baukörpern und dem sie umgebenden Raum sowie ihren Benutzern in einer zukünftigen, medial noch stärker durchwirkten Stadt.

Leider verführen heute die neuen technischen Möglichkeiten sowohl Auftraggeber als auch Gestalter noch zu häufig zu inadäquaten, bezugslosen Inszenierungen von Gebäuden. Oft werden mit farbigem Licht architektonische Oberflächen zu „permanenten Spektakeln" gemacht. Die Integration von Medienfassaden in ein Gebäude verlangt, dass gleichzeitig über System, Inhalt und deren langfristige Wirkung auf den Stadtraum nachgedacht wird. Gelingt jedoch die Gestaltung, werten Gebäude mit medialen Oberflächen den Stadtraum ästhetisch auf, ohne ihn zu „übertönen", und tragen zur persönlichen Identifikation mit einem Ort bei.

The extension of the car museum takes up Schwanzer's concept of the built-in environment. Inside the buildings shapes, openings and pathways make up urban spaces. Thus the interior surfaces are treated as façades, and as media façades they refer to the exterior. The 'dynamic wall-material' is a combination of cinematic technology (LEDs) and classical façade materials (satined glass) and creates a vibrant, architectural surface (fig3).

Der Erweiterungsbau nimmt Schwanzers Konzept des umbauten Stadtraums auf, wobei im Gebäudeinneren Volumen, Plätze und Wege einen urbanen Raum nachbilden. Folgerichtig werden Wandoberflächen als Fassaden konzipiert, die als Medienfassaden im Inneren des Gebäudes auf den Außenraum verweisen. Das „dynamische Wandmaterial" ist eine Kombination aus cineastischer Technologie (LED) mit einem klassischen Fassadenmaterial (satiniertem Glas) und schafft eine dynamische architektonische Oberfläche (abb3).

The façades are predominantly auto-active. At intervals, they react to visitors and, through their presence, draw them into the overall appearance of the museum. (fig4)

Die Fassaden sind in erster Linie autoaktiv. Zeitweise reagieren sie auf die Besucher und beziehen diese durch ihre Präsenz in die Erscheinung des Museums ein (abb4).

In order to distinguish the various BMW Trias buildings along their axis, a further media façade was designed for the factory bordering the museum. To convey the industrial character of the factory where cars are actually built, a mechatronic façade was designed. It is made of a grid of vertically aligned metal plates that can be posted into slots. A vertical 'scanner' equipped with electromagnets, moves horizontally across the façade, lifting individual plates out of or slotting them into their slots, according to the motif of the picture being made. The result is a mechanical façade that is continuously changing (fig5).

Zur besseren Identifizierung der einzelnen BMW Trias Gebäude wurde entlang einer Achse eine weitere mediale Fassade für das sich an das Museum anschließende Werk entworfen. Um den industriellen Charakter der Werkhalle als Produktionsort zu betonen, wurde eine mechatronische, dynamische Oberfläche konzipiert, die aus einem Raster vertikal abstehender und in Schlitzen versenkbarer Metallplättchen besteht. Ein vertikaler „Scanner", der in der gleichen Auflösung wie das Blättchenraster mit ansteuerbaren Elektromagneten versehen ist, bewegt sich horizontal über die Fassade. Dieser zieht die einzelnen Blättchen aus den Schlitzen bzw. versenkt diese in den Schlitzen entsprechend einem Bildmotiv. Eine mechanische, sich über die Zeit langsam verändernde Fassade entsteht (abb5).

Collaboration / Arbeitgemeinschaft: **Atelier Brückner (architecture and scenography), ART+COM (mediatecture and media) und Integral, Ruedi Baur (graphics)**

(fig5)

46

Project: City Hall Extension Location: Frankfurt am Main I Architects: Bolles + Wilson, Münster

City Hall Silhouette

Die Neuinterpretation der lokalen Historie

The reinterpretation of local history

Location: Bremen | **Architects:** Barkow Leibinger Architekten, Berlin

Project: Bremen Shopping Centre

Crystalline Cocoon

Altes Kaufhaus mit Stadtterrasse neu verpackt

Freshly wrapped urban terrace over old department store

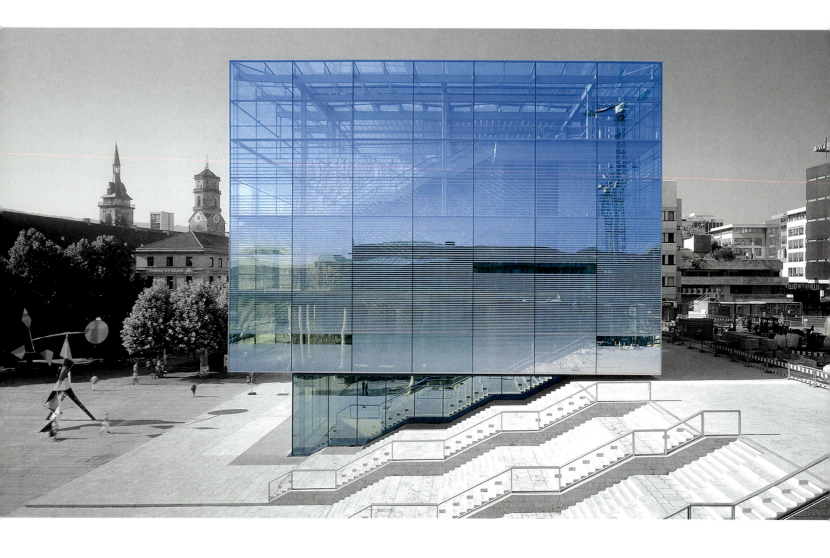

Readjusted Traffic Structure

Wiedergewinnung des Stadtraumes

Retrieving urban space

Project: Stuttgart Museum of Art   Location: Stuttgart | Architects: Hascher + Jehle Architektur, Berlin

Project: Museum of Fine Arts | Location: Leipzig | Architects: Hufnagel Pütz Rafaelian Architekten, Berlin

Visual Space Junction

49

Perforierter Kubus als Keim der Stadtverdichtung

Perforated cube as a seed for urban densification

Life's a Beach

Urbane Gravitationsfelder

Fields of urban gravitation

Urban beaches will be booming again this summer, and they'll certainly boom regardless of the temperature and also whether there is a river in the city or not. Seen from the beach the city becomes the sea; threatening, unpredictable, wild. This topos, temporary and fleeing though it may be, fits in with the pictures and images currently being used to promote cities. Cities like Hamburg, Frankfurt or Leipzig are presented as vital places offering one thing in particular alongside their monuments, high-tech locations and museums: a heightening of the senses. A lively night-life, creative scenes and a multi-cultural atmosphere seem to be the ticket that will admit them to the league that the big boys like London and New York play in. City tourism has become an adventure holiday in Germany too now. The monster that motivated critical voices 100 years ago to confront the urban swamp with neat-and-tidy garden cities is now part of the city marketing repertoire. Interpreting the city as the sea also means

Regina Bittner

Urbane Strände werden auch in diesem Sommer wieder Hochkonjunktur haben, und das sicherlich ungeachtet der Temperaturen und auch unabhängig von der Tatsache, ob es einen Fluss in der Stadt gibt oder nicht. Vom Strand aus betrachtet wird die Stadt zum Meer, bedrohlich, unberechenbar, wild. Dieser Topos, so temporär und flüchtig er auch sein mag, korrespondiert mit Bildern und Images, mit denen neuerdings Städte angeboten werden. Städte wie Hamburg, Frankfurt oder Leipzig werden als vitale Orte präsentiert, die neben ihren Denkmälern, Hightech-Standorten und Museen vor allem eines bieten: Sinnessteigerung. Ein vitales Nachtleben, kreative Szenen und ein multikulturelles Flair zu haben, scheint die Eintrittskarte für die Liga zu sein, in der auch Metropolen wie London und New York spielen.

understanding it as a phenomenon in a state of constant change. Berlin is one of the large German cities whose way of presenting itself, from marketing strategies to scientific analysis, has one outstanding characteristic: change.

Has this unmanageable quality of cities, something that used to feature in discussions about the city in crisis years ago, been reassessed and declared an attraction? Or was this talk motivated by the failure of a specific urban model: the ordered urban model of Fordism, which defined the city as a clearly ordered system. Town planning, architecture and regional planning developed a regulated institutionalised urban space. The city was conceived as a container with a clear pattern of order imposed on it: an ordered network of connections consisting of centre, periphery and regional involvements. The urban landscape was a rhythmic sequence of owner-occupied hotch-potch with its attendant gender-specific infrastructures and social systems, grouped around town centres that had been swept completely clean. But despite a suburbanisation in the form of urban islands of staged urban quality and gigantic green-field logistics and service sites, the city is now once more being offered in pictures and discourses as the preferred space for living together as social beings and as a strategic location for innovation.

Cities have also become the crystallisation points for population movement and for action options within the spectrum of social transformation from demographic change to trans-national migration: society is getting older, people are moving into cities because medical care, shopping, social life and culture can be reached within in the smallest possible area and by travelling the shortest possible distance. Families move into cities because women and men have jobs, but they can have children as well. Young creative service providers, artists and academics have been in the cities for a long time because they are the focus for international scenes and the communications and connections that they need for their careers. And migrants want to be in cities because that's where the trans-national networks offering temporary work have materialised; in barber's shops, restaurants and kiosks.

But what kind of urban model are we looking at here? People do not move into cities because they are defined by a specific territory as an accumulation of buildings, streets, institutions, cultural practices and symbolic aspects, or because they want to live in a specific locality associated with a specific way of life. The fact is that in the post-industrial urban landscape the distinction between town and country has become obsolete. Urban quality has no location and is subject-bound, in short it is a lifestyle pattern. (1)

So if urban quality is available anywhere, why should anyone move into a city? In the case of the city we are talking about, the city that is becoming attractive again, it is not about a uniform structure any more, but about a highly differentiated space: a dynamic and acentric heterogeneous plural network in motion made up of structures with different ranges and fragments of varying origin. Today cities are tied into complex spatial contexts that point out beyond their physical confines. City and space are increasingly out of tune with each other.

In this respect, the city as the sea is a metaphor for which we can find parallels in urban-theoretical discussions about the city as an "open system", as a dynamic structure. Urban beaches are places that offer an image of urban change expressed through the image of the sea. Thus they can be considered exemplary for the specific meaning of images in the context of the increasing invisibility of the

Städtetourismus ist auch in Deutschland inzwischen ein Erlebnisangebot. Der Moloch, der noch 100 Jahre zuvor die Großstadtkritik motivierte, dem urbanen Sumpf mit züchtigen Gartenstädten zu begegnen, gehört heute zum Repertoire des Stadtmarketing.

Die Stadt als Meer zu lesen, heißt auch, Stadt als ein in ständigem Wandel begriffenes Phänomen zu begreifen. Berlin gehört zu den Metropolen in Deutschland, deren Selbstdarstellung von Marketingstrategien bis zu wissenschaftlichen Analysen ein herausragendes Merkmal aufweist: Und das ist der Wandel.

Ist die Unübersichtlichkeit der Städte – eine Figur, die noch vor Jahren das Reden über die Krise der Stadt bestimmt hat – umgewertet worden in eine Attraktion?

Oder war diese Rede eher vom Scheitern eines spezifischen Stadtmodells motiviert: Das geordnete Stadtmodell des Fordismus, mit dem die Stadt als System mit klarer Ordnung beschrieben wurde. Stadtplanung, Architektur und Raumplanung entwickelten einen geregelten institutionalisierten städtischen Raum. Die Stadt wurde als Behälter konzipiert, dem ein klares Ordnungsmuster auferlegt war: Ein geordnetes Beziehungsgeflecht – bestehend aus Zentrum, Peripherie und regionalen Einbindungen. Die Stadtlandschaft setzte sich aus der rhythmischen Abfolge von endlosem Eigenheimbrei mit dazugehöriger genderspezifischer Infra- und Sozialstruktur sowie leergefegten Innenstädten zusammen. Aber ungeachtet der Fortsetzung der Suburbanisierung mit anderen Mitteln in Gestalt von urbanen Inseln inszenierter Urbanität und riesigen Logistik- und Dienstleistungsarealen auf der grünen Wiese ist es heute wieder die Stadt, die in den Bildern und Diskursen als der bevorzugte Raum gesellschaftlichen Zusammenlebens sowie als strategischer Ort von Innovation gehandelt wird. Mehr noch, es sind die Städte, die im Spektrum gesellschaftlicher Transformationen von demografischem Wandel bis transnationaler Migration zum Kristallisationspunkt von Wanderungsbewegungen und vielfältigen Handlungsoptionen werden:

Die Gesellschaft wird älter, die Leute ziehen in die Stadt, weil medizinische Versorgung, Einkaufen, Geselligkeit und Kultur hier auf engstem Raum und mit kurzen Wegen zu erreichen sind. Familien ziehen in die Stadt, weil Frauen und Männer berufstätig sein und trotzdem Kinder haben können. Junge Kreative, Dienstleister, Künstler und Akademiker sind schon lange in der Stadt, weil es der Ort ist, an dem sich die für ihre Karrieren notwendigen internationalen Szenen und kommunikativen Zusammenhänge bündeln. Und Migranten wollen in die Stadt, weil nur dort die transnationalen Netzwerke in Barbershops, Restaurants und Kiosken eingelagert sind, die temporäre Arbeitsmöglichkeiten bieten.

Aber um welches Stadtmodell handelt es sich dabei?

Die Leute ziehen nicht in eine Stadt, weil diese durch ein spezifisches Territorium als Ansammlung von Bauten, Straßen, Institutionen, kulturellen Praktiken und Symbolisierungen definiert ist bzw. weil sie in einer besonderen Lokalität mit spezifischer Lebensweise leben wollen. Denn in der postindustriellen Stadtlandschaft ist die Unterscheidung zwischen Stadt und Land obsolet geworden, Urbanität ist ortlos und subjektgebunden, kurzum ein Lebensstilmuster. (1)

Wenn Urbanität überall zu haben ist, warum sollte man also in die Stadt ziehen?

Bei der Stadt, von der die Rede ist und die zum erneuten Anziehungspunkt wird, handelt es sich nicht mehr um ein einheitliches Gebilde, sondern um einen vielfältig differenzierten Raum: Ein dynamisches und azentrisches, heterogenes, plurales Netz in Bewegung, das sich aus Strukturen unter-

1) Cf. authors including Walter Siebel: Die europäische Stadt, Frankfurt am Main 2004

(1) vgl. u.a. Walter Siebel: Die europäische Stadt, Frankfurt am Main 2004

city. Images make a major contribution to organizing and regulating post-industrial urban change processes. Secondly these facilities can be understood as topoi of an urban model that is linked with particular demands made on its occupants' behaviour. Here the extent to which the city as the sea becomes a projection screen for designs for a creative entrepreneurial city will also be addressed. Thirdly this essay considers the question of cities' permanent convertibility, one with urban beach image overtones – of the city as the sea.

URBAN IMAGES

The post-industrial structural transformation of urban quality is accompanied by a paradox. On the one hand, increasing mobility, migration movements, out-sourcing production and services and global popular cultures have meant that urban metropolises have become increasingly ambiguous. Wildly proliferating structures with qualities that are not easy to define precisely have come into being. Consequently they are undergoing a visibility crisis. The post-industrial city is an arrangement that is becoming increasingly dispersed and polycentric, and its undefinable qualities need to hit back by finding images that help discern a social-spatial context.

On the other hand, relativisation of place in a spirit of unambiguous recognisability results in intensive image production, and this is essentially a direct reaction to the decreasing importance of physical space. It is not just that images can be used to make lost spatial connections recognisable from the outside inwards, as it were, but that they are aiming outwards in order to secure the attention of international investors, potential occupants and tourists for the city. At the same time, mass international distribution of city images now has a massive influence on the way cities are planned, regulated and designed, so anything now seen as urban relates, to a large extent, to media-distributed ideas about density and urban quality. This is intensified by the fact that globally active companies and international chains place themselves in cities, thus contributing to an international levelling and standardization of urban images. Shopping malls, retail worlds and pleasure parks are spatial typologies that organize urban space through images. Here we are dealing with thematic worlds that have led firstly to greater importance for symbolic and cultural resources in the post-industrial city, and secondly are increasingly linked with the fact that urban space is being tailored to suit consumer practices. Thematic worlds are theatrical structures that lay the transformation of cities open to experience.

These are scenarios of consumption based on experience: a living city is put on show, though possibly in one dimension only. Cultural resources are mobilised, partly from the city's or the region's historical repertoire, and are now lending local colour to the shopping experience. But historical set-pieces are not just window-dressing for themed worlds; local history and local culture are generally important for making cities visible. Cities try to put their unmistakable image together by mixing "Appelwoi" (the local cider) and "Mainhatten" in Frankfurt or "August the Strong" and "glass manufacture" in Dresden. Particularly glorious episodes are selectively picked out from the city's history in order to design specific futures. Historical reconstructions in the form of the Stadtschloss in Berlin or the timber-frame houses in Frankfurt are not just aimed at streams of tourists, political elites use them as well; it is about images that make collective identifications of urban space possible, a strategy that is brought even more strongly into play the more confusing and polarized the city's social and spatial connections become. This makes it possible to satisfy the local population's need to find their bearings for living in a particular world, needs that arise from the everyday urban impositions

schiedlicher Reichweite und Fragmenten unterschiedlichsten Ursprungs zusammensetzt. Städte sind heute in komplexe räumliche Zusammenhänge eingebunden, die über den physischen Raum hinausweisen. Stadt und Raum stimmen immer weniger überein.

Die Stadt als Meer ist insofern eine Metapher, zu der sich Parallelen in stadttheoretischen Diskursen zur Stadt als „open system", als dynamisches Gebilde finden lassen. Urbane Strände sind Orte, von denen aus der städtische Wandel im Bild vom Meer zur Anschauung kommt. Sie können damit erstens als exemplarisch gelten für die spezifische Bedeutung von Bildern im Kontext der zunehmenden Unsichtbarkeit der Stadt. Bilder tragen wesentlich dazu bei, postindustrielle urbane Wandlungsprozesse zu organisieren und zu regulieren. Und zweitens können diese Einrichtungen als Topoi eines Stadtmodells verstanden werden, das mit besonderen Verhaltensanforderungen an seine Bewohner verkoppelt ist. Inwiefern die Stadt als Meer zur Projektionsfläche von Entwürfen einer kreativen, unternehmerischen Stadt wird, soll dabei diskutiert werden. Drittens setzt sich der Beitrag mit der Frage nach den Grenzen der permanenten Konvertierbarkeit von Städten auseinander, was in dem Bild vom urbanen Strand, der Stadt als Meer mitschwingt.

STADTBILDER

Der postindustrielle Strukturwandel des Städtischen ist von einem Paradoxon begleitet. Einerseits haben zunehmende Mobilität, Wanderungsbewegungen, Auslagerung von Produktion und Dienstleistungen und globale Populärkultur dazu geführt, dass städtische Metropolen immer uneindeutiger werden. Wuchernde Gebilde mit unklaren Qualitäten sind entstanden. Eine Krise ihrer Sichtbarkeit ist die Folge. Die postindustrielle Stadt ist eine immer disperser und polyzentrischer werdende Anordnung, deren undefinierbare Eigenschaften im Gegenzug Bilder bedürfen, um einen sozialräumlichen Zusammenhang zu erkennen.

Die Relativierung des Ortes im Sinne von eindeutiger Erkennbarkeit hat auf der anderen Seite eine intensive Bildproduktion zur Folge, die im Grunde eine direkte Reaktion auf die abnehmende Bedeutung des physischen Raumes ist.

Über Bilder können nicht nur verloren gegangene räumliche Zusammenhänge quasi nach innen erkennbar gemacht werden, sie zielen vor allem nach außen, um der Stadt einen Platz in der Aufmerksamkeit internationaler Investoren, potenzieller Einwohner und Touristen zu sichern. Zugleich hat die massenhafte internationale Verbreitung der Bilder von Städten heute massiven Einfluss darauf, wie Städte geplant, reguliert und gestaltet werden. Was heute als urban empfunden wird, hat insofern viel mit medial verbreiteten Dichte- und Urbanitätsvorstellungen zu tun. Verschärfend kommt hinzu, dass es weltweit agierende Firmen und internationale Ketten sind, die sich in den Städten platzieren. Sie tragen damit zu einer internationalen Nivellierung und Normalisierung von Stadtbildern bei. Shoppingmalls, Einkaufswelten und Vergnügungsparks sind Raumtypologien, die den städtischen Raum über Bilder organisieren. Es handelt sich dabei um Themenwelten, die in der postindustriellen Stadt zum einen zum Bedeutungszuwachs symbolischer und kultureller Ressourcen geführt haben, die zum anderen mehr und mehr mit einer Zuschneidung des städtischen Raumes auf Konsumpraktiken verbunden sind. Themenwelten sind bühnenhafte Anordnungen, in der die Transformation der Städte erlebbar wird. Es handelt sich um Szenerien eines erfahrungsbasierten Konsums, in denen, wie eindimensional auch immer, eine lebendige Stadt inszeniert wird. Kulturelle Ressourcen werden dabei mobilisiert, die zum Teil aus dem Repertoire der Geschichte der Stadt bzw. Region stammen und nun das Einkaufserlebnis lokal kolorieren. Aber historische Versatzstücke dienen nicht nur der Bühnenausstattung der Themenwelten; lokale Geschichte und Kultur ist insgesamt ein wichtiger Einsatz bei der Sichtbarmachung von Städten. Es ist die Mischung aus „Appelwoi" und „Mainhattan" in Frankfurt, aus „August dem Starken" und „Gläserner Manufaktur" in Dresden, aus dem Städte ihr unverwechselbares Image versuchen herzustellen. Selektiv werden besondere, nämlich ruhmreiche Ausschnitte der Geschichte der Stadt herausgegriffen um damit spezifische Zukünfte zu entwerfen. Historische Rekonstruktionen in Gestalt des Stadtschlosses

associated with structural change. Certain historical set-pieces are activated in order to justify notified breaks with local historical lines of tradition.

Festivals and events plays just as large a part here as iconic or historicising architecture and urban designs. Potsdamer Platz draws its particular symbolic content precisely from the fact that it invokes 1920s Berlin: Berlin was presenting itself as "the most modern city in the world" even then. This self-image as a metropolis of European progress whose ultra-rapid growth and speedy rise up the league table of world cities was precisely what allowed its lack of scepticism about modernity - even though it was so close to Paris. This image was activated particularly after 1990 in the iconography of Potsdamer Platz in order to symbolically underpin Berlin's rise as an international services metropolis. (2) The extent to which iconic architecture can convey urban structural change can also be discussed when taking the Federal Environment Office in Dessau as an example. Can one of the "most innovative buildings of the 21st century" provide an image for the future for one of the East German cities that has been hardest hit by de-industrialisation and thus prolong the Modernist tradition of the 1920s into the present?

URBAN SCENES

Urban beaches do not just provide images, they are also "locations", temporary places representing the nodes within the network-like and flexible spatial practices of specific urban milieus, whose innovative entrepreneurial practices now operate as trademarks of cities' creativity, dynamism and innovative ability. The existence of such locations in Berlin, for example, derives from the presence of a "creative class" in the form of artists, culture producers and academics, but also of financial service providers, business people and managers. Great metropolises all over the world are competing for their presence now. The creative classes do not light upon certain cities for their particular architectural features, local culture or existing infrastructure, nor for their economic prosperity. The only attractive feature is these cities' cultural heterogeneity, their ability to innovate and be tolerant. (3) Berlin provides an excellent example of the fact that the innovation potential of these special features is linked with the transformation potential of certain urban spaces. In the 1990s, the city was an Eldorado for spatial occupation practices because of its reunification-related open structure. The creatives accepted the intermediate state of locations that had not yet been evaluated, and generated a communicative practice emphasizing the potentiality of these empty spaces. "The stress is shifting to the city in the subjunctive, to the city of the conditional form." (4) Cultural entrepreneurs, architects, designers and artists used a variety of strategies to compete for symbolic attention: offices communicated via parties or operated by intervening in public matters, thus inventing their own commissions, they were catalysts, agents and designers of urban change, all in one. Their practices were essentially performance-related, and often described as a new situationism; they also pointed to the fact that the city cannot be presented as a uniform structure. Their work was usually site-

in Berlin oder der Fachwerkhäuser in Frankfurt haben nicht nur die Touristenströme im Auge, politische Eliten zielen damit auch nach innen; es geht um Bilder, die kollektive stadträumliche Identifikationen ermöglichen – eine Strategie, die umso stärker mobilisiert wird, je unübersichtlicher und polarisierter die sozialräumlichen Zusammenhänge der Stadt werden. Damit können lebensweltliche Orientierungsbedürfnisse befriedigt werden, die aus den mit dem Strukturwandel verknüpften Zumutungen im städtischen Alltag erwachsen. Bestimmte historische Versatzstücke werden aktiviert, um avisierte Umbrüche mit lokalen historischen Traditionslinien zu begründen.

Festivals und Events spielen dabei eine ebenso große Rolle wie ikonische bzw. historisierende Architekturen und Stadtgestaltungen. Der Potsdamer Platz bezieht seinen besonderen symbolischen Gehalt gerade aus der Referenz zu dem Berlin der 20er Jahre des letzten Jahrhunderts: Berlin stellte sich damals schon als „modernste Stadt der Welt" aus. Dieses Selbstbild als Metropole des Fortschritts in Europa, deren rasantes Wachstum und schneller Aufstieg in die Liga der Weltstädte gerade seine mangelnde Modernitätsskepsis – auch in Angrenzung zu Paris – erlaubte, wurde nach 1990 insbesondere in der Ikonografie des Potsdamer Platzes aktiviert, um den Aufstieg Berlins als internationale Dienstleistungsmetropole symbolisch zu untermauern. (2) Wieweit ikonische Architekturen den städtischen Strukturwandel vermitteln können, lässt sich auch am Umweltbundesamt in Dessau diskutieren. Kann einer der „innovativsten Bauten des 21.Jahrhunderts" ein Bild für die Zukunft einer von Deindustrialisierung am meisten betroffenen Städte in Ostdeutschland liefern und damit die Modernetradition der 20er Jahre in die Gegenwart verlängern?

STADTSZENEN

Urbane Strände liefern nicht nur Bilder, sie sind auch „Locations": Temporäre Orte, die Knoten innerhalb der netzartigen und flexiblen Raumpraktiken von spezifischen städtischen Milieus darstellen, deren innovative unternehmerische Praktiken heute als Markenzeichen der Kreativität, Dynamik und Innovationsfähigkeit von Städten firmieren. Die Existenz solcher Locations z.B. in Berlin ist auf die Anwesenheit einer „kreativen Klasse" in Gestalt von Künstlern, Kulturproduzenten, Akademikern aber auch Finanzdienstleistern, Geschäftsleuten und Managern zurückführen. Um deren Präsenz konkurrieren mittlerweile die großen Metropolen rund um den Globus. Kreative Klassen suchen bestimmte Städte dabei weder um ihrer baulichen Besonderheiten, lokalen Kultur oder vorhandenen Infrastruktur willen auf noch aufgrund ihrer ökonomischen Prosperität. Anziehend allein ist die kulturelle Heterogenität, Innovationsfähigkeit und Toleranz dieser Städte. (3) Dass das Innovationspotenzial dieser besonderen Akteure in Zusammenhang mit dem Transformationspotenzial bestimmter städtischer Räume steht, ließ sich exemplarisch in Berlin beobachten. In den 90er Jahren bot die Stadt mit ihrer vereinigungsbedingt offenen Struktur für die räumlichen Besetzungspraktiken dieser Akteure ein Eldorado. Aus dem Zwischenzustand dieser noch nicht verwerteten Orte generierten sie eine kommunikative Praxis, die die Potenzialität dieser Leerräume betonte. „Der Akzent verschiebt sich auf die Stadt im Konjunktiv, auf die Stadt in der Möglichkeitsform." (4) Kulturunternehmer, Architekten, Designer und Künstler konkurrierten um symbolische Aufmerksamkeit mit unterschiedlichen Strategien: Büros kommunizierten über Parties oder agierten mit Interventionen in der städtischen Öffentlichkeit und erfanden dabei ihre eigenen Aufträge: Sie waren Katalysatoren, Agenten und Gestalter des urbanen Wandels in einem. Ihre eher performativen Praktiken, die oft als neuer Situationismus bezeichnet

53

2) Michael Makropoulus/Joachim Fischer (ed.): Potsdamer Platz Soziologische Theorien zu einem Ort der Moderne, Munich 2004
3) Richard Florida: Cities and the Creative Class, New York 2005
4) Nikolaus Kuhnert/Susanne Schindler: "Off-Architektur", in: archplus 166 "Off Architektur", Oktober 2003, p. 14

2) Michael Makropoulus/Joachim Fischer (Hg.): Potsdamer Platz. Soziologische Theorien zu einem Ort der Moderne, München 2004
3) Richard Florida: Cities and the Creative Class, New York 2005
4) Nikolaus Kuhnert/Susanne Schindler: „Off-Architektur", in: archplus 166 „Off Architektur", Oktober 2003, S.14

specific, and they preferred a subjective approach to the city based on the impossibility of objectifying space production or space interpretation. These protagonist groups are also tied into specific networks with international connections, permitting successful transfer of their products, services and information between cities. This spatial capital is one of their real resources, along with knowledge and creativity.

The special characteristic of "world cities" is that cultural locations, materials and images are produced here that not only come from the city itself, but resonate beyond it. (5) To this extent beaches are not only places in the city, but also point well beyond Berlin's physical confines, locating it in a "new geography of creativity". At the same time this creative city demands that its protagonists are actively involved in transforming it. The Swedish anthropologist Ulf Hannerz talks of a "working out culture" that is not addressing business people, creative people and knowledge producers alone.

The economic practices of migrants with their trans-national networks also have their cultural value enhanced in this context. The rise of protagonist groups like migrants, culture producers and artists is linked with the post-industrial deregulation of the city: city-dwellers are increasingly seen and promoted as the city's entrepreneurs. Further, the transformation into an entrepreneurial city is accompanied by "lining up" city-dwellers who see themselves as entrepreneurial protagonists. (6) In this respect the activities of the likes of Raumlabor, Urban Catalyst or Raumtaktik – to name but a few – with their parties, exhibitions and projects operate in the field of tension between the demands of transformation and scope for action in the entrepreneurial city. These players' logic suggests that the city is a space of boundless possibilities and that this space is linked with a permanent challenge to be personally active. Like the sea viewed from the beach, that is always tempting us to set out for new and faraway shores, however risky and insecure they may be.

LIMITED CONVERTIBILITY

Beaches are oases in a city that is experienced as chaotic and uncontrollable. Here the city is laid open to contemplation, here you can take a break from the everyday behavioural impositions of personal urban enterprise. Would it not be possible to see urban beaches as spatial figures in this respect, figures in which images, fantasies and ways of dealing with people and things come together with the post-industrial city?

But the boom in urban beaches has nothing to do with the presence of creative urbanites whose lives are conducted in a way that is mainly determinant, in Max Weber's sense. Urban beaches are signatures, conventional mapping symbols indicating membership of a "geography of creativity" and in this respect a good example of Berlin's relocation on the global map. Are these not the beginnings of a new typology for globally distributed, staged urban quality, to be found in London and Zurich as well? Don't these "locations", temporary and versatile as they are, reflect the pictures and images of media-distributed ideas of urban life in the post-industrial metropolis?

So are they in fact nothing but "touch down areas for globally circulating artefacts"? (7) It is worth drawing a German/German comparison to answer this question. The planning authorities in Mannheim have started adapting the banks of the Rhine to fashionable trends. There is very little unemployment here, and young people in particular seem to lack the mapping symbols of a risky "working out culture", despite its polarizing effects. In Berlin the beaches were elements of the biotope, of the "scene" that had come into

werden, weisen auch auf die Nicht-Repräsentierbarkeit der Stadt als einheitliches Gebilde hin. In zumeist ortsbezogenen Arbeiten bevorzugen sie einen subjektiven Zugang zur Stadt, der die Unmöglichkeit einer objektivierten Raumproduktion und Raumdeutung zum Thema hat.

Dabei sind diese Akteursgruppen eingebunden in spezifische Netzwerke internationaler Reichweite, die den erfolgreichen Transfer ihrer Produkte, Dienstleistungen und Informationen zwischen Städten erlauben. Dieses Raumkapital gehört neben Wissen und Kreativität zu ihrer eigentlichen Ressource. Es ist das besondere Charakteristikum so genannter „world cities", dass hier kulturelle Orte, Materialien und Bilder produziert werden, die zwar aus der jeweiligen Stadt kommen, aber vor allem über sie hinaus strahlen. (5) Insofern sind die Strände zwar Orte in der Stadt, die aber zugleich weit über den physischen Raum Berlins hinausweisen bzw. diesen in einer „new geography of creativity" verorten. Zugleich ist aber in diese creative city die Anforderung an die Akteure eingebaut, sich aktiv an der Transformation dieser Stadt zu beteiligen. Der schwedische Anthropologe Ulf Hannerz spricht von einer „working out culture" , die nicht nur an Geschäftsleute, Kreative und Wissensproduzenten adressiert ist. Auch die ökonomischen Praktiken von Migranten mit ihren transnationalen Netzwerken erleben in diesem Kontext eine kulturelle Aufwertung. Der Aufstieg von den genannten Akteursgruppen, wie Migranten, Kulturproduzenten und Künstlern steht in Zusammenhang mit der postindustriellen Deregulierung der Stadt: Stadtbewohner werden dabei zunehmend als Unternehmer der Stadt gedacht und gefordert. Mehr noch, die Transformation zur unternehmerischen Stadt ist von einer „Formierung von Stadtbewohnern begleitet, die sich als unternehmerische Akteure verstehen". (6) Insofern bewegen sich die Aktivitäten von raumlabor, Urban Catalysts oder raumtaktik mit ihren Parties, Ausstellungen und Projekten – um nur einige zu nennen – in dem Spannungsfeld zwischen Transformationsanforderungen und Handlungsspielräumen in der unternehmerischen Stadt.

In der Logik dieser Akteure ist die Stadt auf der einen Seite ein grenzenloser Möglichkeitsraum, der aber auf der anderen Seite mit der permanenten Aufforderung zur Selbstaktivität verkoppelt ist. Wie das Meer, das vom Strand aus gesehen immer wieder zum Aufbruch zu neuen Ufern lockt, so unsicher und riskant das auch sein mag?

BEGRENZTE KONVERTIERBARKEIT

Strände sind Oasen in einer als chaotisch und unkontrollierbar erlebten Stadt. Hier wird die Stadt zur Anschauung gebracht, hier lässt sich von den alltäglichen Verhaltenszumutungen des städtischen Selbstunternehmertums ausruhen. Könnten Urbane Strände nicht insofern als räumliche Figuren verstanden werden, in denen sich die Bilder, Imaginationen und Umgangsweisen mit der postindustriellen Stadt bündeln?

Die Konjunktur urbaner Strände hat aber nicht nur mit der Anwesenheit kreativer Urbaniten zu tun, deren Lebensführung im Sinne von Max Weber wenigstens vornehmlich bestimmend geworden ist. Urbane Strände sind Signaturen für die Zugehörigkeit zu einer „Geography of creativity" und sind insofern ein gutes Beispiel für die Neuverortung Berlins auf der globalen Landkarte. Formiert sich hier nicht eine neue Typologie global verbreiteter inszenierter Urbanität, die auch in London und Zürich zu finden ist? Folgen diese „Locations", so temporär und wandelbar sie sind, nicht doch den Bildern und Images medial verbreiteter Vorstellung vom urbanen Leben in der postindustriellen Metropole?

Stellen sie also nur „touch down areas für global zirkulierende Artefacte" dar? (7) Um diese Frage zu beantworten, lohnt sich ein innerdeutscher Vergleich. In Mannheim bemüht sich inzwischen das Stadtplanungsamt, das Rheinufer modischen Trends anzupassen. Hier, wo die Arbeitslosigkeit verschwindend gering ist, scheinen vor allem junge Leute die Signaturen einer risikoreichen „working out culture", auch mit ihren sozial polarisierenden Effekten zu vermissen. In Berlin waren die Strände Elemente des Biotops, der „Szene", die im Zuge von Wiedervereinigung, postindustriellem Strukturwandel und Hauptstadtwerdung entstanden war. Die Stadt schien für einen kurzen historischen Moment einen grenzenlosen Möglichkeitsraum für unterschiedlichste Formen prekären Unternehmertums zu bieten, ja forderte

being in the course of reunification, post-industrial transformation and becoming the capital. For a short historical moment the city seemed to be able to offer boundless scope and possibilities for a whole variety of forms of precarious entrepreneurialism, indeed it demanded them. But the beaches in Dresden are not such scenes of urban "hip-ness". River and city are part of Dresden people's collective memory, not just as a picture that the newly rebuilt Frauenkirche has completed again, but as in the everyday practice of inline skating, picnics and beer gardens. The different contexts in which the fashion for beaches has condensed itself indicate the boundaries of each city's convertibility. If urban beaches are spatial manifestations of post-industrial urbanisation, then it is always the local contexts that first make them into meaningful places for city-dwellers. Here we are not talking about dominant protagonists working as producers to create a special atmosphere for the city in question. It is "the way a city behaves" that makes a crucial contribution to the direction of city transformations. Thus we are talking about the disposition of a city, asserting "that certain developments suggest themselves more readily to cities, on the grounds of biographical consolidation, and others feel more remote." (8) The local quality of a city can be understood less as a closed spatial unit of physical territory and more as a place of local community with an independent culture in each case. New modes for fixing location other than direct local anchoring can be observed in cities. Local quality means something much more like a special way of being structured, a specific way of having come into being that contributes to the fact that we still seek out cities for their smells, moods and sensual realities.

Possibly the sea metaphor is misleading in this respect. Cities are not faceless indeterminate surfaces resolving into a universal structure of currents, they are open systems, each structured in a particular way, made up of spatial relations with widely differing scope. It is not necessary to have historicising ground plans or façade designs to create cities as places that are meaningfully organized spatial contexts for urban life together. They are much more like relational places, "meeting places", in which local presences and multiple positions vis-à-vis other places are superimposed. Perhaps it is precisely this multi-positional quality that presents such a challenge to creating urban architectures today. The new Leipzig Museum of Fine Art is an example of this location production strategy. The urban space cuts through this building in a complex fashion. The different floors are like stages opening on to the city, and at the same time exhibiting it and thus making it possible to perceive it visually. Quite different views of Leipzig are available from here, from the Platte to the Markt to the heavens. All kinds of spatial connections come into being and seem to come together in the museum like an "urban spatial node". The time-space connections of the apparently disordered entanglement of the city can be made out from here and it is a soothing sight.

dieses heraus. In Dresden hingegen sind Strände weniger Schauplätze urbaner „hippness". Fluss und Stadt gehören im kollektiven Gedächtnis der Stadtbewohner zusammen, nicht nur als Bild, das durch die Frauenkirche wieder komplettiert wurde, sondern als alltägliche Praxis von Inlineskating, Picknick bis Biergarten.

55

Die unterschiedlichen Kontexte, in die die Strandmode eingelagert ist, deuten auf die Grenzen der Konvertierbarkeit von Städten. Wenn es sich bei urbanen Stränden also um räumliche Manifestationen postindustrieller Urbanisierung handelt, dann sind es die jeweils lokalen Kontexte, die diese erst zu bedeutungsvollen Orten für die Stadtbewohner machen. Dabei geht es nicht nur um die dominanten Akteure, die als Produzenten eine besondere Atmosphäre der jeweiligen Stadt herstellen. Sondern es ist „die Art und Weise, wie sich eine Stadt verhält", die entscheidend dazu beiträgt, in welche Richtung Städte sich transformieren. Die Rede ist deshalb inzwischen vom Habitus einer Stadt, womit behauptet wird, „dass auch Städten aufgrund biografischer Verfestigung bestimmte Entwicklungslinien näher liegen, andere ferner stehen." (8) Das Lokale einer Stadt wäre dabei weniger als eine geschlossene räumliche Einheit von physischem Territorium, lokaler Gemeinschaft mit jeweils eigenständiger Kultur zu verstehen. Anstelle der Unmittelbarkeit lokaler Verankerung sind neue Modi der Verortung in der Stadt zu beobachten. Lokalität meint eher eine besondere Strukturiertheit, eine spezifische Art von Gewordensein, die dazu beiträgt, dass wir Städte immer noch um ihrer Gerüche, Stimmungen und sinnlichen Wirklichkeiten willen aufsuchen.

Insofern ist vielleicht die Metapher vom Meer irreführend. Denn Städte sind keine gesichtslosen, wabernden Flächen, die in einer universellen Struktur von Strömen aufgehen. Gleichwohl sind sie offene Systeme, die auf jeweils besondere Weise strukturiert sind und die sich aus räumlichen Relationen ganz unterschiedlicher Reichweite zusammensetzen. Um Städte als Orte, also als sinnhaft organisierte räumliche Zusammenhänge urbanen Zusammenlebens zu gestalten, braucht es keine historisierenden Grundrisse oder Fassadengestaltungen. Vielmehr sind es relationale Orte, „meeting places", in dem sich lokale Präsenzen, multiple Positionierungen gegenüber anderen Orten und stadträumliche Zusammenhänge überlagern. Vielleicht stellt gerade diese Multipositionalität für die Gestaltung urbaner Architekturen heute eine Herausforderung dar. Beispielhaft für solche eine Strategie der Ortsproduktion kann das Leipziger Museum für Bildende Künste gelten. Der städtische Raum durchschneidet dieses Gebäude auf vielschichtige Weise. Die Geschosse sind wie Bühnen, die sich zur Stadt öffnen und diese zugleich ausstellen und so zur Anschauung bringen. Von hier aus hat man ganz unterschiedliche Perspektiven auf Leipzig, von der Platte über den Markt bis zum Himmel. Mannigfaltige räumliche Beziehungen stellen sich her und scheinen sich im Museum wie in einem „urbanen Raumknoten" zu bündeln. Von hier aus lassen sich die zeiträumlichen Zusammenhänge des scheinbar ungeordneten Geflechts Stadt erkennen; ein beruhigender Anblick.

5) Cf. Ulf Hannerz: "Thinking about Culture in Cities", in: Leon Deben et.al. (eds.): Understanding Amsterdam. Essays on Economic Vitality, City Life and Urban Form, Amsterdam 2000. pp. 161-178
6) Cf. Alexa Färber: "Vom Kommen, Bleiben und Gehen", in: Hotel Berlin. Formen urbaner Mobilität und Verortung, Ethnografische und Ethnologische Beiträge issue 37/2005 p. 11
7) Helmut Berking/Martina Löw: "Über Städte als Wissensobjekt der Soziologie", in: Helmut Berking/Martina Löw (eds.): Die Wirklichkeit der Städte, Baden Baden 2005, p. 18
8) Rolf Lindner: "Urban Anthropology", in: Helmut Berking, Martina Löw (eds.), Die Wirklichkeit der Städte, Baden Baden 2005, p. 64

5) vgl. Ulf Hannerz: „Thinking about Culture in Cities", in: Leon Deben et.al. (eds.), Understanding Amsterdam. Essays on Economic Vitality, City Life and Urban Form, Amsterdam 2000, S. 161-178
6) vgl. Alexa Färber: „Vom Kommen, Bleiben und Gehen", in: Hotel Berlin. Formen urbaner Mobilität und Verortung, Ethnografische und Ethnologische Beiträge Heft 37/2005, S. 11
7) Helmut Berking, Martina Löw: „Über Städte als Wissensobjekt der Soziologie", in: Helmut Berking, Martina Löw (Hrsg.): Die Wirklichkeit der Städte, Baden Baden 2005, S. 18
8) Rolf Lindner: „Urban Anthropology", in: Helmut Berking, Martina Löw (Hrsg.): Die Wirklichkeit der Städte, Baden Baden 2005, S. 64

Horst W. J. Rittel, Melvin M. Weber

Dilemmas in a General Theory of Planning

Dilemmas in einer allgemeinen Theorie der Planung

Most research about creativity and problem-solving attitudes addresses "tame" problems because they are so easy to deal with and check. Regrettably, very little is known about tackling "wicked" problems, or about people who actually deal with them because "wicked" problems cannot be simulated experimentally. But all major planning problems are in fact wicked, and the first generation system theory approach is only suitable for more or less tame problems (e.g. for a quadratic equation or a material problem, a chemical analysis or an operations research optimisation problem).

Der Großteil der Forschung über Kreativität und Problemlösungsverhalten befasst sich mit „zahmen" Problemen, weil sie so einfach zu behandeln und zu kontrollieren sind. Bedauerlicherweise weiß man nur wenig über die Behandlung von „bösartigen" Problemen oder über die Personen, die sich eigentlich damit befassen, denn „bösartige" Probleme können nicht in einer Versuchsanordnung simuliert werden. Alle wesentlichen Planungsprobleme sind jedoch bösartig, und der systemtheoretische Ansatz der ersten Generation ist nur für mehr oder weniger zahme Probleme geeignet (z.B. für eine quadratische Gleichung oder ein Sachproblem, eine chemische Analyse oder ein Optimierungsproblem beim Operations Research).

01

ES GIBT KEINE DEFINITIVE FORMULIERUNG FÜR EIN BÖSARTIGES PROBLEM.

Um ein Problem ausreichend genau zu formulieren, müsste man dem Problemlöser alle Informationen zur Verfügung stellen, die er dazu benötigt. Sie wächst jedoch ständig und unvermutet im Verlauf des Lösungsprozesses und beeinflusst so die Problemsicht. Der wachsende Pluralismus der heutigen Öffentlichkeit führt dazu, dass verschiedene Gruppen von Individuen unterschiedliche Werte haben – was den einen zufriedenstellt, ist für den anderen schrecklich, was für den einen eine Problemlösung bedeutet, erzeugt für den anderen gerade das Problem.

THERE IS NO DEFINITIVE FORMULATION OF A WICKED PROBLEM.

To formulate a problem precisely enough, the problem-solver must have access to all the necessary information that he/she needs. But this information increases constantly and unexpectedly in the course of the solution process, and thus affects the approach to the problem. Growing pluralism of the contemporary public leads to a situation where different groups of individuals hold different values - something that satisfies one person my be abhorrent to another, and something that represents the solution of a problem for one is in fact a problem generator for another.

FÜR BÖSARTIGE PROBLEME GIBT ES KEINE „STOPP-REGEL".

Wenn man eine Gleichung hat und auf etwas wie x=y kommt, weiß man, dass man es geschafft hat. Aber bei einem bösartigen Problem ist das nicht so. Bei Planungsproblemen hört man auf, weil man keine Zeit, kein Geld oder keine Geduld mehr hat; aber das hat mit der Logik des Problems nichts zu tun; man kann immer versuchen, es besser zu machen.

02

WICKED PROBLEMS HAVE NO STOPPING RULE.

If you have an equation and reach a solution like x = y, you know that you have solved it. But this is not the case with a wicked problem. With planning problems, you stop because you have no more time, no more money or no more patience; but that has nothing to do with the logic of the problem; you can always try to do it better.

FÜR BÖSARTIGE PROBLEME IST RICHTIG/FALSCH NICHT ANWENDBAR.

Wenn für ein zahmes Problem eine Lösung gefunden ist, kann man sie überprüfen, ihr eines der Attribute „richtig" oder „falsch" zuweisen und Fehler oder Irrtümer genau bestimmen. Bei bösartigen Problemen ist das nicht so: Es gibt weder ein System von Kriterien noch Regeln, die einem sagen, was richtig oder falsch ist. Man kann nur sagen: „Ich glaube, das ist ganz gut, auch wenn du findest, es sei nicht so."

03

SOLUTIONS TO WICKED PROBLEMS ARE NOT TRUE-OR-FALSE, BUT GOOD-OR-BAD.

If a solution is found for a tame problem you can check it and classify it as "right" or "wrong", and mistakes or errors can be defined precisely. This is not the case with wicked problems: There is no system of criteria and there are no rules to tell you what is right or wrong. You can only say "I think that is quite good", even if you don't really think it is.

04 THERE IS NO IMMEDIATE AND NO ULTIMATE TEST OF A SOLUTION TO A WICKED PROBLEM; everything is possible, everything is a case of principles and imagination. For a tame problem there is a finite list of permissable operations. Take a chess problem, for example: there are twenty possible moves at the beginning of a game of chess.

BÖSARTIGE PROBLEME HABEN KEINE ERSCHÖPFENDE, AUFZÄHLBARE MENGE POTENZIELLER LÖSUNGEN; alles ist möglich, alles ist eine Sache der Grundsätze und der Fantasie. Für zahme Probleme gibt es eine erschöpfende Liste erlaubter Operationen. Nehmen wir als Beispiel ein Schachproblem: Zu Beginn eines Schachspiels hat man die Wahl zwischen 20 Zügen.

EVERY WICKED PROBLEM CAN BE CONSIDERED TO BE A SYMPTOM OF ANOTHER PROBLEM, and you can never be sure whether you are addressing the problem at the right level, because of course no one should try to cure symptoms, since curing symptoms can make the actual illness worse.

JEDES BÖSARTIGE PROBLEM KANN ALS SYMPTOM EINES ANDEREN PROBLEMS BETRACHTET WERDEN, und man ist nie sicher, dass man das Problem auf dem richtigen Niveau angeht, weil natürlich niemand versuchen sollte, Symptome zu kurieren, da das Kurieren von Symptomen die eigentliche Krankheit verschlimmern kann.

05

06 THERE IS NO INSTANT OR FINAL WAY OF EXAMINING A WICKED PROBLEM because every measure taken for solving the problem can have consequences over the course of time – next year perhaps there will be a different consequence, and this might affect how you assess your plan a great deal. In addition, the consequences of the solution might cause entirely undesirable reactions that outweigh the intended advantages, or those that have already been achieved.

FÜR EIN BÖSARTIGES PROBLEM GIBT ES WEDER EINE SOFORTIGE NOCH EINE ENDGÜLTIGE ÜBERPRÜFUNGSMÖGLICHKEIT, weil jede Maßnahme, die zur Lösung des Problems durchgeführt wurde, im Laufe der Zeit Konsequenzen haben kann – nächstes Jahr gibt es vielleicht eine andere Konsequenz, die sehr viel dazu beiträgt, wie Sie Ihren Plan beurteilen. Darüber hinaus werden die Konsequenzen der Lösung vielleicht völlig unerwünschte Reaktionen hervorrufen, die gegenüber den beabsichtigten oder bis dahin erreichten Vorteilen überwiegen.

07 EVERY SOLUTION TO A WICKED PROBLEM IS A "ONE-SHOT OPERATION". You cannot undo something that you have made in a first attempt; every attempt counts, and has considerable consequences. You can't build a factory, see how it works, knock it down again and keep rebuilding it until it works. This would influence many people's lives irreversibly, and large sums of money would have been spent. There is no trial and error. There is no way of experimenting with how to tackle wicked problems.

JEDE LÖSUNG EINES BÖSARTIGEN PROBLEMS IST EINE „ONE-SHOT-OPERATION". Man kann nicht ungeschehen machen, was man beim ersten Versuch gemacht hat; jeder Versuch zählt und hat Konsequenzen: Man kann nicht eine Fabrik bauen, schauen, wie sie funktioniert, sie wieder abreißen und immer wieder neu aufbauen, bis sie funktioniert. Das Leben vieler Menschen wird unumkehrbar beeinflusst und große Geldsummen werden ausgegeben. Es gibt nicht die Methode „Versuch und Irrtum". Es gibt kein Experimentieren beim Umgang mit bösartigen Problemen.

EVERY WICKED PROBLEM IS ESSENTIALLY UNIQUE. This is disturbing to the extent that it is not possible to learn for the next time; you cannot simply transfer successful solutions from the past to the future.

08 JEDES BÖSARTIGE PROBLEM IST WESENTLICH EINZIGARTIG. Das ist insofern störend, als man nicht für das nächste Mal lernen kann; man kann erfolgreiche Strategien nicht einfach aus der Vergangenheit in die Zukunft übertragen.

In contrast with the "tame problem solver", who may lose or win a chess game without being called to account or is allowed to set up a false hypothesis that someone else can refute, **THE WICKED PROBLEM-SOLVER HAS NO RIGHT TO BE WRONG:** He is responsible for his actions.

09

Im Gegensatz zum „Zahme-Probleme-Löser", der, ohne dafür zur Rechenschaft gezogen zu werden, ein Schachspiel verlieren oder gewinnen oder eine falsche Hypothese aufstellen darf, die von irgendjemandem widerlegt wird, HAT DER „BÖSARTIGE-PROBLEME-LÖSER" KEIN RECHT AUF IRRTUM. Er ist verantwortlich für das, was er tut.

Excerpts from / Auszüge aus: Policy Sciences 4 (1973), pp. 155-169, Elsevier Scientific Publishing Company, Amsterdam
On the planning crisis: System analysis of the "first and second generation", Bedriftsøkonomen Nr. 8/Oct. 1972

Hovering Habitats

Wohndecks über dem Flachdach

Flat roof pied à terre

Project: Urban Studio | Location: Cologne | Architects: Wiel Arets Architects, Maastricht, The Netherlands

Horst Opaschowski in conversation with Armand Gruentuch, Almut Ernst and Lukas Feireiss

Horst Opaschowski im Gespäch mit Armand Gruentuch, Almut Ernst und Lukas Feireiss

On the Future of the German City

Zur Zukunft der Stadt in Deutschland

Horst Opaschowski, Professor of Education at Hamburg University, is a prominent futurologist who has been advising politicians for decades. The sharp-penned opinion-maker and founder of the "B.A.T. Freizeitforschungsinsituts" (Leisure Research Institute) has also coined numerous terms for the discourse on mass-society in his theses on the subjects of immigration, work and unemployment. He sees the architects of the future increasingly in the roles of social service providers and integration politicians.

What does the city and life in the city mean to you?

For me, the city means short distances from home to work, and short waits for public transport which in turn means living in a central location. For me urban life at its best is something of a modern "Open, Sesame!" with shops, fashionable places and street cafés. But it also has cultural and educational institutions within easy reach and connections with social

infrastructures from tenant and debt-counselling to drug-advice centres. Only the city is capable of providing this diversity – today and even more so in the future. This is why I say: the future will be – urban!

You are regarded as one of the most credible and objective German future researchers and pioneering scientific thinkers. For over thirty years now, you have provoked people in business and industry, politics, scientific academia and the media with your theses and prognoses. In your book published in 2005, the title of which translates as 'Better life, more beautiful home-living? Life in the city of the future', you also address the future of German cities. What is the current state of cities in Germany? What socio-political, economic, historical and cultural challenges – pointing to both past and future – are they confronted with today?

Life in the city can also mean loneliness in the city – despite the telephone and other telecommunication devices. The urbanity of one group can

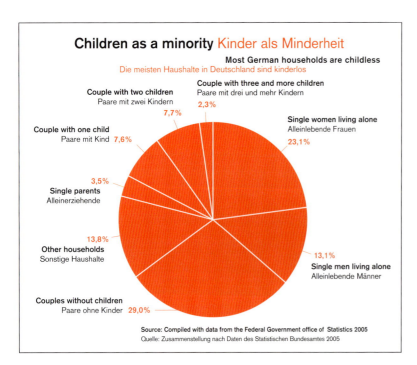

Children as a minority Kinder als Minderheit

Most German households are childless
Die meisten Haushalte in Deutschland sind kinderlos

Couple with three and more children
Paare mit drei und mehr Kindern
2,3%

Couple with two children
Paare mit zwei Kindern
7,7%

Couple with one child
Paare mit Kind **7,6%**

Single women living alone
Alleinlebende Frauen
23,1%

3,5%
Single parents
Alleinerziehende

13,8%
Other households
Sonstige Haushalte

13,1%
Single men living alone
Alleinlebende Männer

Couples without children
Paare ohne Kinder **29,0%**

Source: Compiled with data from the Federal Government office of Statistics 2005
Quelle: Zusammenstellung nach Daten des Statistischen Bundesamtes 2005

Horst Opaschowski, Professor für Erziehungswissenschaft der Universität Hamburg, berät seit Jahrzehnten als prominenter Zukunftswissenschaftler die Politik. Mit seinen Thesen zu den Themen Zuwanderung, Arbeit und Arbeitslosigkeit (Ende der Vollbeschäftigung) etc. hat der pointiert schreibende Meinungsmacher und Gründer des „B.A.T. Freizeitforschungsinsituts" zudem zahlreiche Wortschöpfungen in den massengesellschaftlichen Diskurs eingebracht. Er sieht Architekten künftig verstärkt in der Rolle als soziale Dienstleister und Integrationspolitiker.

Was bedeutet Stadt und städtisches Leben für Sie?

Stadt heißt für mich: Wohnort der kurzen Wege und Wartezeiten, also wohnungsnah arbeiten und in zentraler Lage leben. Und städtisches Leben erinnert mich in seiner schönsten Form an ein modernes „Sesam-öffne-dich!": Shopping, Szene, Straßencafés, aber auch gut erreichbare Kultur- und Bildungseinrichtungen in Verbindung mit sozialer Infrastruktur – von der Mieter- über die Schuldner- bis zur Drogenberatung. Diese Angebotsvielfalt kann nur die Stadt leisten – heute und erst recht in Zukunft. Deshalb sage ich: Zukunft findet Stadt!

Sie gelten als einer der glaubwürdigsten und objektivsten Zukunftsforscher und als wissenschaftlicher Vordenker Deutsch-

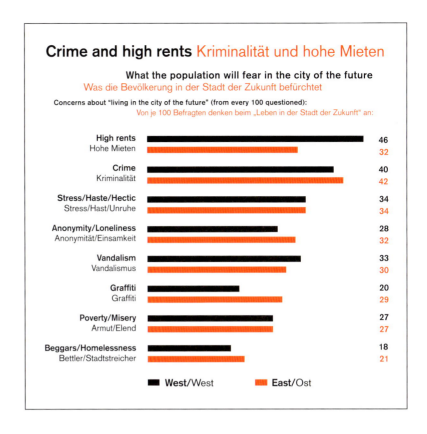

Crime and high rents Kriminalität und hohe Mieten

What the population will fear in the city of the future
Was die Bevölkerung in der Stadt der Zukunft befürchtet

Concerns about "living in the city of the future" (from every 100 questioned):
Von je 100 Befragten denken beim „Leben in der Stadt der Zukunft" an:

	West/West	East/Ost
High rents / Hohe Mieten	46	32
Crime / Kriminalität	40	42
Stress/Haste/Hectic / Stress/Hast/Unruhe	34	34
Anonymity/Loneliness / Anonymität/Einsamkeit	28	32
Vandalism / Vandalismus	33	30
Graffiti / Graffiti	20	29
Poverty/Misery / Armut/Elend	27	27
Beggars/Homelessness / Bettler/Stadtstreicher	18	21

■ West/West   ■ East/Ost

result in the anonymity of another. In industrialised countries, almost three quarters of the population live in cities. There is a great danger that the much propagated guiding image of 'urban expansion' will lose its human measure. This could finally stretch the city to breaking point between poverty and unemployment, migration and isolation of individuals.

What developments do you foresee will happen in German cities over the next years and decades?

Fewer, older, more colourful. That will be our future urban life, meaning there will be fewer children and young people, more grey-haired elderly citizens and a colourful mixture of Germans and immigrants from foreign cultures. When I asked the mayor of a community whether they would then abandon more youth centres and build more housing suited to the elderly, he said, 'We will convert kindergartens into day-care centres for the elderly. The toys are there anyway…seriously!' The social polarisation between young and old, but also between Germans and immigrants, will increase.

In order to respond constructively to these new challenges, they not only have to be recognised early on, but also communicated. What do you suggest should be done?

lands. Seit über dreißig Jahren provozieren Sie mit Ihren Thesen und Prognosen Wirtschaft, Politik, Wissenschaften und Medien. In Ihrem 2005 erschienenen Buch „Besser leben, schöner wohnen? Leben in der Stadt der Zukunft" setzen Sie sich nun auch mit der Zukunft der Städte in Deutschland auseinander.

Wie aber sieht die gegenwärtige Situation in den Städten Deutschlands aus und mit welchen sozio-politischen, wirtschaftlichen und historisch-kulturellen Anforderungen an Vergangenheit und Zukunft sehen sich die Städte heute konfrontiert?

Stadtleben kann auch Stadteinsamkeit bedeuten – trotz Telefon und Telekommunikation. Die Urbanität der einen kann die Anonymität der anderen zur Folge haben. In den Industrieländern leben heute fast drei Viertel der Bevölkerung in der Stadt. Die Gefahr ist groß, dass das vielfach propagierte Leitbild der „wachsenden Stadt" das menschliche Maß verliert. Es kann zur Zerreißprobe zwischen Armut und Arbeitslosigkeit, Migration und Vereinzelung kommen.

Welche Entwicklungen zeichnen sich Ihrer Meinung nach in der Stadtentwicklung in Deutschland in den nächsten Jahren bzw. Jahrzehnten ab?

Weniger. Älter. Bunter. So sieht das Leben in der Stadt der Zukunft aus. Das Stadtbild wird geprägt durch weniger Kinder und Jugendliche, mehr ältere Grauköpfe und ein buntes Gemisch von Einheimischen und Zuwanderern aus fremden Kulturen. Auf meine Frage „Bauen Kommunen dann verstärkt Jugendzentren ab und mehr altersgerechte Wohnungen für Senioren auf?" antwortete mir der Bürgermeister einer Gemeinde: „Aus Kindergärten machen wir Altentagesstätten. Spielzeug ist ohnehin da…" Das ist ernst gemeint.

Die soziale Polarisierung zwischen Jung und Alt, aber auch zwischen Einheimischen und Einwanderern wird zunehmen.

Um diese neuen Herausforderungen konstruktiv anzugehen, müssen diese nicht nur frühzeitig erkannt, sondern auch vermittelt werden. Welche Maßnahmen schlagen Sie hierbei vor?

Das Leitbild der Zukunft kann nur die „Soziale Stadt" sein – von der Hilfe zur Selbsthilfe bis zur Schaffung stabiler nachbarschaftlicher sozialer Netze. Wir wissen: In Großstädten und Ballungszentren ist die Bereitschaft zum Engagement in sozialen Institutionen am geringsten. Aktivitäten im Verein, in Kirche und Gemeinde, in Verbänden, Parteien und Gewerkschaften haben für Städter nur eine marginale Bedeutung. Viel wichtiger ist für Städter das Geben-und-Nehmen-Prinzip: Ich helfe dir, damit auch du mir hilfst. Gemeint sind Hilfeleistungen unter Nachbarn, unter Freunden und Verwandten. Die Kommunalpolitik soll eine solche „Selbsthilfegesellschaft" fördern und Gelegenheitsstrukturen für informelle und ganz persönliche Hilfeleistungen schaffen, ohne die Menschen „einzuverleiben" oder „in die Pflicht zu nehmen." Jeder Bürger soll in Zukunft davon überzeugt sein: „Es gibt nichts Gutes - es sei denn, man tut es."

Ihren zahlreichen Arbeiten zu gesamtgesellschaftlichen Wandlungsprozessen liegt immer der einzelne Mensch zugrunde: „Die Welt im Wandel – der Mensch im Mittelpunkt." Was zeichnet das Weltbild des Stadtmenschen heute aus? Welche Bedürfnisse und Wünsche werden dabei formuliert und inwieweit entsprechen diese noch der gesellschaftlichen Wirklichkeit?

Städter wollen alles und vor allem sich selbst erleben, Kommunikation und Kulinarik genießen. Sie wünschen sich ein städtisches Umfeld, in dem sie sich wohlfühlen, aber auch gebraucht und gefordert werden kön-

62

The guiding image for the future can only be the one of the 'social city' which helps people to help themselves and fosters the creation of stable neighbourly social networks. We know very well that people living in large cities and conurbations are the least prepared to do voluntary work in social institutions. Activities in charities and other associations, church parishes and communities, professional federations, political parties and trade unions are only of marginal importance for city dwellers. Much more important is the give-and-take principle: I will help you so that you will help me. This applies to help from neighbours, friends and relatives. Community politics should promote this kind of self-help society and create opportunities for informal and personal assistance without people being roped in and forced to discharge their responsibilities. Every citizen should simply be convinced that there is no good except the good one does oneself.

Your many publications on general processes of changing societies always seem to have mankind at the centre, e.g. the title which translates as 'A changing world – man at the centre'. What characterises the urban dweller's world view today? What needs and desires does he/she formulate and to what degree do these match social realities?

City dwellers want to experience life to the full and particularly to be aware of themselves and enjoy communication and culinary delights. They long for an urban environment where they can live happily, but are also needed and challenged. Today's and tomorrow's urbanists want to live in the thick of life and be open for new forms of family or communal living. Grandsons and granddaughters, childless couples and singles wish to be included into the community of a residential building as if they were adopted. This generates new adoptive families – and also ensures people's safety and security. City dwellers want to live a self-determined life – but not on their own. This seems a bit like squaring the circle, but they will not get such a concept of life for nothing. They will have to put some effort into it themselves and become the architects, planners and designers of their own notions of home and of life.

Do you think the developments you have described are specifically German phenomena, or do they represent trends that can also be found in other European countries and overseas? What is common to all of them and what differences are there?

In a nutshell, world population figures continue to rise. The German

nen. Die Urbanisten von heute und morgen wollen „mittendrin" und „mitten im Leben" wohnen und offen für neue Lebensformen und Hausgemeinschaften sein. Enkel-, Kinder- und Familienlose wollen wie durch Adoption in die Hausgemeinschaft aufgenommen werden. So entstehen neue Wahlfamilien und Wahlverwandtschaften – auch zur eigenen Sicherheit und Geborgenheit. „Stadtmenschen" wollen ein selbstbestimmtes Leben führen – aber nicht allein. Das erinnert ein wenig an die Quadratur des Kreises. Ein solches Lebenskonzept bekommen sie aber nicht geschenkt. Sie müssen schon selbst etwas dafür tun und sich zu Architekten, Planern und Gestaltern ihrer Wohn- und Lebenskonzepte machen.

Stellen die von Ihnen skizzierten Entwicklungen ein speziell deutsches Phänomen dar oder handelt es sich hier um Entwicklungstendenzen die auch in anderen europäischen und außereuropäischen Ländern nachgezeichnet werden können? Wo lassen sich Gemeinsamkeiten und Unterschiede aufzeigen?

Auf den Punkt gebracht: Die Weltbevölkerung wandert und wächst. Deutschlands Bevölkerung hingegen altert und schrumpft. Das macht den wesentlichen Unterschied aus. Dennoch gibt es eine weltweite Gemeinsamkeit: Immer mehr Menschen zieht es in die Stadt. Fast zwei Drittel der Weltbevölkerung werden in dreißig Jahren Städter sein. Die Frage stellt sich: Wie viele Menschen können die Städte dann noch (er-)tragen, ohne dass es zu massiven Problemen kommt – von der Luftverschmutzung bis zur Wohnungsnot. Das 21. Jahrhundert kann ein Jahrhundert der Megastädte werden.

Auf der Webseite des 1979 von Ihnen gegründeten und seitdem von Ihnen geleiteten Freizeitforschungsinstitut heißt es: „Zukunft ist Herkunft. Nur wer zurückblickt, kann auch nach vorne schauen." Was bedeutet dies Ihrer Ansicht nach in Hinblick auf Städtebau und Architektur?

Seit jeher träumen die Menschen vom guten, vom schönen Leben in der Stadt. Denken Sie nur an den utopischen Roman „Neu-Atlantis" von Francis Bacon aus dem 16. Jahrhundert, der die Vision einer „schön gebauten Stadt" zwischen Wohlstand und Wohlbefinden zeichnet. Stadtleben ist seit Jahrhunderten ein Synonym für Sehnsucht, Mythos und auch Utopie. Allerdings verschieben sich die Leitbilder: In den 60er Jahren träumten wir noch von der autogerechten Stadt. In Zukunft geht es mehr um die lebenswerte Stadt, die Antworten auf die Frage gibt, wofür es sich zu leben lohnt.

Wie verstehen Sie den Ausspruch: „Die Zukunft entscheidet sich in den Städten"?

Schon der biblische Prophet Jeremias verkündete 650 v.Chr.: „Suchet der Stadt Bestes, denn wenn's ihr wohlgeht, so geht's auch euch wohl." Dies gilt auch und gerade für die Zukunft. Ein urbanes Zeitalter liegt vor uns und immer mehr Menschen identifizieren sich mit dem urbanen Lebensstil. Nur wenn die Lebensqualität in den Städten gewährleistet ist, ist auch der soziale Frieden im ganzen Land garantiert. Das meint auch der Spruch des Deutschen Städtetages: „Ohne Städte ist kein Staat zu machen."

Entgegen dem in den Sozialwissenschaften wiederholt prognostizierten Niedergang der Städte scheinen Sie sich kritisch für einen urbanen Optimismus einzusetzen. Worin sehen sie diesen begründet?

A modern "open, sesame" Ein modernes „Sesam-öffne-dich"

How the population want to live in the future
Wie die Bevölkerung in Zukunft leben und wohnen will

Out of every 100 asked the following wished for:
Von je 100 Befragten wünschen sich:

a living place with short distances to travel / Wohnort der kurzen Wege	46
affordable, centrally located living spaces / Bezahlbarer Wohnraum in zentraler Lage	33
a living place with like-minded people / Wohnanlage mit Menschen gleicher Interessen	26
working close to home / Wohnortnah arbeiten	13
communities comprising several generations / Mehr-Generationen-Wohngemeinschaft	12
serviced apartment / Service-Mietwohnung	10
rented apartments rather than owned apartments / Mietwohnung statt Eigentumswohnung	10

Growing cities Wachsende Städte

Population development in German cities with more than
100,000 inhabitants between 2002 and 2020 (growth in percent)

Bevölkerungsentwicklung in deutschen Städten mit mehr als
100.000 Einwohner im Zeitraum 2000 bis 2020 (Wachstum in Prozent)

City	Growth
Heidelberg	+0,6
Potsdam	+0,9
Stuttgart	+1,8
Munich/München	+1,9
Fürth	+2,1
Cologne/Köln	+2,1
Hamburg	+2,2
Trier	+2,3
Frankfurt am Main	+2,5
Darmstadt	+2,7
Wiesbaden	+4,1
Offenbach am Main	+5,8
Ulm	+6,0
Freiburg im Breisgau	+6,7
Ingolstadt	+8,0
Regensburg	+11,3

BBR-population predictions 2002-2020 (Bonn 2005)   BBR-Bevölkerungsprognose 2002-2020 (Bonn 2005)

population, however, is ageing and shrinking. That is the major difference. Still there is a common trend around the world: more and more people are moving to the cities. Thirty years from now, two thirds of the world population will be city dwellers. The question is, how many more people will the cities be able to cope with without facing massive problems – from air pollution to housing shortages? The 21st century might yet become the century of megalopolises.

The website of the Leisure Research Institute that you founded in 1979, and still direct today, says: 'Future means Origins. Only those who look back, can also look forward…' What does this mean when applied to urban planning and architecture?

For centuries people have dreamt of the good life in the city. You only have to think of Francis Bacon's Utopian novel 'The New Atlantis' [pub. 1627] in which he set down his vision of a 'city beautifully built' between wealth and well-being. For centuries urban life has been seen as synonym for all we ever wished for; the urban myth as a kind of Utopia. However, paradigms do change. Whereas in the 1960s we dreamt of the automobile city, in the future we will be more concerned with the inhabitable city which answers our questions about what to live for.

How do you interpret the statement, 'The future will be decided in the cities'?

Even the prophet of the Old Testament Jeremiah proclaimed in 650 BC: 'But seek the welfare of the city […] for in its welfare you will find your welfare.' (Jer. 29,7) This also, particularly, applies to the future. An urban age lies ahead of us and an increasing number of people identify with an urban lifestyle. Only when the quality of life is secured, will social peace be secured as well through-out the country. This is what the Deutscher

Städtetag (German conference of city governments) meant with its slogan 'Ohne Städte ist kein Staat zu machen' [No state can be made without cities. Staat machen, literally 'to make state' also means to do something in great style – translator's note].

By campaigning for critical optimism in regard to the city, you seem to oppose the social scientists who have repeatedly foretold the decline of cities. Where do you see reasons for optimism?

Whereas years ago many people left the cities, recently many of them have returned. They longed for the vibrant life on public squares and in open spaces and in a sense wanted to buy or rent an urban lifestyle. The city guarantees a threefold value of living: the value of salaries, the value of living and the value of leisure activities. The place where you like to live is the place where you like to work as well. All this justifies my demand: let us say goodbye to urban pessimism. Urban living again means urban experience!

What roles do both existing and new architectural and/or urban structures play in this, do you think?

Faith in technology must no longer be confused with future-orientation or seminal quality. Plans for the future must be diverse. They must focus more than has been the case so far on social dimensions, especially on designing buildings for children, families and the elderly. Architects and urban planners should improve the quality of urban environments so that inhabitants will no longer wish to leave and at the same time provide inducements for potential newcomers who wish to establish careers in the city.

Where do you believe the tasks and responsibilities of contemporary architecture and urbanism lie?

From now on, architects and urbanists will increasingly have to see themselves as integrative politicians and as such aim to prevent the concentrated formation of island and parallel societies. They must become providers of socially oriented services and prove their economic efficiency by the social compatibility of their structures. For me, the three top priorities of architecture and urbanism are: firstly more innercity interventions than building in the open countryside; secondly, more concepts of life than building projects, thirdly, more life-style renting than buying owner-occupied flats.

Viele Menschen hatten in den letzten Jahren ihre Stadt verlassen – und kehren jetzt wieder zurück. Sie sehnen sich nach bewegtem Leben inmitten von Plätzen, Räumen und Flächen und wollen regelrecht einen urbanen Lebensstil kaufen oder mieten. Die Stadt garantiert einen dreifachen Lebenswert: Lohnwert, Wohnwert und Freizeitwert. Wo man gerne leben will, will man auch gerne arbeiten. Dies alles berechtigt mich zu der Forderung: Lasst uns Abschied nehmen vom urbanen Pessimismus. Stadtleben heißt wieder Stadt erleben!

Welche Bedeutung messen Sie dabei vorhandenen und neu geschaffenen architektonischen und/oder städtebaulichen Strukturen bei?

Technologiegläubigkeit darf nicht länger mit Zukunftsfähigkeit verwechselt werden. Zukunftsplanung muss variantenreich sein und mehr als bisher soziale Dimensionen im Blick haben und insbesondere mit der Kinder-, Familien- und Seniorenfreundlichkeit ernst machen. Architekten und Stadtplaner sollen beides ermöglichen: Lebensqualität für Bewohner schaffen, die nicht mehr wegziehen wollen, und Anreize für Zuzügler schaffen, die sich eine neue berufliche Zukunft bauen wollen.

Worin liegt Ihrer Ansicht nach die Aufgabe und Verantwortung von Architektur und Städtebau heute?

Architekten und Städteplaner werden sich in Zukunft zunehmend als Integrationspolitiker verstehen müssen, um konzentrierte Inselbildungen und Parallelgesellschaften zu verhindern. Sie müssen zu sozialen Dienstleistern werden und ihre Wirtschaftlichkeit durch Sozialverträglichkeit beweisen. Die drei wichtigsten Prioritäten von Architektur und Städtebau lauten: 1. Mehr Innenstadtförderung als Bauen auf der grünen Wiese 2. Mehr Lebenskonzepte als Bauprojekte 3. Mehr Lebensstilmiete als Wohnungskauf.

Project: Hessisches Staatstheater - Provisorial Theatre Entrance in a Garage   **Location:** Darmstadt | **Architects:** Prof. Arno Lederer + Jórunn Ragnarsdóttir + Marc Oei, Stuttgart

Feet over Wheels

Vom autogerechten Gebäude zum stadtfreundlichen Theater

From car-centric building to city-friendly theatre

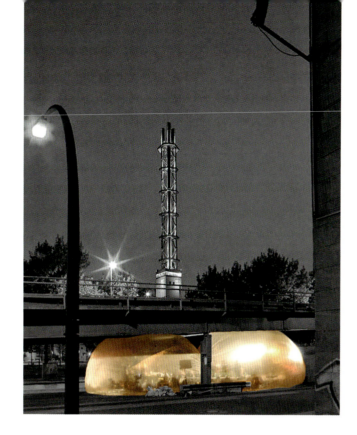

Project: Küchenmonument   **Location:** Berlin / Duisburg / Mühlreim | **Architects:** Raumlabor, Berlin

Blow Out

Festessen im Restraum

Banqueting in left over spaces

The Interiority of the Urban

Insideout – a dance theatre piece by Sasha Waltz

Innenleben des Städtischen

Insideout – ein Tanztheaterstück
von Sasha Waltz

Sasha Waltz's dance theatre piece "insideout" can be read as a parable for modern life – a life that is prototypically formed by the modern metropolis according to the early German sociologist Georg Simmel. It raises persistent questions about the relationship between historical heritage, origins and identity, social and individual values and their antagonisms and contradictions that shape very specific lifestyles and identities. In this respect insideout can also be seen as a narrative about the modern city in which personal life as the driving force behind community life is something that has to be constantly re-created in countless agreements.

Accordingly the starting point for the piece was drawn from autobiographical experiences of each company member. The performers were engaged in the emergence of the piece by making their origins and backgrounds part of the artistic process. The events on stage follow this micro-history in a very personal way; they are so diverse as to resist being incorporated into a coherent narrative. Consequently the choreography of the piece develops simultaneously in all parts of the stage area, and with only minimal focusing. The dramaturgy seems to evolve in a far distance, impacting like shock waves on the protagonists' actions. But it is precisely this distance from the actual origins that brings the elements together and condenses the events: everything seems to be linked not because of arbitrary proximity, but through subtle meanings. Thus fundamental ideas about living together become visible in the performers' personal backgrounds, and the urban factor of insideout is to be found precisely in the dense tissue of mutual references.

Stephan Becker, Anh-Linh Ngo

Das Tanztheaterstück „insideout" von Sasha Waltz kann als eine Parabel für das Leben in der Moderne gelesen werden. Dieses Leben, das Georg Simmel prototypisch in der Großstadt verwirklicht sieht, wirft permanent Fragen nach dem Verhältnis von historischem Erbe, Herkunft und Identität, gesellschaftlichen und individuellen Werten sowie deren Gegensätzlichkeiten und Widersprüche auf, die ganz spezifische Lebensstile und Identitäten prägen. Insofern lässt sich „insideout" auch als Erzählung über die Stadt auffassen: das persönliche Leben als Triebfeder des Gemeinsamen, das in unzähligen Abmachungen immer wieder neu entstehen muss.

Dementsprechend waren der Ausgangspunkt des Stücks die autobiografischen Erfahrungen der einzelnen Mitglieder der Compagnie. In persönlichen Interviews konnten sich die Darsteller mit ihrer Herkunft und ihren Hintergründen in die künstlerische Entstehung des Stücks einbringen. Die Geschehnisse auf der Bühne folgen auf sehr persönliche Weise dieser Mikrohistorie und widersetzen sich in ihrer Vielfältigkeit der Vereinnahmung durch eine kohärente Erzählung. Folgerichtig entwickelt sich das Stück choreografisch zeitgleich in allen Räumen des Bühnenraums und der Fokus wird nur minimal geführt. Lediglich in der Ferne scheint es eine Dramaturgie zu geben, deren Auswirkungen wie Schockwellen in den Handlungen der Akteure sichtbar werden. Doch gerade durch diesen Abstand zum eigentlichen Ursprung treffen sich die Elemente und verdichten sich die Geschehnisse: Alles scheint nicht nur aufgrund willkürlicher Nähe, sondern durch subtile Bedeutungen verknüpft zu sein. So werden in den persönlichen Hintergründen der Schauspieler auch grundsätzliche Ideen vom Zusammenleben sichtbar und gerade im dichten Geflecht gegenseitiger Bezüge liegt das städtische Moment von insideout.

Das Fragmentarische und die Vielschichtigkeit des Lebens spiegeln sich in dem atmosphärisch dichten Bühnenkonzept von Sasha Waltz und Thomas Schenk. Die Intensität des Stücks entsteht somit auch aus dem Bühnenraum selbst, der analog zu den vielfältigen Erfahrungen der Darsteller eine Vielzahl von Räumen mit ganz unterschiedlichen atmosphärischen Qualitäten bietet. Gleich einem Flaneur durchwan-

dert der Zuschauer die Raumbühne, die wie eine Stadt mit engen Gassen, Treppen, intimen Räumen und offenen Plätzen angelegt ist. So gibt es die Weite des Blicks, durch den die architektonischen Fragmente zu modernen Gebäuden zu werden scheinen, die dank großer Fenster Einblicke in ihre Innenräume gewähren. Zugleich verengt sich der Raum an anderer Stelle und wird fast dörflich in der Ansammlung kleinerer, verschlossener Objekte. Der Besucher ist eingeladen, sich das Geschehen selbst zu erschließen und sich frei zwischen der Architektur und den Darstellern zu bewegen.

Die unterschiedlichen räumlichen Konfigurationen wirken sich unterschiedlich auf die Rolle aus, die der Zuschauer dabei einnimmt: Der unbeteiligte Flaneur in den Gassen wird in den meist nur wenige Menschen fassenden Architekturen durch offene Schlitze und Fenster zum unerbittlichen Voyeur. In solchen Momenten wird er im Wortsinne der Eindringlichkeit seiner eigenen Rolle bewusst und die Grenze zwischen Anteilnahme, blasierter Gleichgültigkeit und schmerzhafter Intimität wird fließend: auch das ein zentrales urbanes Motiv. Trotzdem, die fast archetypischen Raumkonfigurationen bleiben niemals abstrakt, sondern bekommen in den biografischen Aspekten des Stücks und den Bewegungen der Darsteller eine große Unmittelbarkeit.

Die Nähe des Bühnenbildes zu tatsächlich gelebten städtischen Räumen ermöglicht den Besuchern immer wieder neue Zugänge, zwingt zugleich aber auch dazu, sich in Relationen zu diesen Konfigurationen zu setzen. Denn anders als sonst im Theater verschwindet der Besucher nicht in der Neutralität der Masse des Zuschauerraums, sondern bleibt Individuum, ohne dass das Stück zu einem peinlichen Mitmachtheater wird. Schnell entstehen so eigene räumliche Vorlieben und die Besucher beginnen in dem Wunsch, das Geschehen zu begreifen, ihre eigenen Choreografien zu entwickeln. Sie folgen mit der Architektur den Wechseln von innen nach außen, von privat und öffentlich, von Intimität und Offenheit. Im Zusammenspiel der intimen Komplexität der Stadtfragmente und den individuellen und persönlichen Bewegungen sowohl der Darsteller wie auch der Zuschauer entfaltet sich die große Wirksamkeit des Stücks, die darin besteht, für einen Moment die Dynamik unter der Oberfläche der üblichen Konventionen des städtischen Zusammenlebens spürbar zu machen.

Sasha Waltz and Thomas Schenk correlate this fragmentary quality and the complexity of life ideally in spatial terms with their atmospherically dense stage set concept. Therefore the piece also derives its intensity from the set itself; like the performers' diverse experiences it offers a wide range of spaces with quite different atmospheric qualities. Spectators wander through the stage space like strollers in a city. Apparently the stage is a city 'en miniature' that has narrow alleyways, steps, intimate spaces and open squares, and there is a breadth of perspective that makes the architectural fragments seem like modern buildings affording views of their interiors thanks to large windows. Then again the space becomes more cramped in other places, and is almost village-like in its accumulation of small, closed objects. Visitors are invited to discover the events for themselves, and to move freely between the architecture and the performers.

The different spatial configurations have different effects on the roles played by the spectators themselves: the uninvolved flaneurs in the streets become merciless voyeurs through the open slits and windows giving insights into the interiors, or by entering the architectural features that accommodate only an intimate number of people. At moments like this they are fully aware of the intrusiveness of their own role and the boundary between sympathetic interest, blasé indifference and painful intimacy becomes fluid: this fluidity is also a central urban motif. Nevertheless, the almost archetypal spatial configurations never remain abstract, but gain great immediacy from the biographical elements of the piece and the performers' movements.

The set's similarity to real urban spaces allows the audience to constantly find new modes of access, but at the same time compels them to relate to the configurations. Because, unlike the usual theatre experience, visitors do not disappear in the neutral mass of the auditorium, but remain individuals, without the piece becoming a kind of pathetic participation theatre. Personal spatial preferences emerge and visitors start to develop their own choreographies in their desire to understand the events. They follow the architecture's shifts from inside to outside; from private to public; from intimate to open. The piece develops its effectiveness from the interaction between the intimate complexity of the urban fragments and the individual and personal movements of both the performers and the spectators. This effectiveness lies in making the dynamics beneath the surface of the usual conventions of urban lifestyles perceptible for a magic moment.

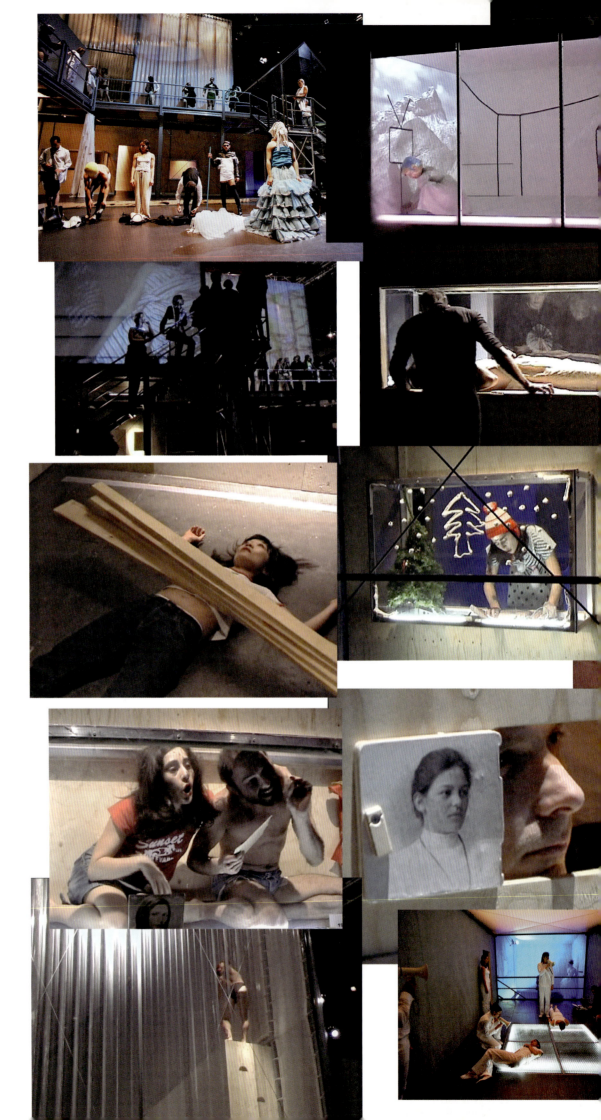

68

Sasha Waltz and Jochen
Sandig founded the dance
company Sasha Waltz &
Guests in 1993. It has since
gained an international repu-
tation as one of the world's
most successful companies.
After a period spent working
closely with the Schaubühne
Berlin, the company has
been independent again
since 2004. From Autumn
2006 Sasha Waltz & Guests
is to move to the newly established "Radialsystem", a
converted former pump station in Berlin.

Sasha Waltz gründete zusammen mit Jochen Sandig 1993
die Tanzcompagnie Sasha
Waltz & Guests, die seitdem
international zu den erfolg-
reichsten Compagnien zählt.
Nach enger Zusammenarbeit
mit der Schaubühne Berlin ist
Sasha Waltz & Guests seit
2004 wieder unabhängig.
Ab Herbst 2006 erhält die
Compagnie im Umbau des
ehemaligen Pumpwerks „Ra-
dialsystem" in Berlin ein neues
Domizil.

Project: 20,000 qm x 5 Jahre   **Location:** Berlin | **Architects:** Urban Catalyst: Philipp Oswalt with Florian Kessel and Matthäus Wirth, Berlin

Activating the Void

Der Keller der Republik als Sandkasten auf Zeit

The cellar of the republic as short-term sandpit

Waiting Lands

Land auf Abruf

In the debate about the European city of the future, particular attention is paid to the question of restructuring inner-cities. Former port, industrial and railway sites are among the few areas close to the centre that are still freely available and thus offer a potential reservoir for urban development. KCAP/ ASTOC uses a variety of strategies for developing such sites, also known a "waiting lands". These strategies can be summed up under the title "The City as Loft".

The notion of the loft occupies a key position in this strategy. It stands for a combined living/work space; a characteristic space of generous dimensions that can be appropriated using minimal but effective interventions. When we develop a loft building in a former port area we say that we have designed a squatted warehouse or a converted grain silo. Buildings in these areas are flexible, with plenty of light, large surface areas and high-ceilinged spaces. Not flexibility in the usual sense, which only results in poor-quality, standard spaces, but a conquerability of powerful, tectonic spaces. In these areas, the term loft is also and primarily applicable to the outdoor space between the buildings. Independent of the specific appearance of the buildings, the context generates a powerful tectonic space, which invites to be occupied with formal and informal action.

There are however many waiting lands that do not possess the conditions for an automatic activation. Theses areas require specific development strategies that will protect the balance of mixed activity against possible homogenisation. Working on a strategy for harbour areas means documenting, interpreting and evaluating the existing structures and devising various development scenarios which are analysed and visualised. Models, ranging from a cautious evolution from the status quo to filling in harbour basins for urban or suburban development, are set alongside each other. The possibility of consolidating valuable port buildings with cultural events or pioneering activities is also being investigated.

With a non-interventionist government policy, the areas would fill up with all kinds of business activity. This, however, would result in vast mono-functional areas lacking in urbanity, something that is no longer acceptable in a modern-day agglomeration already facing considerable structural problems.

In the 1970s, Henri Lefebvre wrote that urbanity evolves from networks, boundaries and differences, and that the friction between these "differences" is expressed in recognition, appreciation, fertilisation and productive

Kees Christiaanse

In der Debatte um die zukünftige europäische Stadt gilt der Frage der Neustrukturierung innerstädtischer Flächen besondere Aufmerksamkeit. Frühere Hafen-, Industrie- und Bahngelände gehören zu den wenigen Flächen in zentrumsnaher Lage, die noch frei verfügbar sind und daher ein potenzielles Reservoir für die Stadtentwicklung darstellen. Für die Entwicklung dieser als „waiting lands" bezeichneten Flächen werden von KCAP/ ASTOC unterschiedliche Strategien angewendet, die sich unter dem Titel „The City as Loft" zusammenfassen lassen.

Das Konzept des Lofts nimmt in dieser Strategie eine Schlüsselstellung ein. Es steht für einen kombinierten Wohn- und Arbeitsraum, typischerweise einen großzügig bemessenen Raum, der sich mit sparsamsten Mitteln wirkungsvoll ausgestalten lässt. Wenn wir einen alten Hafenspeicher umbauen, nennen wir unseren Entwurf ein besetztes Lagerhaus oder einen umgenutzten Kornspeicher. Bauten in Hafenbezirken sind flexibel, haben helle, hohe Räume und große zusammenhängende Nutzflächen. Flexibilität hat für uns nicht die übliche Bedeutung, die nur in Standardräumen von schlechter Qualität resultiert, sondern bezeichnet die Fähigkeit kraftvoller tektonischer Räume, sich erobern zu lassen. In diesem Sinne lässt sich der Begriff Loft auch konzeptuell für den Städtebau nutzbar machen. Er bezieht sich auf eine veränderungsoffene Stadt, deren vorhandene Strukturen und Außenbereiche zwischen den Gebäuden zu einer neuen kreativen Nutzung einladen. Unabhängig vom Aussehen der jeweiligen Bauten erzeugt der Kontext einen eindrucksvollen tektonischen Raum, der formell oder informell bespielt werden kann.

Es gibt jedoch viel mehr „Brachen", die einerseits zu weit vom Zentrum entfernt sind, um ein städtisches Hafenviertel zu bilden, sich aber andererseits zu nahe am Zentrum befinden, um der Peripherie zugeordnet werden zu können. Diese Areale erfordern besondere Entwicklungsstrategien, die das Gleichgewicht vielfältiger Aktivitäten vor einer möglichen Homogenisierung bewahren.

Eine Strategie für Hafengebiete zu erarbeiten, läuft darauf hinaus, die vorhandenen Bauwerke zunächst zu dokumentieren, zu interpretieren und zu evaluieren und anschließend verschiedene Entwicklungsszenarios zu entwerfen, die dann analysiert und visualisiert werden. Modelle, die sich von einer behutsamen Weiterentwicklung des Status quo bis zur Zuschüttung von Hafenbecken für eine städtische oder vorstädtische Bebauung erstrecken, werden nebeneinander gestellt. Die Möglichkeit, wertvolle Hafengebäude für kulturelle Veranstaltungen oder für innovative, wegbereitende Aktivitäten zu nutzen, wird ebenfalls berücksichtigt.

transformation. In port areas that are no longer used for port-related activities and that have been colonised by new activities, such differences are able to evolve, providing a fertile medium for cultural renewal. Any strategy for such areas should therefore create conditions in which the friction of 'differences' can arise and provide impetus for productive transformation. A "simultaneous chess" strategy accordingly involves drawing up a complete inventory of existing structures and activities as well as of all possible activation potentials in an area:

>> The development of a sustainable urban structure, based on the existing street layout and extended with new, impulsive structural lines; >> An almost obsessive inventory of existing structures, such as quays, bridges and cranes. This obsession results in a conservative attitude towards the traces present in the area, as an identification instrument to measure historical embedding; >> A particular inventory of surfaces and textures which are retained if usable or stored in a materials databank for later use elsewhere in the area; >> An inventory and analysis of existing functions, subdivided into categories such as redundant, transferable or improvable; >> A catalogue of all possible actors and stakeholders in the area, including event organizers, housing developers, established industrial companies, business start-ups, landowners and commercial and public investors.

Proceeding from this open condition, all possible actions and projects are initiated simultaneously (simultaneous chess). In such areas, this simultaneous and coordinated mobilisation of all forces is the only way to launch a sustainable transformation process leading to urban social quality within a broad functional mix.

Because of this strategy, such an area makes a finished impression at each phase in its development, which is an essential quality for urban agglomerations with a large number of "waiting lands".

These situations show how urban planning is no longer an off-the-peg profession that people can be trained to perform, but a discipline that must be defined and invented by its practitioners and that is as complex as the waiting lands themselves. Urban planners can no longer sit behind their desks until a commission comes their way; projects of this kind must be exhaustively identified, defined and conquered on one's own initiative.

Bei einer sich jeglicher Interventionen enthaltenden Politik der Behörden würden sich in diesen Arealen alle möglichen geschäftlichen Aktivitäten entfalten. Das Ergebnis wären jedoch ausgedehnte monofunktionale Areale, denen es an Urbanität mangelt – etwas, das in einem modernen, bereits mit beträchtlichen Strukturproblemen konfrontierten Ballungsgebiet nicht mehr hinnehmbar ist.

In den 1970er Jahren schrieb Henri Lefebvre, dass sich Urbanität aus Vernetzungen, Grenzen und Unterschieden entwickle und dass sich die Reibung zwischen diesen Unterschieden in Erkenntnis, Anerkennung, Befruchtung und produktiver Transformation niederschlage. In Hafenarealen, die nicht mehr ihrem ursprünglichen Zweck dienen, sondern für neue Aktivitäten genutzt werden, können sich solche Unterschiede entwickeln und dabei ein fruchtbares Medium für eine kulturelle Erneuerung bieten. Jede Strategie für solche Areale sollte daher Bedingungen schaffen, in denen die Reibung von Unterschieden ermöglicht wird, die dann der Auslöser für eine produktive Transformation ist. Eine Simultanschach-Strategie beinhaltet demnach die Erstellung eines vollständigen Verzeichnisses nicht nur der vorhandenen Bauwerke und Aktivitäten, sondern auch aller möglichen Aktivierungspotenziale in einem Areal:

>> Die Entwicklung einer nachhaltigen urbanen Struktur, die auf dem vorhandenen Straßenplan basiert und diesen um neue, impulsive strukturelle Linien erweitert; >> Ein fast schon obsessives Verzeichnis der vorhandenen Bauwerke wie zum Beispiel Kaianlagen, Brücken und Kräne. Diese Obsession resultiert in einer bewahrenden Einstellung gegenüber den im Areal vorhandenen Spuren der Vergangenheit, als ein Identifizierungsinstrument für eine Maßnahme der historischen Einbettung; >> Ein besonderes Verzeichnis der Oberflächen und Texturen, die, falls sie brauchbar sind, bewahrt oder in einer Materialien-Datenbank gespeichert werden, um sie später an anderer Stelle im Areal zu verwenden; >> Ein Verzeichnis und eine Analyse der vorhandenen Funktionen, unterteilt nach Kategorien wie redundant, übernehmbar oder verbesserungsfähig. >> Ein Katalog aller möglichen Akteure und Interessengruppen in dem Areal, darunter Veranstaltungsorganisatoren, Wohnungsbauunternehmen, etablierte Industriefirmen, Existenzgründer, Landbesitzer sowie private und öffentliche Investoren.

Ausgehend von diesem offenen Zustand werden alle möglichen Aktivitäten und Projekte simultan initiiert („Simultanschach"). In solchen Arealen ist diese simultane und koordinierte Mobilisierung aller Kräfte die einzige Möglichkeit, um einen nachhaltigen Transformationsprozess in Gang zu setzen, der zu einer urbanen sozialen Qualität innerhalb einer breiten funktionalen Mischung führt.

Wegen dieser Strategie erweckt so ein Areal in jeder Phase seiner Entwicklung einen vollendeten Eindruck – was eine essenzielle Eigenschaft städtischer Ballungsgebiete mit einer hohen Anzahl von Brachen ist.

Diese Situationen offenbaren, dass Stadtplanung nicht mehr ein Nullachtfünfzehn-Beruf ist, den man ein für alle Mal erlernen kann, sondern eine Disziplin, die von denjenigen, die sie ausüben, definiert und erfunden werden muss und die so komplex ist wie die Brachen selbst. Stadtplaner können nicht mehr an ihren Schreibtischen sitzen, bis sie mit einem Auftrag betraut werden; Projekte dieser Art müssen gründlich identifiziert, definiert und mit viel Eigeninitiative bewältigt werden.

Project: Kultur Bunker   **Location:** Frankfurt am Main   **Architects:** INDEX Architekten, Frankfurt am Main

Cultural Cargo Dock

Bunkeraufstockung als kultureller Katalysator im Stadthafen

Bunker add-on as a city harbour cultural catalyst

Massimiliano Gioni in conversation with Doreen Mende

Massimiliano Gioni im Gespräch mit Doreen Mende

Berlin, Auguststraße

Discovering city spaces for the 4th berlin biennial for contemporary art

Die Entdeckung des Stadtraumes für die 4. berlin biennale für zeitgenössische kunst

Massimiliano Gioni curated the 4th berlin biennial for contemporary art, a project of the KW Institute for Contemporary Art, together with Maurizio Cattelan and Ali Subotnik. They caused a stir by choosing twelve exhibition venues along Auguststraße in Berlin-Mitte instead of the traditional white cube gallery space. This consistent use of existing infrastructures and spaces meant that the whole section of the street became a museum.

What led you to the decision to leave institutional or museum-like spaces and set the main part of the 4th Berlin Biennial in one street, choosing the spaces of everyday life and reality for the exhibition?

It began by looking around in Berlin. It soon became clear to us that museum spaces or more institutional settings don't really participate in the world and in the languages of contemporary art as they are lived by artists and their audiences here. Contemporary art is experienced in much more varied situations, such as temporary exhibitions in apartments or artists' studios, independent galleries and non-profit spaces etc. Therefore we felt it necessary to move away from the bourgeois model of the museum, and to try and tune in with a much more complex, free and interesting way of producing and looking at art. Another important element of the exhibition and of our relationship to the city of Berlin is its mythology that relies heavily (for better or worse) on the idea of available space, which still acts as a magnet for artists in Germany and internationally. So we started very simply looking around for spaces all over the city and in different neighborhoods. Eventually we came across the former Jewish school building on Auguststraße in Mitte.

The former Jewish school, one of the main venues of the Biennale in direct neighborhood of the KW Berlin, was unused for a period of ten years. Which aspects were curatorially relevant for you when working in a historically charged building and furthermore extending the show into the street Auguststraße?

The school was rich with so many layers of history. Some of these layers appeared to be absolutely crucial to the history of Germany and, even more so, to the history of humanity. So the school really revealed itself as a strong place we wanted to work with. There was resistance from some people we consulted: we realised that many German visitors thought that they had already seen so many exhibitions in empty buildings, that they were rather jaded by it. But even with these reactions we felt that there was something interesting and worthwhile exploring. German visitors to the school often spoke of the smell of the building; they said it smelt like the GDR. We figured that this was not just a reaction to the fact that other shows had been organised in derelict buildings: we felt – and maybe we were wrong – that there was a certain coldness in the building because somehow it also evoked a series of traumas or situations that had been often discussed and yet, understandably, never completely cleared. That's probably also why we came to the decision to basically not touch anything in the building. We wanted to stress that the

Massimiliano Gioni kuratierte dieses Jahr mit seinen Mitaktivisten Maurizio Cattelan und Ali Subotnik die 4. berlin biennale für zeitgenössische kunst, ein Projekt der KW Institute for Contemporary Art. Aufsehen erregte die Auswahl der zwölf Ausstellungsorte entlang der Auguststraße in Berlin-Mitte. Die konsequente Nutzung schon vorhandener Infrastrukturen und Räume führte zur Musealisierung des gesamten Straßenzuges.

Wie kam es zu Eurer Entscheidung, den institutionellen Raum des Museums zu verlassen und den Hauptteil der 4. Berlin Biennale in eine Straße sowie an Orte des alltäglichen Lebens zu verlagern?

Zuerst einmal haben wir uns in Berlin umgesehen. Uns wurde schnell klar, dass Ausstellungsräume in Museen oder ähnlichen Einrichtungen nicht wirklich Teil haben an der Welt und an den Ausdrucksweisen zeitgenössischer Kunst, wie sie von Künstlern in Berlin praktiziert und von ihrem Publikum erlebt wird. Die Rezeption zeitgenössischer Kunst geschieht an sehr unterschiedlichen Orten – von temporären Ausstellungen in Wohnungen oder Künstlerateliers über Kunstgalerien bis hin zu Räumen gemeinnütziger Organisationen. Deshalb hielten wir es für notwendig, uns von dem bildungsbürgerlichen Modell des Museums zu verabschieden und uns auf eine Art der Ausstellung und Produktion von Kunst zu verlegen, die sehr viel komplexer, freier und interessanter ist. Als wir darüber nachzudenken begannen, suchten wir überall in der Stadt nach verschiedenen Räumen, die zugänglich waren.

Das ist ein weiterer wichtiger Aspekt der Ausstellung und unserer Beziehung zur Stadt Berlin. Der ganze Mythos Berlins beruht zu einem wesentlichen Teil auf der Vorstellung, dass leer stehende Räume (mit allen Vor- und Nachteilen) verfügbar sind und neu interpretiert werden können. Wenn Berlin auf deutsche und ausländische Künstler auch heute noch wie ein Magnet wirkt, dann hat das zum großen Teil mit den vielen freien Flächen in der Stadt zu tun. Deshalb sahen wir uns überall, in allen Bezirken, nach solchen Räumen um und entdeckten schließlich in der Auguststraße die ehemalige Jüdische Schule.

Die über einen Zeitraum von zehn Jahren ungenutzte Jüdische Schule, einer der Hauptorte der Biennale in unmittelbarer Nachbarschaft zu den KW Berlin, wurde wieder zugänglich. Welche Aspekte waren aus kuratorischer Sicht wichtig für Euch, mit einem historisch aufgeladenen Gebäude zu arbeiten und darüber hinaus die Ausstellung auf die Auguststraße zu erweitern?

Wir fanden in der Schule so vielschichtige Spuren der Vergangenheit und waren der Meinung, dass einige dieser historischen Schichten absolut entscheidend für Deutschland, ja sogar für die ganze Menschheit gewesen sind. Die Schule erwies sich als ein starker, aussagekräftiger Ort, mit dem wir wirklich arbeiten wollten. Einige Leute, die wir um ihre Meinung zu unserem Ausstellungsvorhaben dort fragten, waren dagegen, weil offenbar schon oft Ausstellungen in leer stehenden Gebäuden stattfanden und viele deutsche Besucher eher genug davon hatten. Trotz dieser Reaktionen gab es für uns Interessantes und Lohnenswertes zu entdecken. Viele Deutsche, die wir durch die Schule führten, machten Bemerkungen über den Geruch des Gebäudes und sagten, es rieche nach DDR. Wir begriffen, dass negative Reaktionen nicht nur darauf beruhten, weil schon viele Ausstellungen in halb verfallenen

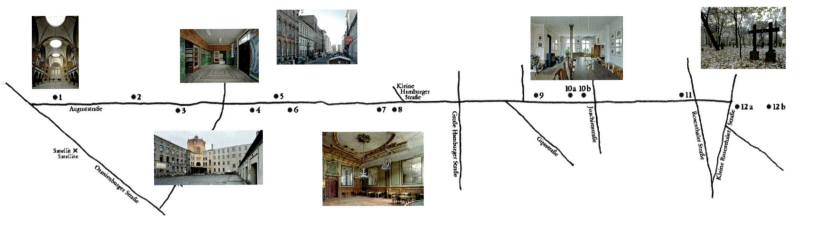

Jewish school was not an empty place that could be reinvented. On the contrary, it was a space full of things, memories, histories, dust and voices. So in a way we were saying that this is the opposite of gentrification, this is about using what's there and preserving it, and it's not about the vacuum, it's actually about things being full, it's about the lives that were here before us. With these elements in mind, and walking up and down Auguststraße thinking about the show, we came up with the idea of using the whole street as both a metaphor, a backdrop, a stage set, and a narrative structure for the exhibition. We started looking for more spaces that were available or could be made available. We spoke to house owners, to neighbours and to different communities and we worked on finding out which spaces could be used for art. Again we tried to focus on buildings and sites that would have a strong symbolic and evocative character. Once again, we were not seeking the emptiness of an abandoned site or the clean vacuum of a gallery, we wanted to find places that were dense with traces of other presences; traces of lives or of different uses.

You planned to stay away from the ideology of the White Cube. I'm not sure whether you succeeded. Is it at all possible to evade the idea of the White Cube - particularly within an international and institutional big show?

It's not that we decided to be against the White Cube per se. In fact we have avoided any reference to this expression in all the communications of the exhibition because we find it a very boring expression. We tried to stay away from the usual standards of biennials such as contemporary art and global sprawl, where everything is connected and leveled out. Instead we wanted to try and see what happens to art when: a) it is presented in very charged environments; b) it is presented in charged environments where the traces of other activities are kept intact; c) it is presented in ways that can also be experienced as intimate and closer. We wanted to work on different scales, creating a biennial that could be very small and intimate at some moments and more open at others. We wanted to remind ourselves, the artists and the public that you don't always need a mammoth or a limousine and that smaller environments are also ok; d) we wanted to see what happens when you see art next to art that is not the art we selected (for example there were private apartments in which we left the paintings and sculptures that the owner liked and had nothing to do with our idea of art); e) We wanted to see what happens to art when it has to measure and confront itself with the everyday, an everyday that can at times be spectacular and other times boring. We wanted to use spaces that were left over, forgotten, not used or looked at. To quote Alfred Hitchcock: "Drama is life with the dull bits cut out …"

Gebäuden stattgefunden hatten. Wir spürten – und vielleicht lagen wir auch falsch – eine gewisse Kühle angesichts dieser Räume, weil diese traumatische Erlebnisse und Situationen wach riefen, die zwar schon oft diskutiert aber nicht wirklich verarbeitet worden waren. Wahrscheinlich war das auch der Grund für unsere Entscheidung, das Gebäude weitgehend so zu lassen, wie es war. Wir wollten damit nicht etwa betonen, dass die Jüdische Schule leer stand und daher völlig neu gefüllt werden konnte, sondern im Gegenteil, dass das Gebäude bereits voll war von Gegenständen, Erinnerungen, Geschichten, Staub und Stimmen. In gewissem Sinne wollten wir sagen: Dies ist das Gegenteil von Aufwertung durch Kunst. Hier es geht darum, das Vorhandene zu nutzen und zu erhalten. Es geht nicht um Leere, sondern um Fülle und um das Leben der Menschen, die vor uns hier waren.

Im Gedanken an all das und an die geplante Ausstellung kam beim Gang durch die Auguststraße die Idee auf, die ganze Straße als Metapher, Hintergrund, Bühnenkulisse und Erzählstruktur der Ausstellung zu nutzen. Also suchten wir Räume, die verfügbar waren oder vorübergehend leer geräumt werden konnten, sprachen mit Hauseigentümern, Nachbarn und verschiedenen Interessensgruppen, um herauszufinden, welche Räume für Kunst genutzt werden konnten. Erneut konzentrierten wir uns auf Gebäude und Grundstücke mit stark geschichtsträchtigem Symbolcharakter, ähnlich wie die Jüdische Schule, und auf Gebäude und Räume, in denen die Schicksale vieler Menschen wieder lebendig werden würden. Wieder suchten wir nicht die Leere verlassener Orte oder das reine Vakuum einer Kunstgalerie, sondern im Gegenteil dicht mit den Spuren früherer Existenzen, Lebensgeschichten oder verschiedener Nutzungen angefüllte Orte.

Gezielt habt Ihr die Ideologie des White Cube, des klassischen weißen Ausstellungsraums, zu vermeiden versucht. Ich bin nicht si-cher, ob Euch das gelungen ist. Ist es überhaupt möglich, sich der Konzeption des White Cube zu entziehen, insbesondere innerhalb einer internationalen Großausstellung?

Wir haben ja nichts gegen den White Cube an sich. Tatsächlich haben wir in allen Mitteilungen über die Ausstellung jede Erwähnung dieses Begriffs vermieden, weil wir den Ausdruck einfach langweilig finden. Weiße Ausstellungsräume und die üblichen Biennale-Standardthemen wie zum Beispiel globale Zersiedelung, bei denen alles zusammenhängt und gleichgemacht wird, haben wir außen vor gelassen.

Stattdessen wollten wir erfahren, was mit Kunst geschieht, wenn sie a) an symbolträchtigen oder belasteten Orten gezeigt wird, b) an belasteten Orten präsentiert wird, an denen die Spuren früheren Lebens noch intakt sind, c) so ausgestellt wird, dass sie intimer wirkt und dem Betrachter näher kommt. Wir wollten in verschiedenen Größenordnungen arbeiten und eine Biennale veranstalten, die in einem Moment ganz klein und intim ist und im nächsten Moment größer, offener. Wir wollten uns selbst, die Künstler und das Publikum daran erinnern, dass man nicht immer etwas Riesiges wie einen Straßenkreuzer braucht, sondern dass auch kleinere Räume okay sind. d) Wir wollten sehen, was passiert, wenn man Kunst neben Kunstwerken sieht, die wir selbst nicht ausgewählt haben. In einigen Wohnungen hatten zum Beispiel die Mieter Bilder oder Plastiken hängen und stehen gelassen, die ihnen gefielen, die aber nichts mit unserer Kunstauffassung zu tun hatten. e) Wir wollten herausfinden, was mit Kunst geschieht, wenn sie mit der Alltagskultur konfrontiert ist und sich mit ihr messen lassen muss, einer Alltagskultur, die spektakulär, aber auch öde sein kann. Alfred Hitchcock hat einmal gesagt: „Kino zeigt das Leben ohne die langweiligen Szenen …"

76

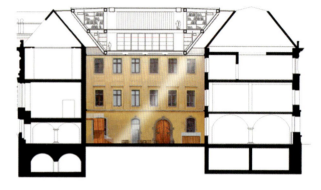

Project: Albertinum   Location: Dresden | Architects: Staab Architekten, Berlin

Ark for Art

Architektonische Tarnkappe für ein
hochwassergeschütztes Kunstdepot

**Architectural invisibility cloak
for a water-tight art depot**

Heart of the House

Raumimplantat für eine Familie

Space implant for a family

Project: Neo Leo / Vertical Living   **Location:** Cologne | **Architects:** Lüderwaldt Verhoff Architekten, Cologne

"What's the city all about?"

„Was ist denn schon dran an einer Stadt?"

Gert Kähler's book "Scifun-City" attempts to explain living and building in the "urban jungle" to children. His city rally navigates through urban complexity, striving to awaken lasting commitment to the built environment by conveying knowledge to the youngest citizens. Kähler is also committed to the "Architecture in Schools" initiative. As a freelance journalist, he has been contributing to the discussion about architecture and town planning in Germany for decades. He has taught at various German universities, and also addresses the subject in school textbooks.

Mr Kähler, in your book "Scifun-City. – Planen, bauen und leben im Großstadtdschungel" [Planing, building and living in the big city jungle, Rowohlt, 2002] your target audience is children of 10 years old and over. You show them how to analyse their urban habitat in a playful and critical way with the aid of numerous pictures and practical examples. How do you make it easier for children to access this subject matter, or to put the question in your own words: „What's the city all about?"

The title "Scifun" prepares them for the fact that town planning is a science, but that our enjoyment of the city has to be renegotiated and mediated all the time. When I'm writing, I try to formulate general questions about the city and its functional connections from a child's point of view. Initially, I try to make children aware of their built environment and to show them ways of influencing it. I want to broaden children's field of vision and make it clear to them that you have to know how something works to be able to change it. I explain the principles of town planning and living together in society, mentioning private and public space, urban infrastructures, political issues like "Who governs the city?". Also the history of city-building and symbolic conventions are explained using concrete examples. I deliberately address the children's impulse to participate directly in their urban environment. The fact is that children realise at a very early age that a city is a complex structure made up of very different components. So for this reason alone they should not leave it all to the adults. Ultimately they want to live in the city as well when they grow up.

Gert Kähler versucht mit dem Buch „Scifun-City" Kindern das Leben und Bauen im „Großstadtdschungel" zu erklären. Die Stadt-Rallye navigiert durch die Komplexität der Stadt und will so bei den jüngsten Bürgern durch Vermittlung von Wissen ein nachhaltiges Engagement für die gebaute Umwelt wecken. Daneben engagiert sich Kähler für die Initiative „Architektur in der Schule". Als Hochschullehrer war er an verschiedenen Universitäten in Deutschland tätig und trägt seit Jahrzehnten als freier Publizist zur Diskussion von Architektur und Stadtplanung in Deutschland bei. Seit einigen Jahren befasst er sich darüber hinaus erfolgreich mit der Vermittlung dieser Themen in Schulbüchern.

Herr Kähler, mit Ihrem Buch „Scifun-City. Planen, bauen und leben im Großstadtdschungel" (2002) wenden Sie sich an Kinder ab 10 Jahren, denen Sie mit Hilfe von zahlreichen Bildern und praktischen Beispielen die spielerisch-kritische Auseinandersetzung mit dem Lebensraum Stadt nahe bringen. Wie erleichtern Sie Kindern den Einstieg in das Themenfeld oder in Ihren eigenen Worten gefragt „Was ist denn schon dran an einer Stadt"?

Der Titel Scifun-City spielt bereits darauf an, dass Stadtplanung eine Wissenschaft ist, dass aber die Freude an Stadt stets neu verhandelt und vermittelt werden muss. Beim Schreiben versuche ich, aus Sicht eines Kindes allgemeine Fragen an die Stadt und ihre Funktionszusammenhänge zu formulieren. In erster Linie gilt es, Kinder gegenüber ihrer gebauten Umwelt zu sensibilisieren und ihnen dabei Möglichkeiten aufzuzeigen, wie sie Einfluss auf diese ausüben können. Es geht mir darum, das Sichtfeld der Kinder zu erweitern und ihnen klarzumachen, dass man wissen muss, wie etwas funktioniert, um es ändern zu können. Prinzipien der Stadtplanung und des gemeinschaftlichen Zusammenlebens wie Privatheit / Öffentlichkeit, die Infrastrukturen der Stadt, politische Zusammenhänge wie 'Wer regiert die Stadt?', aber auch Stadtbaugeschichte und Zeichenkonventionen werden anhand konkreter Beispiele erläutert. Der Impuls zur aktiven Teilnahme an der Stadtentwicklung wird gezielt angesprochen. Denn Kinder erkennen bereits früh, dass Stadt ein komplexes Gefüge unterschiedlichster Bestandteile darstellt. Allein deshalb schon sollten sie sie nicht den Erwachsenen allein überlassen. Schließlich wollen sie, wenn sie erwachsen sind, auch noch in der Stadt wohnen.

Tatsächlich laden Sie die Kinder zur direkten Einflussnahme und Gestaltung der städtischen Umwelt ein. Ihr Buch liest sich dabei wie eine Einführung in die Grundregeln demokratischen Zusammenlebens. Der Fokus Ihrer Beschäftigung mit der Stadt scheint stärker auf den Bewohnern der Stadt und weniger auf deren architektonischer oder städtebaulicher Umsetzung zu liegen. Was zeichnet also Stadt für Sie aus?

"Lesezeichen für Salbke", Magdeburg, KARO
with architektur+netzwerk, Leipzig
On the derelict site of a former public library a
"bookmark" was created. The shelving system
made from beer crates was filled up with books
by local residents. The shape of this improvised
spatial sculpture resulted from a local workshop
that included children as well as adults.
Auf der Brachfläche der früheren Ortsbibliothek
entstand ein „Lesezeichen". Das Regalsystem
aus Bierkisten wurde von den Anwohnern selbst
mit Büchern gefüllt. Die Form der improvisierten
Raumskulptur basiert auf einem Vor-Ort-Work-
shop, an dem u.a. Kinder beteiligt waren.

Gert Kähler im Gespräch mit Armand Gruentuch, Almut Ernst und Lukas Feireiss
Gert Kähler in conversation with Armand Gruentuch, Almut Ernst and Lukas Feireiss

And you certainly do invite children to influence and design their urban environment directly. Your book reads like an introduction to the basic rules of living together democratically. Your concern with the city seems to focus more on the people who live there and less on the way it is handled in terms of architecture and urban development. What makes the city so special for you?

Right at the beginning of the book I make it clear that merely putting up buildings and constructing roads is not enough to create a city. "City" means, above all, people living in the same place and feeling they belong together. And they do their living in a built environment. When explaining the basic building blocks of a functioning city I distinguish between its inhabitants' activities, their civil behaviour modes ("civis" means "citizen"!) and architecture and town planning in the traditional sense. This raises questions such as: How do they behave in relation to each other? Do they follow rules? How do they deal with the weaker people in society: children, homeless people, foreigners? Is the only person who is worth something in a city the strongest person, the one who has built the biggest or the tallest house? And yet it is the physical component of the city that usually comes to mind first: the buildings and streets, the schools and theatres, the railway lines and tramlines – everything that for its part makes

it possible for people to be active in the city. I think it is important to make it clear to children that each individual represents an important building block in the overall structure of the city, where the city user is part of a community in which the individuals are dependent on each other. A group of people who see their existence consisting of work, leisure, recreation and living together best realised in the city as system.

In this respect, given your focus on the people who inhabit a city, it seems logical for you to turn to young readers and to understand education as an urban development practice mode.

Correct, because if I want to change something, I have to be in a position to have my say about it. That's why I see architectural education in the sphere of building culture, and urban development education in urban development culture, as the first step towards long-term change. It is only when planning disciplines are made comprehensible to a wider public that real participation can take place in the long term, and decisions that are today largely dealt with by experts as technical questions can be discussed democratically. Fundamentally I encourage children to take responsibility and concern themselves with their city's future. It is not so much about them building a city themselves as about building on the existing city structure and contributing to the city's long and successful history.

Bereits zu Beginn des Buches mache ich deutlich, dass nur das Bauen von Häusern und Straßen nicht ausreicht, um eine Stadt zu kreieren. Stadt – das sind vor allem Menschen, die an einem Ort leben, dem Sie sich zugehörig fühlen. Und dieses Leben findet in einer gebauten Umgebung statt. Ich unterscheide bei der Erläuterung der Grundbausteine einer funktionierende Stadt zwischen den Aktivitäten der Bewohner, deren zivilen Umgangsformen („civis" heißt „Stadt"!) sowie der Architektur und Stadtplanung im herkömmlichen Sinne. Dabei werden Fragen aufgeworfen wie z.B.: Wie gehen sie miteinander um? Befolgen sie Regeln? Wie behandeln sie die Schwächeren in der Gesellschaft – die Kinder, die Obdachlosen, die Ausländer? Gilt nur der etwas in der Stadt, der am stärksten ist, der das größte oder das höchste Haus gebaut hat? Uns kommt jedoch meist der physische Teil der Stadt als erstes in den Sinn: Das sind die Häuser und Straßen, die Schulgebäude und Theater, die Bahngleise und Straßenbahnschienen – alles, was wiederum die Aktivitäten der Menschen in der Stadt erst möglich macht. Ich halte es für wichtig, den Kindern klarzumachen, dass jeder Einzelne einen wichtigen Baustein im Gesamtgefüge Stadt darstellt, in welcher der Stadtbenutzer Teil einer Gemeinschaft ist, in der wiederum die Einzelnen voneinander

abhängig sind. Eine Gruppe von Menschen, die ihre Existenz aus Arbeit, Freizeit, Erholung und Zusammenleben am besten im System Stadt verwirklicht sieht.

Mit diesem Fokus auf die Akteure der Stadt erscheint es folgerichtig, dass Sie sich an eine junge Leserschaft wenden und Bildung als ein Modus der städtebaulichen Praxis begreifen.

Richtig, denn wenn ich etwas verändern will, muss ich in der Lage sein, mitzureden. Daher sehe ich im Bereich der Baukultur die architektonische Bildung und in der Stadtbaukultur die städtebauliche Bildung als ein erster Schritt zu langfristigen Veränderungen an. Erst wenn die Planungsdisziplinen einer erweiterten Öffentlichkeit verständlich gemacht werden, kann langfristig gesehen wirkliche Partizipation stattfinden und Entscheidungen, die heute weitgehend als technische Fragen von Fachleuten getroffen werden, demokratisch diskutiert werden. Grundsätzlich ermuntere ich die Kinder dazu, Verantwortung zu übernehmen und sich selbst um ihre Stadt der Zukunft zu kümmern. Dabei geht es weniger darum, eine Stadt selber zu bauen, als vielmehr darum, die bestehende Stadt weiterzubauen und zur langen und erfolgreichen Geschichte der Stadt beizutragen.

81

Vertical Labyrinth

Spielplatz im Kirchenschiff

Playground in a nave

Project: MACHmit! Children's Museum   **Location:** Berlin | **Architects:** Klaus Block, Berlin

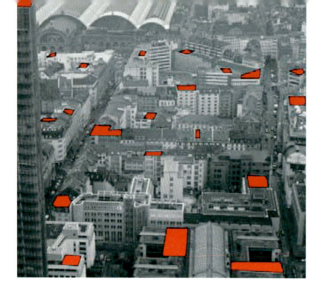

82

Project: Idea Laboratory   **Location:** Frankfurt am Main | **Architects:** bb22 architekten + stadtplaner, Frankfurt am Main

Inner City Laboratory

Masterplan der Möglichkeiten

Opportunity masterplan

Game cube with
unconventional layout

A
New
Set
of
Rules

Project: Playground Niebuhrstraße | Location: Berlin | Architects: TOPOTEK 1, Berlin

Project: City Odours **Location:** Germany | **Artist:** Sissel Tolaas, Berlin

Smell Matters

Unsichtbare Spuren der Stadt

Invisible traces of the city

"Es scheint, dass die Verbannung des Geruchs aus dem kulturellen Diskurs – Gerüche waren für die Moderne kein Thema – durch dessen Ausarbeitung im kommerziellen Diskurs ersetzt worden ist. Marketing-Experten haben entdeckt, was Akademiker und andere Kulturträger ignoriert haben: GERÜCHE SIND VON BEDEUTUNG." (Sissel Tolaas)

"It seems that the elimination of smell from the cultural discourse – smells are not a topic of discussion in modernity – has been replaced by its elaboration through commercial discourse. Marketers have discovered what academics and other arbiters of culture have ignored: SMELL MATTERS TO PEOPLE." (Sissel Tolaas)

The Atmosphere of a City

Die Atmosphäre einer Stadt

Gernot Böhme

The Paris Metro once boasted a very special scent. You could have taken me to Paris while I was sound asleep and I would have awoken knowing exactly where I was. Now I'd give anything if someone could just find a way to get me a bottle of that fragrance. I'd breathe it in and instantly I'd distinguish the Paris of yesteryear just like Marcel Proust recognised his Cambrais from a Madeleine cake. Paris has changed. It's more technical, cleaner. These days one must draw upon something other than an odour to identify the place. Perhaps my Parisian perfume was the last whiff of that particular stench, the one so delightfully portrayed by Alain Corbin in his book "The Foul and the Fragrant" (1982), which, since the beginning of the nineteenth century, was expelled from the city by its sensitive citizens in wave after wave of deodorisation. It may in fact be the case that younger people recognise completely different odours while I, in a fit of nostalgia, refuse to take them in.

Indeed, it is still true that cities, districts, neighbourhoods, and landscapes all have their scents – despite modern sewage systems, ventilation, and deodorisation. It is thus still possible to entrust the nose to decide whether one is standing in Eastern or Western Berlin. It may no longer have anything to do with two-stroke engine fuel, but most certainly with the East's burning of brown coal briquettes. In other places, it has to do with the dampness of the earth, or with stones, or the particular variety of trees that grow in the city, or that one can smell the sea, or the kind of petrol being pumped, or the kinds of transportation devices themselves, or of course the city's people and their lifestyles and nutritional habits. Smells are an essential element of the atmosphere of a city – perhaps the most essential of all, since no other sense can claim to be quite as atmospheric as the phenomena of smells. Haphazardly spewed into the vastness, they enfold, swath, enshroud, and allow no escape. They establish the most dramatic of all environmental qualities, wherever a person finds himself. Smells make it possible to identify places and to identify oneself with a place.

„Eine Stadt ohne Geruch ist
wie ein Mensch ohne Charakter."

**"A city without a scent is like
a person without a personality"**

Mitscherlich (1966)

Früher hatte die Metro in Paris einen ganz besonderen Geruch. Man hätte mich im Schlaf nach Paris versetzen können, und ich hätte an diesem Geruch erkannt, wo ich bin. Heute würde ich etwas darum geben, wenn mir jemand noch einmal ein Fläschchen von diesem Geruch verschaffen könnte. Ich würde daran schnuppern und aus diesem Geruch jenes Paris von damals herausschnüffeln – wie Marcel Proust sein Cambrais aus dem Madelaine-Kuchen. Paris ist anders geworden, viel technischer, cleaner, und man muss es wohl heute an etwas Anderem erkennen als am Geruch. Vielleicht war ja mein Paris-Geruch noch der letzte Hauch jener Miasmen, die nach der schönen Darstellung von Alain Corbin in seinem Buch „Pesthauch und Blütenduft" (1982) von den empfindsam gewordenen Bürgern seit Anfang des 19. Jahrhunderts in mehreren Desodorierungswellen aus der Stadt vertrieben wurden.

Aber vielleicht sind es heute nur andere Gerüche, an denen nun Andere, Jüngere ihr Paris erkennen, während ich in nostalgischer Laune mich weigere, sie aufzunehmen. Denn dass Städte, Quartiere, Gegenden und Landschaften ihre Gerüche haben, gilt auch heute – trotz Schwemmkanalisation, Ventilation, Desodorierung. So kann man noch immer mit der Nase entscheiden, ob man sich in Ost- oder West-Berlin befindet. Das liegt zwar nicht mehr am Zweitakter-Benzin, wohl aber an der Verwendung von Braunkohlenbriketts im Osten. Anderswo liegt es an der Erde, wenn sie feucht wird, oder an Steinen oder an bestimmten Bäumen, die in der Stadt wachsen, oder dass man das Meer riecht, am verwendeten Benzin, an den Verkehrsmitteln überhaupt und natürlich an den Menschen und ihren Lebens- und Essgewohnheiten. Die Gerüche sind ein wesentliches Element der Atmosphäre einer Stadt, vielleicht sogar das wesentlichste, denn Gerüche sind wie kaum ein anderes Sinnesphänomen atmosphärisch: Unbestimmt in die Weite ergossen, hüllen sie ein, sind unausweichlich, sie sind jene Qualität der Umgebung, die am tiefgreifendsten durch das Befinden spüren lässt, wo man sich befindet. Gerüche machen es möglich, Orte zu identifizieren und sich mit Orten zu identifizieren.

Excerpts from / Auszüge aus:
"Die Atmosphäre einer Stadt", in: Gernot Böhme, Architektur und Atmosphäre, **published autumn 2006** / erscheint im Herbst, Wilhelm Fink Verlag, Stuttgart

The "As Found" Principle

The story of the "Convertible City" begins – one could claim – in Aix-en-Provence, in the summer of 1953. The British architects Alison and Peter Smithson presented their "Urban Re-Identification" panels (CIAM grille) there at the 9ᵗʰ CIAM congress, offering stern criticism of the prevailing functionalist city model, with all its social and anthropological deficits. The Smithsons set the more phenomenological criteria of house, street, neighbourhood and metropolis against the four functionalistic categories cited in the "Charter of Athens": living, working, recreation and circulation.

Their approach was illustrated by Nigel Henderson's photographs of street life in the East End of London, and by their urban development ideas, which later became well-known as "Cluster City". Henderson's pictures of children playing in the street, and thus the act of addressing the situation "as found", were intended to offer a different perception of reality and an appropriate approach to dealing with emerging problems. The Smithsons used their urban development diagrams to show how new urban structures evolved in harmony with the existing city, becoming integrated within an overall urban programme by exchanging ideas with it.

Thomas Schregenberger

Die Geschichte der „Convertible City" – so könnte man behaupten – beginnt im Sommer 1953 in Aix-en-Provence. Dort präsentierten die britischen Architekten Alison und Peter Smithson auf dem 9. CIAM-Kongress ihre „Urban Re-Identification" Tafeln (CIAM-Grille), eine harte Kritik am damaligen funktionalistischen Stadtmodell, mit seinen gesellschaftlichen und anthropologischen Defiziten. Den vier funktionalistischen Kategorien der „Charta von Athen": Wohnen, Arbeiten, Erholung und Verkehr setzten die Smithsons die eher phänomenologischen Kategorien Haus, Straße, Bezirk und Stadt entgegen.

Illustriert wurde ihre Haltung durch Fotografien von Nigel Henderson über das Straßenleben im Londoner East End und durch ihre städtebaulichen Konzepte, welche später unter dem Namen Cluster-City bekannt wurden. Hendersons Bilder von auf der Straße spielenden Kindern, und damit die Auseinandersetzung mit dem Vorgefundenen – „as found" – sollte eine veränderte Wahrnehmung der Wirklichkeit und eine adäquate Bearbeitung der anstehenden Probleme bieten. Mit ihren städtebaulichen Diagrammen zeigten die Smithsons auf, wie neue Stadtstrukturen sich im Einklang mit der bestehenden Stadt entwickeln und im Austausch mit ihr zu einer stadträumlichen Gesamtheit verweben.

Hinter dieser Zuwendung zur realen und existierenden Stadt und ihren räumlichen und gesellschaftlichen Qualitäten steckte eine entschiedene Distanzierung von den abstrakten und elitären Parallelwelten des modernen Städtebaus. An ihre Stelle setzten sie die Suche nach einem Dialog zwischen aktuellem Städtebau und bestehender Stadt.

Upper Lawn Pavilion,
Fonthill, 1959-1961,
Alison and Peter
Smithson, London >>
Skipping, Chisenhale
Road, 1951, Gillian
Alexander, London

With this attention to the real and existing city and its spatial and social qualities they were firmly distancing themselves from the abstract and élitist parallel worlds of modern urban development, which they replaced with a search for a dialogue between current urban development and the existing city.

Even back then, the Smithsons began using the term "as found" to describe this approach to the problem and their attitude to the existing city, to the everyday and the ordinary. They did not in fact begin to write about it until 1990 (1) but they had been using the term long before in discussions with their friends like the artist Eduardo Paolozzi, the aforementioned Nigel Henderson and, of course, the onlooker Reyner Banham. All the works produced by this group in those years,their buildings and designs, collages and sculptures, photographs and texts, and not least their exhibition installations, were originally inspired by the term as found.

As found tends to carry some negative associations; it was most unusual to see it as a characteristic offering positive qualities. It is usually thought of disparagingly in the sense of "been there, done that", "same as ever" or "old hat". So it was also to this group's credit that they suddenly started to identify the positive qualities of what has always been there and thus open up a background that also shows things, people who make them and the manufacturing process in a particular light.

Diese Denk- und Vorgehensweise und diese Haltung gegenüber dem Bestehenden, Alltäglichen und Gewöhnlichen nannten die Smithsons schon damals as found.

Alison und Peter Smithson schrieben zwar erst 1990 (1) davon, hatten den Begriff jedoch schon lange vorher zusammen mit ihren Freunden wie dem Künstler Eduardo Paolozzi, dem Fotografen Nigel Henderson und natürlich dem Zaungast Reyner Banham verwendet. Die Werke, die diese Gruppe in jenen Jahren hervorbrachte, ihre Bauten und Entwürfe, ihre Collagen und Skulpturen, ihre Fotografien und Texte und nicht zuletzt ihre Ausstellungsinstallationen haben in der Bezeichnung des as found ihr gemeinsames Ursprungsmotiv.

As found bedeutet „wie gefunden", „wie aufgefunden" oder „wie vorgefunden" und es war durchaus ungewöhnlich, in einer solchen Eigenschaft nach den positiven Qualitäten zu suchen. Denn meist wird es im Sinne von „schon da gewesen", „wie gehabt" oder „Schnee von gestern" entwertend gedacht. Darin lag also auch das Verdienst dieser Gruppe, nun plötzlich das Positive des schon Dagewesenen zu behaupten und damit einen Hintergrund aufzuspannen, der den Dingen, den Personen, die sie herstellen, und dem Prozess der Herstellung selbst eine bestimmte Tendenz verleiht.

Denn as found ist die Tendenz, sich mit dem, was da ist, auseinanderzusetzen, das Vorhandene zu erkennen, seinen Spuren mit Interesse zu folgen. Dieses Interesse liegt in der Erfahrung begründet, dass man gerade auf diesen Wegen zu neuen Erkenntnissen und „Formen" kommt. As found ist eine Sache des Selbstvertrauens. Letztlich bedeutet der Begriff, etwas radikal zur Kenntnis zu nehmen; und ist damit womöglich die umgekehrte Entsprechung zum „interesselosen Wohlgefallen" der Aufklärung. Denn dieses inthronisierte die Ästhetik des Idealismus und dachte auf das Absolute hin, während der as-found-Ansatz alles, womit er zu tun hat, nur in Relationen bestimmen kann und will. So ist er ästhetisch innerhalb einer realistischen Ein-

from left to right/ von links nach rechts: "Living Bunker", Cologne, Luczak Architekten, Cologne >>"Bitumen Palace", Cologne, Boris Sieverts, Cologne >> "PLATOON office", Berlin, PLATOON, Berlin >> "House Bonnin", Eichstätt, HildundK Architekten, Munich >> "Hotel Continental", Aachen, Tatsurou Bashi (Tazro Niscino), Cologne

As found represents an inclination to address what is there, to acknowledge what already exists, and to take an interest in the clues it offers. This interest is based on the experience that that this is precisely the right path to take in order to acquire new insights and "forms". As found is a matter of self-confidence. Ultimately the term means taking note of something radically, and that may well be the converse of the Enlightenment's "benign neglect", a movement that enthroned the aesthetics of idealism and inclined towards the absolute, while the as found approach can only, and only intends to define everything it touches in relative terms. So it is positioned aesthetically within a realistic attitude to the world. Ethically it admires and respects everything that is. Insight encourages the approach's interest in what "reality" is. Aesthetic is not only beautiful, ethical is not only good, cognitive, insightful is not only true.

But what do we mean by taking note of something radically? What does that imply for the weeds in the garden, the dents in the car, the graffiti on the walls of buildings? There are various reactions, The cathartic: pull up anything that doesn't belong, knock out the dents or paint over the graffiti. The pragmatic-idealistic: try to imagine the damage is not there. Then the as found approach would be to ask: why are they called weeds? Could a weed also be seen as a plant? Was the wall really more attractive before?

This attitude reveals certain qualities within things: directness , immediacy, roughness and material presence. As found means dealing with the here and now, with things that are real and ordinary, solid and tangibly present. It is an invitation to follow the trail of what is there already. It is an approach that neutralises an existing set of values first and then effectively recharges them from that position. As found requires a specific evaluation dependent on the concrete case. It is an independent path to the substance of a work.

As found involves being attentive, respect for what is there, and making something of something, with all your heart in the job. It is the technique of reaction. Rather than charging urgently ahead and imposing a theme, the theme is to be developed.

Faced with the evanescent excess of conceivable resources, as found contains the subversive possibility of using intelligent restriction to find a foothold and a sense of commitment . It sees a situation's limitations as opportunities and not as confining possibilities. The eye is compelled to look in a different way and to concentrate on what is nearby; by doing this it will prove to be looking at the unexpected inventive power and spaciousness of the world - as found.

stellung zur Welt verortet. Ethisch ist seine Hochachtung vor dem, was ist. Erkenntnis fördert sein Interesse für das, was „Wirklichkeit" ist. Das Ästhetische ist nicht nur das Schöne, das Ethische nicht nur das Gute, das Erkenntnismäßige nicht nur das Wahre.

Doch was heißt es, etwas radikal zur Kenntnis zu nehmen? Was heißt das für das Unkraut im Garten, für die Beulen im Auto, für die Graffitis an den Hauswänden? Es gibt verschiedene Reaktionen. Die kathartische: Das Ungehörige jäten, ausbeulen oder überstreichen. Die pragmatisch-idealistische: versuchen, die Schäden wegzudenken. Die as-found-Haltung wäre etwa, zu fragen: Warum nennt man das Unkraut? Könnte man im Unkraut auch eine Pflanze sehen? War die Wand vorher wirklich schöner?

Diese Haltung und die Eigenschaften der Dinge, die sie an den Tag bringt, sind die der Direktheit, der Unvermitteltheit, des Rohen, der materiellen Präsenz. As found, das ist die Beschäftigung mit dem Hier und Jetzt, mit dem Realen und Gewöhnlichen, mit dem Handfesten und Wirklichen. Es ist der Vorschlag, den Spuren des Vorhandenen zu folgen. Es ist ein Ansatz, der ein bestehendes Wertgefüge zunächst neutralisiert und von dort aus gleichsam neu auflädt. As found bedingt eine spezifische Bewertung in Abhängigkeit vom konkreten Fall. Es ist ein eigener Weg zur Substanz eines Werkes.

Im as found liegt angesichts der zerfließenden Überfülle an denkbaren Mitteln eine subversive Möglichkeit, in der intelligenten Beschränkung Halt und Verbindlichkeit zu finden. Es versteht die Begrenztheit einer Situation als Chance und nicht als Einengung der Möglichkeiten. Der Blick wird gezwungen, sich umzuwenden und sich auf das Naheliegende zu konzentrieren; und bei dieser Umkehrung wird er sich immer wieder als ein Blick auf die unerwartete Erfindungskraft und Geräumigkeit der vorgefundenen Welt erweisen.

from left to right/ von links nach rechts: "Das Silo", Hamburg-Harburg, bhl Architekten, Hamburg >> "Netzuniversität Ost", Johanna Bornkamm, Berlin >> Youth hostel Bremen, Raumzeit, Berlin >> "Radialsystem", Center for performing arts, Berlin, Gerhard Spangenberg Architekt, Berlin

AS FOUND TODAY

The as found approach was first important in England in the 1950s, but it can also be understood as a starting-point for addressing the problems of today. Even though the historical situation is completely different, now as then, as found means dealing with the "inertia" and "resistance" of what already exists. And the result is not a vision of the great lack of friction between the past and the future, but the question of the necessary obstinacy in dealing with what is there.

To what extent can we relate the dynamics of the fifties and early sixties to today? There is something incredibly liberating about the approach of allowing yourself to the stimulated by clues from the past and then develop new insights from them. It means emancipation from every attempted insinuation that requires all emotions to be thoroughly remoulded against the background of ambitious aims. In contrast with this, as found offers stubbornly discovering the ostensibly unimportant and the gift of making something personally important out of this. It makes it possible to question conventional value structures in a friendly and subversive way and, perhaps even aggressively, rejecting second-hand experiences. If there is immediacy, then it is here. See for yourself, understand for yourself. Find something that was not already obvious and now that it has been found let it develop impact as an idea and in its material quality. This is a fascinating process. It leads to exciting discoveries and often makes something new out of almost nothing.

Alison and Peter Smithson's Upper Lawn Pavilion is an outstanding example of this dis-covering. (2) As found, and linked with this the Smithsons' way of thinking, appears to relate to the concept of the "Convertible City" and Grüntuch und Ernst's "extension" of the German Pavilion.

It is all about connecting up with the place and its history, about discovering what is already there, with all its opportunities and potentials. It is about perceiving and being aware of things and the de- and re-valuing process. And not least it is about passion for the task.

AS FOUND HEUTE

Die Haltung des as found wurde zunächst im England der fünfziger Jahre wichtig, zugleich lässt sie sich aber auch als Ansatz zur Auseinandersetzung mit den Problemen von heute verstehen. Auch wenn die geschichtlichen Voraussetzungen gänzlich verschieden sind, handelt as found damals wie heute vom Umgang mit der „Trägheit" und dem „Widerstand" des Bestehenden. Und am Ende steht nicht die Vision der großen Reibungslosigkeit von Vergangenheit und Zukunft, sondern die Frage nach dem notwendigen Eigensinn im Umgang mit dem Vorhandenen.

Inwiefern lässt sich die Dynamik der fünfziger und frühen sechziger Jahre in einen Bezug zu heute setzen? Die Haltung, sich von den Spuren des Vorhandenen anregen und zu neuen Erkenntnissen führen zu lassen, hat etwas ungemein Befreiendes. Sie ermöglicht die Emanzipation gegenüber allen Einflüsterungsversuchen, die vor dem Hintergrund großer neuer Ziele die Durchmodellierung aller Emotionen verlangen. As found bedeutet demgegenüber die eigenwillige Aufdeckung von angeblich Unwichtigem und die Gabe, daraus etwas persönlich Wichtiges zu machen. Es ermöglicht eine freundlich-subversive, vielleicht auch eine aggressive Hinterfragung des konventionellen Wertgefüges und den entschiedenen Verzicht auf Secondhand-Erlebnisse. Wenn es Unmittelbarkeit gibt, dann hier. Selber merken, selber verstehen. Etwas finden, was nicht schon offenkundig war, was aber, nachdem es nun gefunden ist, als Idee und in seiner Materialität eine Ausstrahlung entwickelt. Dieser Prozess ist faszinierend. Er führt zu aufregenden Entdeckungen und macht oft aus fast Nichts etwas Neues.

Ein hervorragendes Beispiel für diese Herangehensweise in der Architektur ist der Upper Lawn Pavillon von Alison und Peter Smithson. (2) As found, und damit verbunden die Denk- und Vorgehensweise der Smithsons, scheint verwandt zu sein mit dem Konzept der „Convertible-City" und der „Erweiterung" des Deutschen Pavillon von Gruentuch und Ernst. Es geht um Beziehungen zum Ort und seiner Geschichte, um die Entdeckung des Vorgefundenen mit ihren Chancen und Potenzialen. Es geht um das bewusste Wahrnehmen der Dinge und um den Prozess des Entwertens und Neubewertens derselben. Und nicht zuletzt geht es auch um die Leidenschaft für die Aufgabe.

1) Alison and Peter Smithson: "The 'As Found' and the 'Found'", in: D. Robbins (ed.): Independent Group. Postwar Britain and the Aesthetics of Plenty, Cambridge, Mass./London 1990, p. 201ff.

2) For more on the Upper Lawn Pavilion: Thomas Schregenberger, Das Prinzip 'as found' in Smithson's Upper Lawn Pavilion, in: Positionen. Architektur 2002/03, FH Liechtenstein 2003; see also: archplus 161, pp. 16-17

1) Alison und Peter Smithson: „The 'As Found' and the 'Found'", in: D. Robbins (Hg.): Independent Group. Postwar Britain and the Aesthetics of Plenty, Cambridge, Mass./London 1990, S. 201ff.

2) Mehr zum Upper Lawn Pavilion: Thomas Schregenberger, Das Prinzip „as found" in Smithson's Upper Lawn Pavilion, in: Positionen. Architektur 2002/03, FH Liechtenstein 2003; siehe auch: archplus 161, S. 16-17

See also / siehe auch: Claude Lichtenstein / Thomas Schregenberger (eds.): As Found. Die Entdeckung des Gewöhnlichen, Zürich 2001

Project: Theaterformen   Location: Braunschweig, Germany | Architects: Kühn Malvezzi, Berlin

Red Carpet Treatment

Temporäres Treppenmonument für das Stadttheater

Monumental temporary entrance to the municipal theatre

Realtime Theatre

92

Öffentlichkeit als Schauspiel

Staging the public

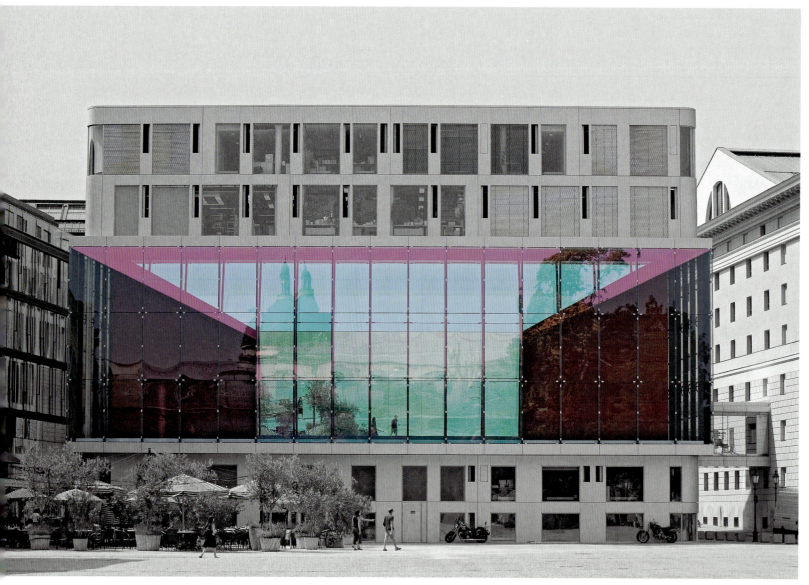

Project: Bühnenfenster   Location: Munich I Artist: Olafur Eliasson, Berlin

Open Invitation

Aufruf zum kulinarischen Ungehorsam

Call for culinary disobedience

Project: Hotel Q   Location: Berlin | Architects: GRAFT Berlin - Los Angeles - Beijing

Glamour Magnet

Eingeschobene Hotellandschaft als kosmopolitische Anlaufstelle

Implanted hotel landscape as a cosmopolitan rendezvous

Project: Permanent breakfast   Location: Germany | Architects: MESS, Kaiserslautern

The City and It Gardens

Die Stadt und ihre Gärten

Nature, country, countryside or garden have long been names for places promising respite from the city's rigours and the everyday life associated with them. Designs by landscape architects and artists still tend to celebrate this contrast. But other designs redefine nature's urban manifestations and create surprising new gardens; Beaches with palm trees are created by city river- banks, and agriculture is coming back to town in some places. The images of today's inner cities are just as diverse as the expectations and desires invested in their often controversial open spaces.

PARKS >> Older municipal parks invite us in to stroll and rest, to contemplate or admire nature at her most beautiful and imposing, and sometimes exotic. The 19th century style people's parks with their beer gardens and boating lakes, sports fields and bathing areas emphasise sociability and communication. Their green, unpretentious functional areas are intended for mass use and offer space for a whole variety of activities, from demonstrations to ball games, from concerts to picnics. Parks are still essential features of towns.

New parks offering this range of possibilities have emerged in recent years in places where derelict sites have opened up in urban or suburban areas, and districts have been replanned or upgraded. Examples of this are the Riemer Park on the site of Munich's Riem airport (design: Latitude Nord, Gilles Vexlard, opened 2005). The Südstadtpark in Fürth on an old military site (Werkgemeinschaft Freiraum, Gerd Aufmkolk, 2004) or the Wiesenpark an der Wuhle in Marzahn, Berlin, where the area surrounding a slab-construction estate has been redesigned on a large scale (Gruppe F, Nikolai Koehler, 2002).

One of the few new parks in a high-density city-centre area is "Park Fiction", the Antonipark in Hamburg's St. Pauli. It has been available to a wider public since documenta 11. In 1994, a group of artists, planners and nearby residents was set up to maintain the last large open space in the city's night-life district, which is also its poorest residential area. The park was realized between 2003 and 2006; it was created by a collective planning process that responded

Susanne Hauser

Die Natur, das Land, die Landschaft oder der Garten sind seit Langem Namen für Orte, die Erholung von der anstrengenden Stadt und dem durch sie bestimmten Alltag versprechen. Nach wie vor zelebrieren landschaftsarchitektonische und künstlerische Entwürfe diesen Gegensatz. Andere Entwürfe aber definieren neue urbane Naturen und erzeugen überraschend neue Gärten. Daneben entstehen Palmenstrände an innerstädtischen Flussufern und an manchen Orten wandert die Landwirtschaft in die Stadt zurück. Die Bilder der heutigen Innenstädte sind ebenso vielfältig wie die Erwartungen und Wünsche an ihre oft umstrittenen Freiräume.

PARKS >> Ältere Stadtparks laden zum Spaziergang und Ausruhen, zur Kontemplation oder zum Staunen vor einer schönen und repräsentativen, manchmal auch exotischen Natur ein. Volksparks mit ihren Biergärten und Ruderteichen, Sportwiesen und Badestellen legen dagegen Wert auf Geselligkeit und Kommunikation. Ihre grünen, unprätentiösen Nutzflächen sind für massenhaften Gebrauch gemacht und bieten Platz für die unterschiedlichsten Aktivitäten, von der Kundgebung bis zum Ballspiel, vom Konzert bis zum Picknick. Parks sind bis heute unverzichtbare Orte in der Stadt.

Neue Parks mit diesem Spektrum an Möglichkeiten sind in den letzten Jahren dort entstanden, wo sich in städtischen oder suburbanen Gebieten Brachen aufgetan haben und die Neuplanung oder Aufwertung von Stadtteilen anstand. Beispiele sind der Riemer Park auf dem alten Gelände des Flughafens München-Riem (Entwurf: Latitude Nord, Gilles Vexlard, eröffnet 2005), der Südstadtpark Fürth auf einem alten Militärgelände (Werkgemeinschaft Freiraum, Gerd Aufmkolk, 2004) oder der Wiesenpark an der Wuhle in Berlin-Marzahn, wo die Umgebung einer Plattenbausiedlung großräumig neu gestaltet wurde (Gruppe F, Nikolai Koehler, 2002).

Einer der wenigen neuen Parks in hochverdichtetem Innenstadtgebiet ist „Park Fiction", der Antonipark in Hamburg-St. Pauli. Er ist einer breiteren Öffentlichkeit seit der documenta 11 bekannt. 1994 hatte sich eine Gruppe von Künstlern, Planern und Anwohnern mit dem Ziel gegründet, die letzte größere Freifläche im Amüsierviertel der Stadt, welches gleichzeitig das ärmste Wohngebiet ist, zu erhalten. Der zwischen 2003 und 2006 realisierte Park entstand in einem kollektiven Planungsprozess, der mit einer Vielzahl von Einzelobjekten auf konkrete Wünsche antwortete. Das Ergebnis ist ein neuer Typus eines Innenstadtparks. In ihm gibt es eine Palmeninsel, den Fliegenden Teppich (ein Mosaik), ein Tulpenfeld, einen Hundegarten mit Zuschauertribüne, drei Open Air Solarien, Nachbarschaftsbeete und öffentliche Kräuterbeete, eine Boule-Insel und den „Bambushain des bescheidenen Politikers" (Anwohnerinitiative „Park Fiction" und arbos Landschaftsarchitekten Greis, Günter Greis).

"Parkscheinautomatenbegrünung",
Berlin / Hamburg, Yutta Saftien, Hamburg

KLEINE GÄRTEN >> Zwei Entwicklungen fallen in Innenstädten auf: Funktionen alter Parks ziehen sich in private Räume zurück oder sie vermischen sich kleinräumig mit anderen städtischen Funktionen. Das geht teilweise mit Privatisierung und der Individualisierung der Pflege und des Zutrittsrechts zu grünen Zonen einher. Eine nicht neue, bekannt exklusive und luxuriöse Variante ist der private Garten auf dem Dach des innerstädtischen Hauses, eine andere, ebenfalls nicht ganz neue Variante ist die Anlage von privatem Grün um innerstädtische Siedlungen.

Auch die Entwicklung neuer öffentlich zugänglicher Frei- und Grünräume findet relativ kleinteilig statt. Sie realisiert sich in einer Diffusion von kleinen grünen Zonen, die auf unterschiedlichste Auffassungen von „Natur" oder „Grün in der Stadt" verweisen. Die Erinnerung an ältere städtische Gärten erscheint in neu interpretierter und manchmal miniaturisierter Form wie im kleinsten der hier vorgestellten Gärten: So hat der Kieler Apotheker Eckhard Kratzenberg vor etwa fünf Jahren begonnen, die Baumscheiben unter den Bäumen vor seiner Apotheke mit Heilkräutern zu bepflanzen und mit Tafeln zu versehen. Diese geben wie in einem botanischen Garten Auskunft über die Pflanzen und ihre Bedeutung.

Manche Gärten zeugen von einem geradezu detektivischen Spürsinn für Nischen und Lücken, in denen neues Grün entstehen kann. Die Düsseldorfer Künstlerin Tita Giese hat beispielsweise ab 2000 vier Restflächen, die am Fußgängerüberweg zwischen Kunstverein und Deichtorhallen in Hamburg durch Verkehrsbauten übrig gelassen wurden, in erstaunliche Gärten verwandelt. Die exotischen Pflanzen erreichten eine Höhe von bis zu sechs Metern, sodass sie auch für die vorüberkommenden Autofahrer hervorragend sichtbar waren. Konzeptionelle Voraussetzung dieses Projektes ist die Auffassung von Pflanzen als Kulturprodukte, deren „natürliches" Vorkommen nicht bedeutsam ist. Wohl aber sind es ihre Wachstumsbedingungen und -prozesse sowie ihre formal-ästhetischen und skulpturalen Eigenschaften. So wuchsen zwischen winterharten Palmen aus China Schilf und verschiedene Bambusarten, und aus Pappelstämmen wucherten drei Sorten Pilze, von denen eine auffallend gelb leuchtete.

to concrete requests with a large number of individual features. The result is a new kind of inner city park. It has an island with palm trees, the Flying Carpet (a mosaic), a tulip field, a dog garden with stand for spectators, three open-air solariums, neighbourhood beds and public herb beds, a boules island and the "modest politician's bamboo grove" ("Park Fiction" residents' initiative and arbos Landschaftsarchitekten Greis, Günter Greis).

SMALL GARDENS >> There have been two striking developments in city centres: functions that used to be performed by old parks are shifting back into private spaces or mingling with other urban functions on a small scale. This is partly associated with privatisation and the individualisation of maintenance and the right of access to green zones. One variant, that are not new but known to be exclusive and luxurious, are the private roof-gardens of inner-city houses, and another, also not altogether new, are private green areas established around inner city housing estates.

New, publicly accessible, open and green spaces are also developing in relatively intricate forms. Small green zones are diffusing, indicating a variety of views on "nature" or "green space in the city". Older municipal gardens are remembered in re-interpreted and sometimes miniaturised form, as in the smallest of the gardens presented here: about five years ago the Kiel pharmacist Eckhard Kratzenberg started to plant the beds round the trees outside his chemist's shop with medicinal herbs and provide them with labels like those in a botanical gardens to give information about the plants and their meaning,

Some gardens demonstrate an almost detective-like eye for niches and gaps in which new green can emerge. For example, the Düsseldorf artist Tita Giese, working from 2000 to 2005, transformed four spaces left vacant by transport construction beside the pedestrian walkway between the Kunstverein and the Deichtorhallen in Hamburg into astonishing gardens. The exotic plants reached a height of up to six metres, so they

were also clearly visible for passing motorists. The essential concept behind this project was seeing plants as cultural products whose "natural" occurrence is not important. What is important is their growing conditions and processes and their formal-aesthetic and sculptural qualities. So reeds and various kinds of bamboo grew alongside hardy palms from China, and three sorts of mushrooms proliferated on poplar trunks, one of them glowing a striking yellow.

TEMPORARY GARDENS >> Some of the most significant urban garden explorations have been realised on a purely temporary basis. One popular pioneering event featured the "Temporary Gardens" that explored the potential of Berlin's urban space from 1997 to 2003 (Sprenger Architekten, Daniel Sprenger; Atelier le Balto, Marc Pouzol). For four days around the first weekend in each July, the organisers showed twenty playful and surprising gardens by landscape architects, artists or students in prominent urban locations. Practical, poetic or ironic comments on the nature of the place in questions were provided by features like deckchairs made of turf rolls (Jens Gartelmann, Klemens Hundertmark, 2000), a miniaturized classical garden (Belvedere 1999), sunflowers in a sewer access shaft (Maike Gevers, Bernd Reinecke, 2001) or the attic storey of a supermarket wreathed with roses (Markus Heller, Daniel Roehr, 2003).

A new annual garden (Atelier le Balto) has been created in the large paved courtyard of the KW Institute for contemporary art in the Mitte district of Berlin ever since the second Kunstbiennale Berlin in spring 2001. In the first years this garden was structured by wooden walkways defining a route through the plants, which looked different with the changing seasons. The first garden was a "tree nursery" with fruit trees, tamarisks, willows, vines and three larger trees. Climbers flowered in 2002 and 600 ornamental Japanese hop plants provided a feast for the eye in 2004.

In Leipzig, the Art Association there continued the "Temporary Artists' Gardens" project, which had been operating since 2001, with an event called "Art and Garden" in 2005. A number of artists decided not to design a garden from the outset, like for example Bertram Weisshaar, who showed "Leipzig as not built" in 2005 and invited visitors to walk round and explore existing gardens, and to look at an open-air seat, a pool and a station platform. André Tempel placed a mysterious structure comprising plastic parts in the fork of a tree, Ralf Witthaus cut spontaneous monuments into the grass in the park by the Schwanenteich with a lawnmower and Ulrike Gärtner marked out a "Parking space for itinerant aliens" by the Schauspielhaus. The result was transportable, disposable and ephemeral garden incidents compatible with the time-scale of the urban event.

RURALISATION >> Urban ways of life have been changing urban space for some time, but in Germany, after agriculture was driven out of town in the 19th century, the reverse process was known only in times of emergency or in financially weak urban districts. Today vegetables are not only grown in allotments, but also in urban

TEMPORÄRE GÄRTEN >> Einige der inhaltsreichsten Erkundungen zum Garten in der Stadt sind nur temporär realisiert worden. Eine populäre Pionierveranstaltung waren die „Temporären Gärten", die von 1997 bis 2003 Potenziale im Berliner Stadtraum erkundet haben (Sprenger Architekten, Daniel Sprenger; Atelier le balto, Marc Pouzol). Die Veranstalter stellten jeweils am ersten Juliwochenende für vier Tage an einem prominenten urbanen Ort zwanzig spielerische und überraschende Gärten von Landschaftsarchitekten, Künstlern oder Studierenden aus. Praktische, poetische oder ironische Kommentare zur Natur des jeweiligen Ortes lieferten unter anderem Liegestühle aus Rollrasen (Jens Gartelmann, Klemens Hundertmark, 2000), ein miniaturisierter klassischer Garten (Belvedere 1999), Sonnenblumen in einem Einstiegsschacht der Kanalisation (Maike Gevers, Bernd Reinecke, 2001) oder ein Kranz aus Rosen auf der Attika eines Supermarktes (Markus Heller, Daniel Roehr, 2003).

Seit der zweiten Kunstbiennale Berlin im Frühjahr 2001 entsteht jedes Jahr im großen gepflasterten Hof des KW Institute for contemporary art in Berlin-Mitte ein neuer Garten (Atelier le balto). Dieser Garten war in den ersten Jahren durch Holzstege strukturiert, die einen Weg durch Pflanzen vorgaben, deren Anblick sich je nach Jahreszeit veränderte. Der erste dieser Gärten war eine „Baumschule" mit Obstbäumen, Tamarisken, Weiden, Weinstöcken und drei größeren Bäumen, 2002 blühten Kletterpflanzen und 2004 waren 600 Japanische Zierhopfen zu bewundern.

In Leipzig hat der dortige Kunstverein 2005 mit der Veranstaltung „Kunst und Garten" das seit 2001 stattfindende Projekt der „Temporären Künstlergärten" fortgesetzt. Manche Künstler verzichteten von vornherein auf die Gestaltung eines Gartens, so Bertram Weißhaar, der 2005 „das nicht gebaute Leipzig" zeigte und zur Spaziergangsforschung in bestehende Gärten, zu einem Freisitz, einem Teich und einem Bahnsteig einlud. André Tempel hat eine rätselhafte Konstruktion aus Kunststoffteilen in einer Astgabel abgelegt, Ralf Witthaus mit dem Rasenmäher spontane Denk-mäler in das Gras des Parks am Schwanenteich gemäht und Ulrike Gärtner am Schauspielhaus einen „Parkplatz für Aliens unterwegs" markiert. Entstanden sind transportable, disponible und ephemere Gartenereignisse, die sich mit dem Zeitmaß des urbanen Events vertragen.

RURALISIERUNG >> Städtische Lebensweisen verändern schon lange den ländlichen Raum, doch die Umkehrung war in Deutschland seit der Vertreibung der Landwirtschaft aus der Stadt im 19. Jahrhundert nur in Notzeiten oder in finanzschwachen Stadtbezirken bekannt. Heute wird Gemüse nicht nur in Schrebergärten, sondern auch in Höfen städtischer Häuser angebaut, Kräuter und Salate werden auf Balkonen und Fensterbänken gezüchtet und Nahrungsmittel in Mietergärten erzeugt. Längst geht diese Entwicklung über das Beispiel des Nutzgartens hinaus, den ein türkischer Mitbürger noch im Schutz der Mauer im äußersten Osten Berlin-Kreuzbergs angelegt hat. Der Garten ist eine der Attraktionen des Bezirkes.

In Gemeinschaftsgärten in Berlin, in denen unter anderem Nahrungsmittel angebaut werden, geht es in unterschiedlicher Gewichtung um die Gewinnung von Grünflächen in hochverdichteten Gebieten, um die Frage, wie bürgerschaftliches Engagement zur Rettung öffentlicher Grünflächen beitragen kann, um sinnvolle Beschäftigung,

ästhetischen Genuss, um das gemeinsame ökologische und auch ökonomische Experiment. Potenziale bieten Baulücken oder Brachflächen. Die an vielen, mittlerweile auch akademischen Orten darüber geführten Diskussionen knüpfen an das Vorbild der New Yorker Community Gardens an.

Auch ein Kunstprojekt ist unter dem Stichwort Rurali-sierung zu nennen. Olaf Nicolai hat 2005 im Rahmen der schon erwähnten Temporären Künstlergärten in Leipzig ein innerstädtisches landwirtschaftliches Projekt realisiert. Er hat bekannte Architekturbüros gebeten, zeitgenössische Bienenhäuser für das Leipziger Stadtgebiet zu entwerfen. Sie werden von Mai bis Oktober mit Bienen besetzt und von Imkern betreut. Das Winterlager befindet sich im Museum der bildenden Künste. Die Entwürfe stammen von sauerbruch hutton (London/Berlin), Ortner & Ortner (Wien), b+ (Köln) und J.P. Kleihues (Berlin).

Wenn auch in Deutschland die Ruralisierung der Innenstädte nur selten Grundbedürfnisse befriedigen muss, so ist es doch auch in Planungen nicht mehr tabu, über Nahrungsmittelproduktion in Städten nachzudenken. Ein im Wettbewerb „Schrumpfende Städte" (2004) ausgezeichnetes Projekt für den Raum Halle hat vielmehr schon eine Transformation und Wiederbelebung verlassener Stadtteile durch eine besondere Art der Ruralisierung vorgeschlagen: Die Grundidee der Autoren, Johannes Touché mit anschlaege.de (Axel Watzke, Christian Lagé, Steffen Schuhmann), war die Umnutzung leerstehender Plattenbauten für die Zucht von Edelpilzen. (vgl. archplus 173, Mai 2005, S. 44 f.)

KEIN FAZIT >> Die magisch-mythischen und ganz-heitlichen Vorstellungen einer Natur, die in den 1970er und 80er Jahren en vogue waren, haben sich ebenso aus der Stadt verabschiedet wie die elegische Liebe der 90er Jahre zur anarchischen Brachenvegetation. Zu den Manifestationen der Convertible City gehören der genießende Gebrauch der alten Parks bis an ihre Leistungsgrenzen, die Auffassung der Natur als von vornherein kulturelles Konstrukt, das urbane Bedürfnisse erfüllt oder nicht, die kurzfristige und spielerische Erzeugung von Idyllen wie politisch und ökonomisch engagierte Versuche zur städtischen Kleinstlandwirtschaft. Insgesamt ergibt sich das Bild einer Entgrenzung der Vorstellungen davon, was Freiraum in Innenstädten bedeuten kann.

Zur lebenswerten Stadt, die als Daueraufenthaltsraum taugt, gehört unbedingt auch die lustvolle Bespielung von Oberflächen. Davon zeugen die Stadtstrände, die im Sommer in nahezu allen größeren Städten mit Fluss- oder Seeufern existieren. Meist sind es private Veranstalter, die in Berlin, Dresden, Düsseldorf, Frankfurt am Main, Köln, Stuttgart oder Würzburg hellen Sand anfahren lassen, Palmen, Liegestühle und eine leistungsfähige Musikanlage aufstellen, DJs buchen und gut bestückte Bars einrichten. Ihnen ist es gelungen, extrem populäre, allgemein zugängliche Erholungsräume mit Natur-Appeal zu erzeugen.

backyards; herbs and salad vegetables are cultivated on balconies and windowsills and food produced in tenants' gardens. This development has long gone beyond the example of the kitchen garden planted while it could still be protected by the Wall at the east end of Berlin's Kreuzberg. This garden is one of the attractions of the district.

Different emphases are placed on different aims in community gardens in Berlin, where food is grown among other things. Sometimes the aim is to create green spaces in densely populated areas, to look at how communal commitment can contribute to rescuing public green areas, to provide scope for meaningful activity, to give aesthetic pleasure, or to conduct joint ecological and even economic experiments. Gaps between buildings and derelict land offer potential. The many discussions held on the subject, even in academic institutions on occasion, link up with the New York Community Gardens model.

There is also an art project that falls under the ruralisation heading: the artist Olaf Nicolai realised an agricultural project as part of the above-mentioned Temporary Artists' Gardens project in Leipzig in 2005. He asked well-known architecture practices to design contemporary beehives for the Leipzig urban area. They are occupied by bees and looked after by beekeepers from May to October. Their winter home is in the Museum of Fine Art. The designs are by sauerbruch hutton (London/Berlin), Ortner & Ortner (Vienna) b+ (Cologne) and J.P. Kleihues (Berlin).

Even though the ruralisation of inner cities seldom has to meet any basic needs in Germany, it is no longer out of the question for town planners to think about food production. On the contrary, an award-winning project for the Halle area in the "Shrinking Cities" competition (2004) has already proposed using ruralisation to transform and revive abandoned urban areas: the authors', Johannes Touché mit anschlaege.de (Axel Watzke, Christian Lagé, Steffen Schuhmann) basic idea was modifying empty slab-construction buildings to use for mushroom cultivation (cf. archplus 173, May 2005, p. 44 f.)

NO SUMMARY >> The magical-mythical and holistic ideas about nature that were in vogue in the 1970s and '80s have bidden the city farewell, and so has the '90s' infatuation with anarchic vegetation on derelict land. Manifestations of the Convertible City include using and enjoying old parks to the limit of their potential, seeing nature as a cultural construct from the outset, that either does or doesn't meet urban needs, creating short-term and playful idylls like politically and economically committed attempts at urban micro-agriculture. All in all we have a picture showing that the barriers are coming down in terms of thinking about what open space in inner cities can mean.

If a city is to be worth living in and viable as a place to enjoy in the long term, then it is essential to treat spaces joyfully. Evidence of this is given by the urban beaches that spring up in summer in almost all cities with river banks or maritime promenades. It is usually private entrepreneurs who ship in the light-coloured sand in Berlin, Dresden, Düsseldorf, Frankfurt am Main, Cologne, Stuttgart or Würzburg, set up palm trees, deckchairs and powerful music systems, book DJs and run well-stocked bars. They have succeeded in creating extremely popular recreational spaces with nature-appeal that are open to all.

"GrüntMit!", Berlin, Frank Daubner, FH Potsdam, www.gruentmit.de

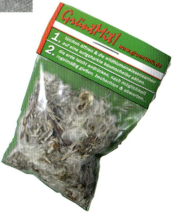

this page from top to bottom, from left to right / diese Seite von oben nach unten, von links nach rechts:
"Wo ist der Garten", Berlin, atelier le balto, Berlin >> "Symbiont", Merzig, 2004, FloSundK, Saarbrücken >> "Südstadtpark Fürth", Werkgemeinschaft Freiraum Landschaftsarchitekten, Nürnberg >> "Baumhaus an der Mauer", Berlin, Osman Kalin, Berlin >> "Pflanzen-projekt auf 4 Restflächen über dem Deichtortunnel", Hamburg 2000, Tita Giese, Düsseldorf >> "Birkenhain Wuhlepark", Berlin, 2005 >> "BAD", Stuttgart 2006, smaq Berlin-Rotterdam

next page from top to bottom, from left to right / nächste Seite von oben nach unten, von links nach rechts:
"Roofterrace", Berlin-Mitte >> "Roofgarden" Berlin >> "Roofgarden Kreuzberg", Berlin >> Roofgarden "Fünf Höfe", Munich, Burger Landschaftsarchitekten >> "Jahrtausendfeld", Leipzig, Schaubühne Lindenfels, Leipzig >> "DIE INSEL", Berlin-Neukölln, Christian Hasucha, Berlin >> "Liegen ist Gebührenfrei", Leipzig Ruth Habermehl mit Chris Schneider, Leipzig >> "Zwischengrün", Leipzig, Ralf Witthaus, Cologne >> "Hans-Baluschek-Park", Landschaftsarchitekten Kiefer, 2003 Berlin >> "Riemer Park" München >> "Park Fiction", Hamburg, Park Fiction & arbos Landschaftsarchitekten Greis, Hamburg

From Necessity to Desire

Brand placement in urban spaces

Vom Bedürfnis zur Begierde

Brand-Placement im urbanen Raum

Berlin, 1999 – the first Niketown opens on the European mainland. First impressions are that Niketown is a department store offering clothing and sporting goods from Nike, enhanced by altars to famous athletes and large-format video spots of current sports stars. But Niketown is more than just a flagship store: It is the starting point for the systematic conquest of urban space by the Nike brand. Nike is perhaps the most prominent representative of a space-oriented advertising strategy that has developed over the past few years into what appears to be an increasingly influential player in urban planning processes. In their approach, iconographic advertising is overridden by a personal brand experience. They employ active intervention to achieve these brand experiences in urban space. But in contrast to standard architectonic and urban planning strategies, building modifications are traded for interventions into the 'mental' structure of a place. It is not the hardware, but the software of a location that is redesigned and implemented in the city. This development has been particularly noticable in Berlin which has become a laboratory for new lifestyles and an ideal testing grounds for urban marketing strategies. The degree of intervention by the strategies observed ranges from transformation of existing locations and the reinterpretation of utilisation options, to disguised operations within spaces and places that are selected with specific target groups in mind. Here are some examples:

TRANSFORMATION >> The "bolzplatz" campaign is a perfect example of the non-constructional transformation of existing spaces. "Bolzplatz" is the German term for a small football field surrounded by a high metal fence, usually part of a children's playground: not a particularly cool location. With the slogan "freedom lies behind bars," Nike not only managed to bring a much cooler association with "prison" into play, but they also expressed a fundamental experience of their young target group: that the city is not a free space. Suddenly, the bolzplatz has become a place to be – almost as cool as a Bronx basketball court. Instead of limiting the campaign to slogans and posters, Nike installed signs on the fences of the bolzplatzes. Public space becomes Nike space. To strengthen the brand experience, the target group was motivated to undertake

Friedrich von Borries, Matthias Böttger

Berlin, 1999, das erste Niketown auf dem europäischen Festland wird eröffnet. Auf den ersten Blick ist Niketown ein Kaufhaus, in dem man Kleidung und Sportzubehör von Nike kaufen kann, angereichert mit Devotionalien berühmter Sportler und großformatigen Videospots aktueller Stars. Doch Niketown ist mehr als ein Flagship-Store: Niketown ist der Ausgangspunkt für die systematische Eroberung des städtischen Raums durch die Marke Nike. Nike ist der vielleicht prominenteste Vertreter einer raumbezogenen Werbestrategie, die sich in den letzten Jahren entwickelt hat und ein immer bedeutender werdender Player in der Stadtgestaltung zu werden scheint. Dabei tritt an die Stelle ikonografischer Werbung das individuell erfahrbare Markenerlebnis. Für diese Markenerlebnisse wird im urbanen Raum gestaltend interveniert. Anders aber als bei herkömmlichen architektonischen und städtebaulichen Strategien stehen dabei nicht bauliche Veränderungen im Vordergrund, sondern eine Intervention in die mentale Struktur eines Ortes. Nicht die Hardware, sondern die Software eines Ortes wird neu entworfen und in die Stadt implementiert. Diese Entwicklung konnte man in den letzten Jahren besonders gut in Berlin beobachten – dem Labor für neue Lebensstile und idealem Testfeld für urbane Marketingstrategien. Der Interventionsgrad der beobachteten Strategien reicht von der Transformation vorhandener Orte über die Reinterpretation für neue Nutzungsmöglichkeiten hin zu verdeckten Operationen an zielgruppenspezifischen Räumen und Orten.

TRANSFORMATION >> Die Bolzplatz-Kampagne ist eine perfekte nicht-bauliche Transformation vorhandener Räume. Bolzplätze sind kleine Fußballfelder, mit hohen Metallzäunen umgeben, meist ein Teil von Kinderspielplätzen. Kein besonders cooler Ort also. Mit dem Slogan „Die Freiheit liegt hinter Gittern" brachte Nike aber nicht nur den wesentlich cooleren Assoziationsraum „Gefängnis" ins Spiel, sondern sprach auch eine Grunderfahrung der jugendlichen Zielgruppe aus: Stadt ist ein unfreier Raum. Plötzlich wird der Bolzplatz ein angesagter Ort, fast so cool wie Basketballplätze in der Bronx. Statt die Kampagne auf Slogan und Plakat zu beschränken, brachte Nike Verbotsschilder an den Zäunen der Bolzplätze an: Der öffentliche Raum wird zum Nike-Raum. Um das Erleben der Marke weiter zu verstärken, wurde die Zielgruppe zur Eigeninitiative animiert. Mit kleinen Stickern, die an Fluchtweg-Schilder erinnern, konnte jeder in seinem Quartier den Weg zum nächsten Bolzplatz ausweisen: Aus dem Konsument wird ein kleiner Erlebnis-Straßenkämpfer.

"Welcome to Niketown", Berlin

REINTERPRETATION >> Einen Schritt weiter ging Adidas mit den City Games. Neue Sportarten sollten erfunden werden. Unter anderem meldeten sich die Turbo-Golfer zu Wort, die Golf nicht auf dem gepflegtem Green, sondern in Brachen und Baustellen spielen. Statt auf Löcher zu zielen, schießen sie die Bälle in alte Fenster und kaputte Autos. Die langweilige Brache wird zum erlebnisintensiven Sportplatz, ohne dass eine bauliche Maßnahme getroffen werden muss. Die Marke macht's! Und die beworbene Zielgruppe wird zum sich selbst um- und bewerbenden Akteur, der sich seine Stadt selbsttätig aneignet.

VERDECKTE OPERATIONEN >> Verdeckte Operationen sind getarnte Werbemaßnahmen, die den Quellcode der Zielgruppe hacken sollen. So initiierte Nike in guter Berlin-Mitte Tradition einen temporären Club. Einzige Werbemaßname in der Location, zu der nur 300 ausgewählte Opinion-Leader mit einem Schlüssel Zugang hatten: Die Räume schmückte eine Fototapete, auf der eine Lovestory erzählt wurde – die Protagonisten trugen auf jedem Bild ein Nike-Kleidungsstück. Die Marke dringt in den Quellcode der Zielgruppe ein.

its own initiatives. With little stickers reminiscent of emergency exit signs, everyone in their 'hood could follow the route to the next bolzplatz: The consumer is transformed into a little street fighter for adventure.

REINTERPRETATION >> Adidas took things a step further with their City Games. The object of the project was to invent new kinds of sports. Among the participants were the Turbo Golfers who, instead of playing on a well-kempt greens, preferred putting on wasteland and building sites. Instead of aiming to get the balls in holes, they like to hit them through old windows and abandoned automobiles. The boring wasteland becomes an adventurous arena without ever having to build anything. The brand does the job! And the courted target group becomes a participant both soliciting and promoting to itself and appropriating its own city .

DISGUISED OPERATION >> Disguised operations are undercover promotions designed to hack into the source code of their target groups. This was how, in good Berlin-Mitte tradition, Nike set up a temporary club in the city. The only promotion at the location, to which only 300 specially selected opinion leaders were given a key, was that the room was decorated with photographic wallpaper telling a love story and the protagonists wore a piece of Nike clothing in every shot. Here the brand penetrates the source code of its target group.

SUBCULTURE as voluntary marketing avant-garde >> These kinds of undercover operations are naturally impossible without cooperating subcultures, – that, incidentally, have always been a marketing avant-garde, both voluntary and involuntary. Meanwhile, brands like Nike and Adidas now tend to operate with rather less subterfuge in the urban milieu: Adidas runs a bar, wittily named "Stripes", and even coffee labels, such as Senseo, are opening up temporary galleries in order to introduce their coffee to customers that happens to be served there almost as an afterthought. For the 2006 World Cup, Nike operated, with local partners in various cities, so-called Nike Casas, in which

SUBKULTUR als (frei-)willige Marketing-Avantgarde >> Diese verdeckten Operationen sind natürlich nicht ohne kooperierende Subkulturen möglich – und die ist ja schon seit jeher eine frei- und unfreiwillige Marketing-Avantgarde. Inzwischen operieren Marken wie Nike und Adidas auch weniger getarnt im urbanen Raum. Adidas betreibt eine Bar mit den sinnigen Namen „Stripes", und sogar Kaffeehersteller wie Senseo eröffnen temporäre Galerien, um ihren dort ganz beiläufig ausgeschenkten Kaffee in der Zielgruppe bekannt zu machen. Zur WM 2006 betreibt Nike in verschiedenen Städten in Zusammenarbeit mit lokalen Partnern so genannte Nike-Casas, in denen im brasilianischen Favela-Look Ghetto-Reenactment kultiviert wird. Gemeinsam mit kooperierenden Subkulturen werden Marken so zum gestaltenden Akteur alltäglichen urbanen Raumes. Auch wenn die einzelnen Aktionen, Orte und Räume vielleicht gelungene Erweiterungen des urbanen Lebens sind, bleiben sie in ihrer eigentlichen Zielsetzung etwas Anderes: Es sind Marketingmaßnahmen, die in den urbanen Raum intervenieren.

BRAND PLACEMENT im urbanen Raum >> Product-Placement nennt man die Marketingstrategie, Konsumprodukte und Marken in Kino- und Fernsehfilmen zu platzieren – welches Auto fährt James Bond? Ganze Serien werden durch diese versteckten Werbefenster finanziert. In den 50er Jahren wurden

a Brazilian favella-look ghetto-re-enactments are cultivated. Together with cooperating subcultures, brands thus become active players in the daily life of the urban space. Even when the individual activities, locations, and spaces manage to become successful enhancements of urban life, in their original conception they still remain something quite different: promotional activities that intervene in urban spaces.

BRAND PLACEMENT in the urban space >> Product placement is the term used to decribe the placement of marketing strategies, consumer products, and brands in films and television. (Which type of car does James Bond drive?) Entire series have been financed by such concealed advertising methods. In the 1950s, advertisers experimented with the use of strategies that appealed solely to the subconscious: How does a consumer react to advertising messages that are cut into films for fractions of a second, for example? Contemporary urban marketing can be understood as a continuation of these experiments, except that now the subliminal advertisement should not be communicated by a picture, but by a "real" experience. Instead of representing the advertising message visually in film and television it is now actually experienced in real space. The temporary transformation of the urban space into a marketing space inscribes the message into the emotional memory; it is no longer bound to a promise, but to an experience. Marketing strategies create places where the target groups feel comfortable and like to spend time, thus connecting pleasant memories with the subliminally communicated product.

These new spaces and locations, which define the atmosphere of the urban network, have been developed according to wholly different criteria from those typical for architects and urban planners. This is because branding does not pursue a linear strategy, so much as a paradoxical one: It does not want to be consciously recognised, but subconsciously decoded. It is a careful balancing act: Which target group can withstand how much branding?

At the heart of this paradoxical functionalism is not need, but desire; the search for exciting experiences and a different life. To fulfil these desires, the city doesn't need to be rebuilt but reread and overlaid with new images. Architects and planners have to learn more about this approach, and develop new instruments not for building but for atmospheric interventions. Otherwise, the city of the future will be nothing more than a playground for advertisers and marketing strategists, who configure urban spaces according to commercial interests and reduce city life solely to the experience of consumerist desires.

go to: www.yellowarrow.net

Werbestrategien diskutiert, die nur das Unterbewusste ansprechen sollten: Wie reagiert ein Konsument, wenn für Sekundenbruchteile Werbebotschaften in Kinofilme eingeschnitten werden? Das heutige urbane Marketing kann man als Fortschreibung dieser Experimente verstehen, nur dass die unterschwellige Werbung nicht durch ein Bild, sondern ein „echtes" Erlebnis vermittelt werden soll. An die Stelle der Verbildlichung einer Werbebotschaft in Film und Fernsehen tritt die Verräumlichung der Werbebotschaft. Die temporäre Transformation urbanen Raumes in einen Markenraum schreibt die Werbebotschaft in das emotionale Gedächtnis ein; sie ist nicht mehr an ein Versprechen, sondern an ein Erlebnis gebunden. Denn die Marketingstrategien erschaffen Orte, in denen sich die Zielgruppe wohl fühlt, gerne Zeit verbringt und so angenehme Erinnerungen an das unterschwellig kommunizierte Produkt knüpft.

Diese neuen Räume und Orte, die die Atmosphäre des urbanen Geflechts bestimmen, sind nach ganz anderen Kriterien entwickelt, als sie bei Architekten und Planern üblich sind. Denn urbanes Branding verfolgt keine lineare Strategie, sondern eine paradoxe. Sie will nicht bewusst erkannt, aber unterbewusst dechiffriert werden. Es ist eine Gratwanderung: Welche Zielgruppe verträgt wie viel Branding?

Im Zentrum dieses paradoxen Funktionalismus stehen keine „Bedürfnisse", sondern Begierden: Die Suche nach spannenden Erlebnissen und einem anderen Leben. Zur Erfüllung dieser Begierden muss die Stadt nicht neu gebaut, sondern neu gelesen und mit neuen Images belegt werden. Architekten und Planer müssen hier dazulernen und neue Instrumente für nicht-bauliche, aber Atmosphäre schaffende Intervention entwickeln. Sonst wird die Stadt in Zukunft nur noch ein Spielfeld für Werber und Marketingstrategen sein, die urbane Räume nach kommerziellen Interessen gestalten und Stadtnutzung auf das Ausleben rein konsumistischer Begierden reduzieren.

Reclaim the Streets

Die Eroberung des Stadtraums

The conquest of urban space

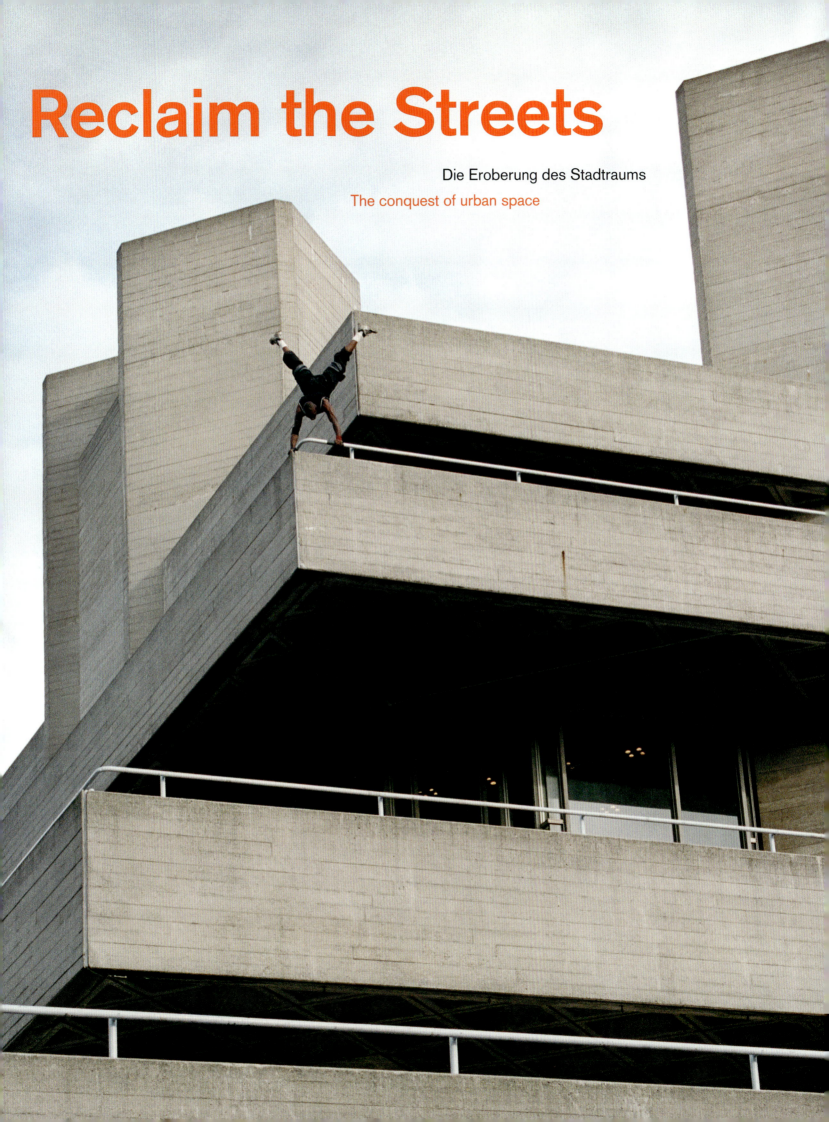

Lukas Feireiss

IMAGINE >> Far beyond the conventions of architecture and territorial planning cities offer a multitude of opportunities for alternative engagements. As the city presents itself to the alert as a playground of possibilities, novel ways of discovering and negotiating the concrete potential of the urban environment emerge.

TACTICAL VICTORY >> Given forms, norms and regulations within the cityscape are commonly subverted in silent resistance. It is the ordinary users and inhabitants of the city who constantly challenge and adapt civic spatial rules and functions to their benefit. The abundance of anti-authoritarian practices in everyday life marks the tactical victory of bottom-up' approaches in comprehending and experiencing the city over functionalistic 'top-down' strategies of traditional urban planning. By adapting and manipulating rather than by accepting or refusing the existing spatial system, it is the users who are exploring and defining new urban territories.

STAND YOUR GROUND >> A radical concept of retrieving urban terrain is advocated by the "Reclaim the Streets" movement. The collective ideal behind the anti-road protest group is the encouragement of community ownership of public spaces and opposition to the corporate forces of globalization and the car as the dominant mode of transport. Their non-violent direct action street-reclaiming events have included occupying major roads and traffic junctions to stage improvised parties; painting DIY cycle lanes overnight on city streets and holding humourous guerrilla gardening festivals on motorways, during which holes were secretly drilled in the tarmac to plant trees. Although these spectacular performances obstruct the regular users of the occupied spaces, these activities are nevertheless understood as the opening up of public spaces that had been previously occupied by motorised traffic. The ultimate goal is to mobilise a critical mass of people and to encourage them to change the urban setting directly by their own actions.

SPACE PIONEER >> Another way of regaining urban environment is through the temporary use of abandoned buildings and vacant spots. With the falling of the Berlin Wall and the quasi-overnight doubling of the city's footprint, extensive area resources were suddenly available. Superfluous infrastructures and questionable property rights triggered a phase of urban exploration. The informal club scene benefited in particular from this development by occupying unusual locations such as former vaults, powerhouses and subway stations as well as urban wasteland along the long neglected banks of the river Spree for their nocturnal activities. The celebration of the perennial interim solution became the status quo of the time, transforming the city into an open laboratory and propagating its experimental spirit way beyond the city limits.

previous page/ vorherige Seite: Parkour, London
top row/obere Reihe: Sportification, Complizen Planungsbüro, Halle >> ZAST & AKIM, New York >> "Railslide", Skateboarder, Berlin
left/ links: Reclaim the Streets, London

HIT AND RUN >> 35 years ago an article in the New York Times about Taki 183, "a Manhattan teenager who writes his name and his street number everywhere he goes" set the stage for the explosion of another spectacular intervention into the built environment: graffiti. Since then, many thousands of young 'writers' have followed in Taki 183's footsteps and made their mark in ever more complex calligraphies across urban landscapes worldwide. With missionary zeal they crusade entire cities, conquering every tag-able surface at hand. In their eyes, their subversive seizure of public space and transport is a David-against-Goliath-showdown between the graffiti artists and the ubiquitous neon and commercial signage covering the city. This illicit battle is engaged at night and the modus operandi of the writers is "hit and run", leaving nothing but traces of a different reading of the city that contest, provoke and sometimes blend into the cityscape.

GO WITH THE FLOW >> The physical topography of the city provides the everyday spaces and structures, to which we adapt ourselves as we move through the city. Like graffiti, the urban practice of skateboarding offers a completely alternative view, or use, of the city that tests the boundaries of the urban environment by threatening conventional definitions of space. A similar approach to skateboarding, where encountering and utilising the shape of the modern city is seen as a mode of operation exists within the relatively new domain of parkour. Parkour or 'freerunning' is a physical discipline of French origin in which participants, so called 'traceurs', attempt to pass obstacles in the built environment in the fastest and most direct manner possible using skills such as jumping, vaulting and climbing, or other more complex techniques. Its goal is to fluidly adapt one's movement to any given restraint. The traceur must be able to see different ways of negotiating the urban terrain. Experiencing architecture thereby less as an object but a process to flow through, she/he not only dissolves the physical constraints of the city but questions and disturbs the very concept of built space.

FREEDOM >> The ability to overcome the confines of the passive experience of urban surroundings and actively explore their hidden potentials opens up the prospect of discovering a world of difference. By actualising the possibilities of space in our built environment the protagonists of these informal urban and cultural practices are actively engaged in a continually refreshing the urban perspective. They challenge contemporary architecture and city planning using minimalist means thus providing alternative and valid critical insights to the understanding of the city.

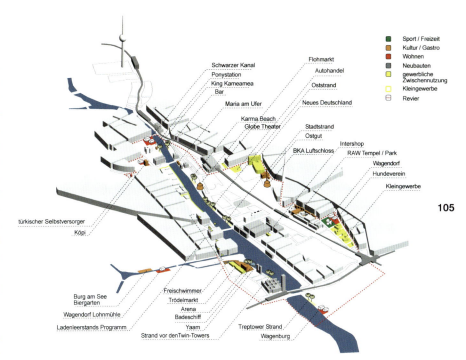

105

"Raumpioniere", cet-0 & studio Urban Catalyst in commission of Senatsverwaltung für Stadtentwicklung Berlin

kreativer Erkundungen und spekulativer Streifzüge durch die Stadt. Insbesondere die informelle Clubszene profitierte von dieser Entwicklung, indem sie sich so außergewöhnlicher Orte, wie etwa alter Tresorräume, Umspannwerke und U-Bahnhöfe sowie Brachflächen entlang der Spree für ihre Veranstaltungen annahm. Die Zelebrierung der permanenten Zwischenlösungen wurde zum Zeitgeist erhoben und verwandelte die Stadt in ein offenes Laboratorium, dessen experimenteller Charakter weit über die Grenzen der Stadt hinaus ausstrahlte.

HIT AND RUN >> Ein vor 35 Jahren in der New York Times erschienener Artikel über Taki 183, „einen Teenager aus Manhattan, der seinen Namen und seine Hausnummer überall hinschreibt", ist Auslöser für die explosionsartige Vermehrung eines weiteren spektakulären Eingriffs in die gebaute Umwelt geworden: Graffiti. Seither folgen Tausende Writer dem Vorbild von Taki 183 und prägen mit zunehmend komplexen Kalligrafien Stadtbilder weltweit. Mit missionarischem Eifer unterziehen Sie auf Ihren Kreuzzügen durch die Stadt ganze Straßenzüge der Aerosol-Zwangstaufe. Die subversive Eroberung öffentlicher Flächen und Verkehrsmittel mutet dabei wie ein ungleiches Kräftemessen zwischen den Graffitikünstlern und den allgegenwärtigen Neonreklamen und Werbeplakaten in der Stadt an. Das Gefecht wird des Nachts ausgetragen, und der modus operandi der Writer lautet „hit and run". Was bleibt, sind Spuren einer anderen Leseweise der Stadt, die diese herausfordert und provoziert.

IM FLUSS DER BEWEGUNG >> Die physische Struktur der Stadt bildet die Grundlage unseres alltäglichen Umgangs mit dem Stadtraum. Skateboarding stellt in der Auslotung der Grenzen dieses Raumes eine alternative Gebrauchsweise der Stadt dar, die zugleich unser herkömmliches Raumverständnis in Frage stellt. Eine vergleichbare Auseinandersetzung mit Form und Gestalt der Stadt findet im Parkour statt. Parkour oder Free running ist eine relativ neue Straßensportart aus Frankreich, bei der deren Teilnehmer, so genannte Traceurs, versuchen, Hindernisse in der gebauten Umwelt auf schnellste und direkteste Weise durch Techniken wie Klettern und Springen zu überwinden. In einer fließenden Bewegung gilt es eigene, durch Körper und Umwelt gesetzte Grenzen zu erkennen und zu überwinden. In dem der Traceur das urbane Terrain dabei stets aufs Neue verhandelt, erlebt er dieses nicht als festgelegten Rahmen, sondern als freiverhandelbaren Prozess. Physische Barrieren werden dabei umgangen, scheinbar festgelegte Funktionen von Orten und Gebäuden aufgebrochen und allgemeine Vorstellungen von Raum in Frage gestellt.

MÖGLICHKEITSSINN >> Die Fähigkeit, die Grenzen im überwiegend passiven Erleben der urbanen Umwelt aufzuheben und deren verborgene Potenziale zu erkunden, öffnet den Blick für eine Welt der Vielfalt. In der Erweiterung stadträumlicher Möglichkeiten tragen die Protagonisten dieser informellen Kulturpraktiken aktiv zur kontinuierlichen Erneuerung des Stadtbildes bei. Mit minimalen Mitteln gelingt es ihnen, die Konditionierungs- bzw. Disziplinierungsmechanismen zeitgenössischer Architektur und Stadtplanung herauszufordern, um dem Gebrauch von Architektur und Stadt einen Mehrwert abzuringen, der auf deren Möglichkeitssinn verweist.

106

Working with Dinosaurs

Die Einverleibung des Industriezeitalters

Annexing the industrial age

Project: Stadtwerke | **Location:** Düsseldorf | **Architects:** Christoph Ingenhoven in Ingenhoven Overdiek und Partner, Düsseldorf

Project: Westhafen Pier | Location: Frankfurt am Main | Architects: Schneider+Schumacher, Frankfurt am Main

On the Edge

Bürowelten zwischen Kraftwerk und Wasserfront

Office bridge between power station and waterfront

Project: Badeschiff / Winterbadeschiff **Location:** Berlin | **Architects:** Susanne Lorenz and AMP arquitectos with Gil Wilk / Gil Wilk Architekten with Thomas Freiwald

Reclaim the River

Ein schwimmender Pool als Brücke zur Spree

A floating pool as a bridge to the Spree

A Sense of Place

Ortssinn

Wim Wenders has addressed – right from the outset of his career – the importance of places as a starting-point for his cinematic creations. He is a master in reading places and their moods like no one else. Wenders' cinematic ideas about conveying urban quality are highly relevant to architects, and his influence on how American and German urban structures are perceived is not to be underestimated. Wim Wenders is currently professor at the "Hochschule für bildende Künste" in Hamburg.

You once talked about the contrast between the city and the desert – the fact that the city is so full that it almost seems empty and the desert is so empty that it seems as though it were crammed full off all the essentials – and that the most fascinating places in cities are the ones without buildings. As our subject is these "wastelands", do tell us about the marginal, desolate elements of wastelands… as places, as spaces with potentiality…

I once arrived in a town I had wanted to visit for a very long time. In fact I had been wanting to see Brasilia for over twenty years. The city was built when I was a boy, and at the time I read all the magazines, newspapers and architecture periodicals I could lay my hands on. I was very taken with this idea of an artificial city in the middle of the jungle! I wanted to be an architect myself at the time. This childhood fascination never left me, and one day in 1985, I actually found myself on my way to Brasilia.

I got there – and was soon bitterly disappointed. I couldn't find what I'd been looking for in the city for all those years, what I had seen in it as a little boy and what I'd hoped for from it for me. When I was walking around there it suddenly seemed absurd that this city had been planned down to the last detail, that for example all the hotels were in one area and all the shops in another. Everything was organized in such a way that it seemed impossible to me to actually to live in this city. Until I suddenly came across this place that Oscar Niemeyer had somehow left out of his plans. He had forgotten it simply because it was under a bridge. Nothing had been planned for this plot, this small, cramped, empty little piece of land had not had a function allotted to it. The only place in the whole city of Brasilia that I liked and thought was beautiful was under a road bridge and was used as a kind of flea market, presumably the last thing the architect wanted to

Wim Wenders hat sich von Anfang an mit der Bedeutung von Orten als Ausgangspunkt seines filmischen Schaffens auseinandergesetzt und beherrscht das Lesen von Orten und deren Stimmungen wie kein Zweiter. Wenders filmische Gedanken zur Vermittlung des Städtischen sind für Architekten von hoher Relevanz, und sein Einfluss in der Wahrnehmung amerikanischer und deutscher Stadtstrukturen ist nicht zu unterschätzen. Derzeit ist Wim Wenders Professor an der Hochschule für bildende Künste in Hamburg.

Sie haben einmal über den Kontrast zwischen der Stadt und der Wüste gesprochen – dass die Stadt so voll ist, dass sie beinahe leer wirkt, und dass die Wüste so leer ist, dass es scheint, als wäre sie mit all den essenziellen Dingen überfüllt – und dass die faszinierendsten Orte in Städten diejenigen ohne Häuser sind. Da unser Thema dieses Brachland ist, diese „Wastelands", erzählen Sie mir doch von Marginalen, vom Desolaten, von den Wastelands – als Orte, als Räume der Möglichkeit…

Ich kam einmal in eine Stadt, die ich schon seit sehr langer Zeit hatte besuchen wollen. In der Tat hatte ich Brasilia schon seit mehr als zwanzig Jahren sehen wollen. Die Stadt wurde erbaut, als ich ein Junge war, und damals las ich alle Magazine, Zeitungen und Architekturzeitschriften, die ich in die Hände bekam. Ich war begeistert von dieser Idee einer künstlichen Stadt mitten im Urwald! Ich wollte damals selbst Architekt werden. Diese Faszination aus meiner Kindheit hat mich nie verlassen, und eines Tages, im Jahr 1985, war es also endlich so weit, dass ich unterwegs war nach Brasilia.

Ich kam dort an – und war bald bitter enttäuscht. Ich konnte nicht finden, was ich in all diesen Jahren in dieser Stadt gesucht hatte, was ich als kleiner Junge in ihr gesehen und mir von ihr erhofft hatte. Als ich dort umherlief, schien es plötzlich absurd, dass diese Stadt von A bis Z durchgeplant war, dass zum Beispiel alle Hotels in einem Viertel waren und alle Geschäfte in einem anderen. Alles war so organisiert, dass es mir unmöglich erschien, in dieser Stadt tatsächlich zu leben. Bis ich diesen einzigen Ort fand, den Oscar Niemeyer irgendwie in seinen Plänen ausgelassen hatte. Er hatte ihn einfach deshalb vergessen, weil er sich unter einer Brücke befand. Für dieses Grundstück war nichts geplant worden, diesem kleinen, engen und leeren Stückchen Land war keine Funktion zugeschrieben worden. Der einzige Ort in der gesamten Stadt Brasilia, der mir gefiel und den ich als schön empfand, lag unter einer Autobrücke und wurde als eine Art Flohmarkt genutzt – vermutlich das Allerletzte, was der Architekt in „seiner Stadt" hatte sehen wollen. Aber hier war er: Ein offener Markt mit Leuten, die alles mögliche Zeug verkauften, mit spielenden Musikern und allen Arten von Imbissbuden. Es war ziemlich chaotisch, aber hier brandete wirklich das Leben. Ich

Wim Wenders in conversation with Alessandra Casu and Ilene Steingut

Wim Wenders, Entrance, Houston, Texas, 1983

see in "his city". But here it was: an open market with people selling all sorts of stuff, with musicians playing and all kinds of snack stalls. It was pretty chaotic, but things really were tumultuously alive here. I spent practically all the rest of my stay in this market because I was completely fed up with organised order. I had never realized so clearly before that there have to be places in cities that are not occupied, but that have to open up suddenly, like clearings in a wood. I like the word we have in German for clearing: "Lichtung", suggesting a place with bright clear light, as does the English "clearing". If you don't leave islands of light and disorder like this the city becomes overloaded, it becomes a closed system.

What was is about Brasilia that so fascinated you as a child?

My enthusiasm about Brasilia was certainly something to do with the fact that I grew up in post-war Germany as a little boy, and everything was so painfully broken there. You have to see that I grew up believing that the whole world was as damaged as my street and my home town. I didn't know anything else. Half the house we lived in was bombed and burnt out. Even so we were lucky: most of the other houses in Düsseldorf had collapsed completely. The street to the right and left of us was nothing but rubble with chimneys sticking up out of it and the tram winding its way through the heaps of debris. I think I was so fascinated with the futuristic vision

of Brasilia because the town had been built in the middle of nowhere, to replace emptiness with fullness. How could there be anything more beautiful that something newly built! I had omnipotence fantasies as a boy that one day I would be able to rebuild entire cities, like the one I lived in. Other children had posters of cowboy heroes or Mickey Mouse on their walls, I had pictures of futuristic architecture. And at that time Brasilia seemed like pure science fiction.

Are you still interested in Futurism?

I am still interested in the future, but not so much in Futurism. But that reminds me about another piece of wasteland I saw recently, in Hong Kong. That really is a cramped city where there is no room at all, especially not for people and least of all for poor people. The poorest are the Filipino women who work in the city as nannies or charwomen. They have Sunday off and then they meet up, thousands of them, and fill up an enormous park in the city centre. There they all sit on the ground on their blankets, chat and eat picnics. And because not even this park is big enough, they colonize the places round about as well: for example, the gigantic forecourt in front of one of the biggest banks in Hong Kong, a kind of open, roofed foyer where you can see the glass lifts travelling high up into the bank. Normally it's teeming with businessmen, of course, but on Sundays the

verbrachte praktisch den gesamten Rest meines Aufenthalts auf diesem Markt, denn ich hatte die organisierte Ordnung außenrum gründlich satt. Nie zuvor war mir so klar geworden, dass es in Städten Orte geben muss, die nicht besetzt werden, sondern die sich wie freie Stellen im Wald plötzlich öffnen müssen. Ich mag das Wort, das wir im Deutschen dafür haben: eine „Lichtung", also ein Ort der Helligkeit. Wenn man keine solchen Inseln des Lichts und der Unordnung lässt, dann überfrachtet man eine Stadt, dann wird sie zu einem geschlossenen System.

Was haben Sie als Kind in Brasilia gesehen, das Sie so fasziniert hat?

Meine Begeisterung für Brasilia hatte sicherlich damit zu tun, dass ich als kleiner Junge im Nachkriegsdeutschland aufwuchs, wo alles so schmerzhaft kaputt war. Sie müssen verstehen, dass ich in dem Glauben aufgewachsen bin, dass die ganze Welt so zerstört wäre wie meine Straße und meine Heimatstadt. Ich kannte ja nichts anderes. Die Hälfte des Hauses, in dem wir lebten, war zerbombt und ausgebrannt. Trotzdem hatten wir noch Glück: Die meisten anderen Häuser in Düsseldorf waren vollständig eingestürzt. Die Straße rechts und links von uns bestand nur noch aus Schutt mit herausstehenden Schornsteinen, die Straßenbahnen schlängelten sich durch die Trümmerberge. Ich glaube, dass ich deswegen von der futuristischen Vision der Stadt Brasilia so fasziniert war: Diese Stadt wurde mitten ins Nichts gebaut, mitten in den Urwald gesetzt, um die Leere durch die Fülle zu ersetzen. Wie sollte es etwas Schöneres geben als das neu Konstruierte! Ich hatte als Junge Allmachtsphantasien, dass ich eines Tages ganze Städte wieder aufbauen würde – so wie die, in der ich lebte. Andere Kinder hatten Poster von Westernhelden oder Mickey

Mouse an ihren Wänden; ich hatte Bilder von futuristischer Architektur. Und Brasilia erschien zu dieser Zeit wie reine Science Fiction.

Sind Sie immer noch am Futurismus interessiert?

Die Zukunft interessiert mich schon noch, aber der Futurismus nicht mehr so sehr. Aber das erinnert mich an ein anderes Stück Brachland, das ich kürzlich gesehen habe, in Hongkong. Das ist eine ausgesprochen enge Stadt, wo es überhaupt keinen Platz gibt, vor allem nicht für Menschen und am allerwenigsten für arme Menschen. Und die Ärmsten sind die philippinischen Frauen, die in der Stadt als Kindermädchen oder Putzfrauen arbeiten. Am Sonntag haben sie frei, und dann treffen sie sich, viele Tausende von ihnen, und besetzen und füllen einen riesigen Park mitten im Stadtzentrum. Da sitzen sie alle auf ihren Decken auf dem Boden, reden und picknicken. Und weil nicht einmal dieser Park ausreicht, bevölkern sie auch die Orte drum herum: Zum Beispiel den gigantischen Vorplatz einer der größten Banken in Hongkong, eine Art offenes, überdachtes Foyer, wo man die gläsernen Aufzüge hoch ins Bankgebäude fahren sieht. Normalerweise wimmelt es da natürlich von Geschäftsmännern, aber sonntags ist der Platz leer und die Aufzüge sind hinter gläsernen Toren geschlossen. Und so sitzen Sonntag für Sonntag eben diese philippinischen Frauen dort, unter dem Dach dieses Bankgebäudes, als wäre es eine Art Kathedrale, und ihre tausend plappernden Stimmen hallen wider wie das Zirpen von tropischen Vögeln in einem gewaltigen Regenwaldbaum. Auch eine Art Lichtung – ein Ort, der von Menschen geschaffen und besetzt wird, die ein Stück Brachland brauchen. (Auch ein Ort, der sich ein wenig nach Science Fiction anfühlt.)

On his travels around the world Wim Wenders always carries an old panorama camera with him. Over the years he has produced many photographs, that speak of places, people and life in their very own temporality. His photographic work can be seen in the travelling exhibtion "Pictures from the Surface of the Earth", the latest station was the Gallery "Scuderie del Quirinale" in Rome. The accompanying publication is published under the same title by Schirmer/Mosel publishers.

Auf seinen Reisen um die Welt hat Wim Wenders stets eine alte Panoramakamera in seinem Reisegepäck. Im Laufe der Zeit sind dabei Momentaufnahmen entstanden, die mit der ihnen eigenen Temporalität von Orten, Menschen und vom Leben erzählen. Unter dem Titel „Bilder von der Oberfläche der Erde" sind diese seit einiger Zeit auf einer Wanderausstellung zu sehen, zuletzt in der Galerie „Scuderie del Quirinale" in Rom. Unter dem gleichnamigen Titel ist im Schirmer/Mosel Verlag die begleitende Publikation erschienen.

Wim Wenders, Two Cars and a Woman Waiting, Houston, Texas, 1983

place is empty and the lifts are shut up behind glass gates. And so these Filipino women sit there Sunday after Sunday under the roof of this bank as though it were a kind of cathedral, and their thousand chattering voices echo around like the chirruping of tropical birds in a massive jungle tree. Another kind of clearing, a place created and used by people who need a bit of wasteland. (Also a place that feels a little like science fiction.)

So what is the relationship between place and identity, and what part is played here by interstitial spaces, the gaps between the categories, like the waste land under the bridge, for example?

"Identity" is a big and powerful word. I prefer to think of it in the simplest of its meanings, as a feeling of belonging…To belong to a place, you have to link it with memories. And to do that you have to have had experiences you remember…It is only the intensity of the memory that counts, only the importance of what you find in your memory. And it is precisely there that your gaps come into play. The "interstitial spaces" par excellence are the spaces between the lines. The proverbial "reading between the lines" is so important because there is nothing where I am reading, because it is just white, because I as the reader have to use my own imagination to fill it in myself, with my own dreams, hopes and fears. And the empty spaces in cities work like that as well. They encourage us to fill them up with ourselves…

I have always wondered what a fundamental difference in the feeling of identity children must share who have grown up in difficult places, in "dangerous parts of town" or, even worse, in the slums – in contrast with children who grow up in privileged inner-city areas, let's say in Paris, London, Berlin or New York, or in the secure leafy suburbs on the outskirts of these cities. Of course "security" comes into play in one case and "exposure" in the other. But does the safety in which the latter children grow up create a different kind of identity from the danger the former are exposed to? Ultimately how do certain places or a certain kind of architecture shape a sense of identity? Or is it just the social structures again? I don't know.

The suburbs are a non-place, they repeat themselves and remain anonymous. But the slums, despite their extreme problems with poverty and a lack of infrastructure, perhaps carry more identity within them despite their apparently peripheral existence.

…I have just recently been back to Paris, and that is a particularly sacrosanct city. I watched some children in a park, and they were not even allowed to walk on the grass. So they go onto these playgrounds with sand strewn over them artificially and here there are just as many adults watching and looking out for them as children playing. But cities are fundamentally invulnerable. A city is built, and that's that. The past lives on permanently in the present, it is set in stone. Now and again a new building is added on, like for example the Pompidou Centre in Paris, and that seems all the more incredible because everything around it is so uniform, built at the same time and in the same style, with the same roof heights, so the new buildings stand out all the more. The Centre Pompidou is a magnificent building. I love it because it is the opposite of all the other buildings in this city, a building that turns its inside outwards, while all the rest of Paris just consists of façades, of outsides, anxiously concealing everything inside…

Wie verhält es sich dann allgemein mit dem Verhältnis von Ort und Identität, und welche Rolle spielen dabei die interstitiellen Räume, die Zwischenräume sozusagen zwischen den Kategorien, wie etwa das „Wasteland" unter der Brücke?

„Identität" ist ein großes und mächtiges Wort. Ich denke es lieber in der einfachsten seiner Bedeutungen, als ein Gefühl der Zugehörigkeit. (…) Um an einen Ort zu gehören, muss man mit ihm Erinnerungen verbinden. Dafür wiederum muss man Erfahrungen gemacht haben, an die man sich erinnert. (…) Nur die Intensität der Erinnerung zählt, nur die Wichtigkeit dessen, was man in seiner Erinnerung findet. Und genau da kommen Ihre Zwischenräume ins Spiel. Die „interstitiellen Räume" par excellence, das sind doch die Leerräume zwischen den Zeilen. Das sprichwörtliche „Zwischen-den-Zeilen-Lesen" ist doch deshalb so bedeutsam, weil da nichts ist, wo ich lese, weil es da bloß weiß ist, weil ich als der Leser das selbst auffüllen muss mit meiner eigenen Imagination, mit meinen eigenen Träumen, Hoffnungen und Ängsten. Auch die Leerräume in den Städten haben so eine Funktion. Sie ermuntern uns, sie mit uns selbst aufzufüllen. (…)

Ich habe mich immer gefragt, was der grundsätzliche Unterschied im Identitätsgefühl sein muss zwischen Kindern, die in schwierigen Orten groß geworden sind, in „gefährlichen Stadtteilen" oder, noch schlimmer, in den Slums – im Gegensatz zu solchen Kindern, die in den privilegierten Vierteln der Innenstädte, sagen wir von Paris, London, Berlin oder New York aufwachsen, oder in den beschützten Villenvierteln am Rand dieser Städte. Natürlich kommen da die „Geborgenheit" auf der einen und die „Ausgesetztheit" auf der anderen ins Spiel. Aber schafft die Sicherheit, mit der diese Kinder aufwachsen, eine grundsätzlich andere Art von Identität als die Gefährdung, mit der jene groß werden? Wie genau prägen bestimmte Orte oder eine bestimmte Architektur das Identitätsgefühl letztlich mit? Oder sind es doch wieder nur die sozialen Strukturen? Ich weiß es nicht.

Die Vorstadt ist ein Nicht-Ort, sie wiederholt sich und bleibt anonym. Die Slums dagegen, trotz ihrer extremen Probleme mit Armut und fehlender Infrastruktur, bergen vielleicht mehr Identität, trotz ihrer scheinbaren Randexistenz.

(…) Gerade erst war ich wieder einmal in Paris, und diese Stadt ist ganz besonders unantastbar. Ich habe den Kindern im Park zugesehen, und man durfte nicht einmal die Rasenflächen betreten. Die gehen dann auf diese Spielplätze mit künstlich aufgeschüttetem Sand; und dort gibt es genauso viele Erwachsene, die zuschauen und aufpassen, wie Kinder, die spielen. Aber Städte sind ganz grundsätzlich unangreifbar. Eine Stadt wird einmal gebaut, und das war's. Die Vergangenheit lebt dauerhaft in der Gegenwart weiter, sie ist in Stein gehauen. Hin und wieder wird ein neues Gebäude dazugestellt, wie z.B. in Paris das Centre Pompidou, und das scheint dann noch unglaublicher, weil alles andere außen herum so einförmig ist, zur selben Zeit und im selben Stil gebaut, mit derselben Dachhöhe, deswegen stechen die neuen Bauwerke noch mehr heraus. Das Centre Pompidou ist ein großartiges Gebäude. Ich liebe es, weil es das Gegenteil von allen

Would Homer in Wings of Desire still seek out Potsdamer Platz today?

I think that Homer would be even more confused now than he was then. And that was only 14 years or so ago. At the time of Wings of Desire he was desperately trying to match his memories to the desert he found there, to this Patagonia in the middle of Berlin. Potsdamer Platz was nothing else for years. But at least he could always imagine what it used to look like before it became a no-man's-land. Potsdamer Platz was once a wonderful place, and our Homer, alias Curt Bois, was one of the first people to drive his car round it. He sat in the cafés and smoked cigars. Potsdamer Platz was the centre point and the heart of this 1920s Berlin, the busiest square in Europe, with hellish traffic all round it. When Homer looks round it in the '80s there's nothing left of that at all. The square he knew has simply disappeared, it's been a piece of waste land, practically since the end of the Second World War…In any case, this wasteland was the second incarnation of Potsdamer Platz: a desert that even had a wall running through it in the end. Today the square exists in its third manifestation. That's why I think that dear old Homer would be even more confused than he was then. I think that he would now not be able simply to resurrect his old square in his imagination, because there are new and different buildings here now. Homer would no longer be able to understand the transformation of Potsdamer Platz as he knew it in the twenties and thirties into the little Tokyo that stands there today. … It is the way in which these buildings are arranged, the way all sorts of different styles stand side by side, combined with gigantic video screens, neon signs, brand names…This whole consumer-oriented, chaotic, bustling, post-modern style is certainly not America, it is pure Tokyo!

Do you like it?

I like Tokyo very much, so I think I could come to like it. But that could be a false conclusion…

Is it a place yet?

At the moment this new Potsdamer Platz is pretty incomprehensible, essentially a series of cheerless, boring façades. But I think it could become a proper place. The very fact there are so many cinemas there, above all the "Arsenal", will help. Why? When you come out of a film you're stepping out of a different world and back into your own, and you suddenly see it with new eyes. (I know there's a bit of wishful thinking there, or at least romanticism about cinema, but sometimes it really is like that…) Coming out of a really good film and experiencing your own city in a different light can be one of the profoundest bonds you can built up with a place…

anderen Häusern in dieser Stadt ist, ein Bauwerk, das seine Innenseite nach außen kehrt, während ganz Paris nur aus Fassaden besteht, aus Außenseiten, die alles in ihrem Inneren ängstlich verbergen. (…)

Würde Homer in „Der Himmel über Berlin" heute immer noch den Potsdamer Platz suchen?

Ich denke, dass Homer heute noch verwirrter wäre als damals. Und das ist auch nur gerade mal 14 Jahre her oder so. Zum Zeitpunkt von „Der Himmel über Berlin" versuchte er verzweifelt, seine Erinnerungen mit der Wüste in Einklang zu bringen, die er dort vorfand, mit diesem Patagonien mitten in Berlin. Etwas anderes war ja der Potsdamer Platz jahrelang nicht. Aber zumindest konnte er sich immer noch vorstellen, wie es dort ausgesehen hatte, bevor es zum Niemandsland wurde. Der Potsdamer Platz war einmal ein wunderschöner Ort, und unser Homer alias Curt Bois war einer der ersten, der mit seinem eigenen Auto dort herumgefahren ist. Er hat sich in die Cafés gesetzt und Zigarren geraucht. Der Potsdamer Platz war der Mittelpunkt und das Herz dieses Berlins der Zwanziger Jahre, der belebteste Platz Europas, mit einem höllischen Verkehr rundherum. Als Homer sich nun in den Achtzigern dort umsieht, ist nichts mehr davon übrig. Der Platz, den er kannte, ist einfach verschwunden – der ist jetzt Brachland, praktisch seit dem Ende des Zweiten Weltkriegs. (…) Auf jeden Fall war dieses Brachland die zweite Inkarnation des Potsdamer Platzes: Eine Wüste, durch die schließlich sogar noch eine Mauer gezogen wurde. Heute existiert der Platz in seiner dritten Erscheinungsform. Deswegen glaube ich ja, dass der gute Homer heute noch verwirrter wäre als damals. Ich glaube, dass er „seinen alten Platz" in seiner Vorstellung jetzt nicht mehr einfach auferstehen lassen könnte, weil es an dieser Stelle eben andere, neue Gebäude gibt. Homer würde die Verwandlung vom Potsdamer Platz, den er in den Zwanziger und Dreißiger Jahren gekannt hatte, zu diesem Little Tokio, das heute an diesem Ort steht, nicht mehr nachvollziehen können.

(…) Es ist die Art, wie diese Bauwerke arrangiert sind, wie dort alle möglichen Stilrichtungen Seite an Seite stehen, verbunden mit riesigen Videoleinwänden, Neonlichtern, Markennamen. (…) Diese ganze konsumorientierte, durcheinandrige, wuselige, post-postmoderne Art ist keineswegs Amerika, das ist reinstes Tokio!

Gefällt es Ihnen?

Weil ich Tokio sehr mag, denke ich, das könnte mir auch gefallen. Aber wahrscheinlich ist das ein Trugschluss. (…)

Ist es schon ein Ort?

Im Moment ist dieser neue Potsdamer Platz noch ziemlich ungreifbar, eine Reihe eher trostloser und langweiliger Fassaden. Aber ich denke, es könnte ein richtiger Ort werden. Allein die Tatsache, dass es dort so viele Kinos gibt, vor allem das „Arsenal", das wird helfen. Warum? Wenn man aus einem Film herauskommt, tritt man gerade aus einer anderen Welt heraus und betritt wieder seine eigene, die man plötzlich mit neuen Augen sieht. (Ich weiß, da ist ein bisschen Wunschdenken dabei, oder zumindest Kinoromantik, aber manchmal ist das ja wirklich so…) Aus einem richtig guten Film zu kommen und seine eigene Stadt wieder aufs Neue zu erfahren, das kann eine der tiefsten Verbindungen sein, die man zu seinem Ort aufbauen kann. (…)

Extracts from / Auszüge aus**:** Wim Wenders, A Sense of Place, Verlag der Autoren, Frankfurt am Main 2005. **Reprinted by kind permission of the publisher.** / Nachdruck mit freundlicher Genehmigung des Verlags.

116

Project: Panzerhalle, Garrison Conversion   Location: Tübingen | Architects: Stadtsanierungsamt, Tübingen

From "Panzerhalle" to Community Hotspot

Konversion einer Kaserne schafft Offenheit für Vielfalt

Converted barracks open up for diversity

Open for Diversity

Die Wiedernutzung von Siedlungsbrachen (nicht mehr genutzte Militär-, Fabrik-, Hafen-, Bahn-, Post- und Wohnungs-bauareale) ist seit den 1990er Jahren eine der wichtigen Aufgaben der Stadtentwicklung. Allerdings werden die mit dieser Aufgabe verbundenen Erwartungen (z.B. Reduzierung des „Flächenverbrauchs") bisher kaum erfüllt, weil die veränderten sozialen und kulturellen Bedürfnisse der Bevölkerung zu wenig Berücksichtigung finden. Kurze Wege im Alltagsleben, unmittelbares Eingehen auf vielfältige Nutzerinteressen bleiben leere Versprechen, solange große Entwickler ihre eigenen kurzfristigen Verwertungsinteressen verfolgen können. Oft entsteht der Eindruck, die künftige Wissensgesellschaft beste-he einzig aus Service-Wohnen, Shopping und immer noch mehr gestapelten Büros.

Wirtschaftssoziologen sprechen vom Scheitern der Hoffnung Jean Fourastiés, der die (nicht rationalisierbaren) Dienst-leistungen als Quelle unerschöpflicher Beschäftigung betrachtete: Es entstehe stattdessen ein neuer Industrialismus, eine McDonaldisierung des tertiären Wirtschaftssektors. Kein Wunder, wenn die Bevölkerung überwiegend nach den Vorstel-lungen des fordistischen Städtebaus in Funktionsgebieten lebt, wo die personale Verknüpfung von Arbeiten und Leben durch die geltenden Bauordnungen geradezu verboten ist. Aber nicht alle Leute betrachten dies als den one best way der Lebensqualität! Wie kann also – z.B. bei der Wiedernutzung vorhandener Stadtbrachen – freie Wahl im Sinne eines fairen Wettbewerbs gegen das fordistische System durchgesetzt werden?

Andreas Feldtkeller

Die Tübinger Südstadt-Planung (eine Militärkonversion auf insgesamt über 60 Hektar Neuordnungsfläche für 6500 Einwohner und 2300 Arbeitsplätze) folgte der originär städtischen Leitidee Offenheit für funktionale Vielfalt. Um dieses Ziel zu erreichen, wurden folgende Eckpunkte festgelegt: Erwerb der Areale durch die Stadt, funktionale Vielfalt und Dichte, kleinräumige Parzellierung, grundsätzliche Erhaltung der Altbauten, Straßen und Plätze als Aufenthaltsräume, vorrangige Vergabe von Bau-grundstücken an private Nutzer und Baugruppen.

Das Ende 1990, Anfang 1991 in der Stadt-verwaltung entwickelte Konzept wurde innerhalb weniger Monate nach eingehender öffentlicher Er-örterung vom Tübinger Gemeinderat beschlossen; es bekam 1992/93 nach einem offenen Architek-tenwettbewerb die passende stadträumliche Dispo-sition und wird seither in kleinen, stetigen Schritten erfolgreich umgesetzt.

Drei Dinge entscheiden den Erfolg: >> (a) das planungsrechtlich und auch faktisch ehrliche Zu-lassen aller kleinen und mittleren Unternehmen (KMU) und aller Selbständigen, die sich ansiedeln wollen, >> (b) die Erhaltung auch solcher Altbau-ten, die längst abgewirtschaftet sind und angeblich dem großzügigen Stadtgrundriss im Wege stehen, >> (c) die Installierung eines fairen Bodenmarkts für alle Nutzer, die am dicht genutzten Quartier In-teresse haben.

Viele Stadtbrachen liegen in unmittelbarer Nach-barschaft zu Arealen des früheren sozialen Woh-nungsbaus; von ihrer kleinteiligen und funktional vielfältigen Wiedernutzung profitieren auch diese oft benachteiligten und wenig beliebten Viertel.

Redeveloping derelict facilities (military, factory, harbour, rail, postal services and housing estates) has been an important element of urban development since the 1990s. However, not all the expectations (e.g. reduction of "land consumption") associated with such projects have been met because too little attention has been paid to people's changed social and cultural needs. The promise of short journeys every day, a direct response to complex user interests, remained empty for as long as major developers were able to pursue their own interests in short-term exploitation. It often seems as though the future information society consists solely of service accommodation, shopping and more and more piled-up offices.

Economic sociologists speak of the failure of Jean Fourastié's hopes. He saw services (that could not be rationalised) as an inexhaustible source of employment: they say that a new industrialism is emerging instead, a McDonaldisation of the tertiary economic sector. And this is hardly surprising when the majority of the population lives on a basis of ideas about Fordist urban development in functional areas where personal linking of work and life is effectively forbidden by the building regulations that apply. But not everyone sees this as the one and only way to better quality of life! So how can (e.g. when re-using existing derelict urban land) free choice be successfully established in the sense of fair competition against the Fordist system?

The plan for Tübingen South (a former military use conversion of 60 hectares of re-ordered land for 6500 occupants and 2300 jobs) followed the originally urban guidelines on openness to functional diversity. To achieve this aim, the following key points were fixed: the town buys the site, functional diversity and density, small-scale parcelling, old buildings to be retained in principle, streets and squares as places in which to spend time, building plots largely distributed to private users and building groups.

This concept was developed by the municipal authorities in late 1990, early 1991, and passed by the Tübingen city council within a few months, after thorough public discussion; the appropriate urban space was allocated in 1992/93, after an open architects' competition, and the scheme has since been successfully implemented in small, steady steps.

Three things are essential for success: >> (a) the honest – in terms of planning law, and of fact – admission of all small and medium-sized businesses and all self-employed people who wish to move in, >> (b) retaining even those old buildings that have long since come to the end of their useful lives and are allegedly in the way of a generous urban ground plan, >> (c) setting up a fair land market for all users who are interested in this densely used quarter.

Many derelict urban areas are immediately adjacent to earlier social housing sites; these quarters, often neglected and unpopular, also benefit from intricate and functionally diverse redevelopment.

Project: wöhmen+ Bögenallee | Location: Hamburg | Architects: blauraum architekten, Hamburg

119

Residential Recharge

Von der Bürozelle zur Wohnbox

Morphing office cells to living rooms

120

Wrap-on and Over

Lofts mit Anlagerung im
denkmalgeschützten Industriebau

**Lofts with add-ons in
a listed industrial building**

Project: Falkenried Lofts   **Location:** Hamburg | **Architects:** BRT Architekten, Hamburg

Re-inventing the City for the Information Society

Dieter Läpple

"Are cities dying?" This question was asked a few years ago by the Harvard-based urban economist Edward Glaeser, and the question was not just intended rhetorically. In countries where industrialisation came early, cities had been losing inhabitants and increasing numbers of jobs for many decades. This "exodus from the cities" was particularly marked in the USA. But in West Germany as well, an apparently unstoppable peripheral migration was turning the monocentric relationship structure of city centre and surrounding areas into an increasingly polycentric urban landscape. It was easy to understand - at least until just a few years ago - the reasons behind these stories of decline and crisis that dominated discussion about cities. Mass unemployment has persisted for decades, with multiple social and social cohabitation problems as a consequence. It is concentrated in the cities, as a result of new forms of international labour distribution and accelerating changes in economies and settlement structures. In the last two decades, developments in the labour market have apparently led not just to increased social inequality and the consolidation of structural poverty, but also to the permanent exclusion of some social groups from regular gainful employment and thus tendentially away from participating in social, cultural and political life. At the same time the social dynamic had increasingly shifted from the city centres into the surrounding area and even into peripheral regions.

The new information technology breakthroughs seemed to seal the fate of the cities once and for all. It was now technically possible to de-couple the functions of everyday life - like work, shopping or entertainment - from their traditional locations on an extensive scale. Much speculation about the knowledge economy's companies and specialists moving out of the city and thus the disintegration of the spatially tied-down city into a "city of bits" were linked with the idea of distance and location being devalued electronically.

Glaeser looked at the cities' confrontation with the new information technologies and asked the question: "Will the 21st century see a decline in urbanisation as rapid as the rise in urbanisation over the 19th and 20th centuries? Or will breakthroughs in information technology and law enforcement transform the blighted inner city of today into the gentrified polis of tomorrow?" (1)

In the first instance it is indisputable that the cities have largely lost their role as privileged centres of industrial production as a result of economic structural change and of new forms within the international division of labour. But this profound transformation of the cities' economic basis did not lead to a dramatic decline in industrial jobs. In fact the structural change led to new and crucial development opportunities for cities. As the traditional industrial systems were transformed, based on the mass production advantages of large

„Are cities dying?" Diese Frage stellte vor einigen Jahren der in Harvard forschende Stadtökonom Edward Glaeser, und die Frage war nicht nur rhetorisch gemeint. In den frühindustrialisierten Ländern hatten Städte über viele Jahrzehnte hinweg Einwohner und auch immer mehr Arbeitsplätze verloren. Besonders ausgeprägt war diese „Stadtflucht" in den USA. Aber auch in Westdeutschland transformierte eine scheinbar unaufhaltsame Randwanderung das monozentrische Beziehungsgefüge von Kernstadt und Umland in eine zunehmend polyzentrische Stadtlandschaft. Die Verfalls- und Krisengeschichten, die die Diskurse über die Stadt dominierten, hatten – zumindest bis vor einigen Jahren – nachvollziehbare Gründe. In der Folge neuer Formen internationaler Arbeitsteilung und eines beschleunigten wirtschafts- und siedlungsstrukturellen Wandels konzentriert sich in den Städten die seit Jahrzehnten anhaltende Massenarbeitslosigkeit, mit ihren vielfältigen sozialen und sozialräumlichen Folgeproblemen. Die Arbeitsmarktentwicklung führte in den letzten zwei Jahrzehnten offensichtlich nicht nur zu einer Verschärfung sozialer Ungleichheit und der Verfestigung struktureller Armut, sondern auch zu einer dauerhaften Ausgrenzung sozialer Gruppen aus einer regelmäßigen Erwerbsarbeit und damit tendenziell auch aus der Teilhabe an dem sozialen, kulturellen und politischen Leben. Gleichzeitig hatte sich die gesellschaftliche Dynamik immer mehr weg von den Kernstädten ins Umland und selbst in periphere Regionen verlagert.

Mit dem Durchbruch der neuen Informationstechnologien schien das Schicksal der Städte endgültig besiegelt zu sein. Denn damit eröffneten sich die technischen Möglichkeiten einer weitgehenden räumlichen Entkopplung alltäglicher Lebensfunktionen – wie Arbeit, Einkaufen oder Unterhaltung – von ihren tradierten Standorten. An die Vorstellung einer elektronischen Entwertung von Entfernung und Standort knüpften sich vielfältige Spekulationen über einen Auszug der Unternehmen und Spezialisten der Wissensökonomie aus der Stadt und damit die Auflösung der räumlich gebundenen Stadt in eine „City of Bits".

Angesichts der Konfrontation der Städte mit den neuen Informationstechnologien stellte Glaeser die Fragen: „Wird das 21. Jahrhundert einen urbanen Verfall erleben, der sich ebenso schnell vollziehen wird, wie der Aufstieg der Städte im 19. und 20. Jahrhundert? Oder wird der Durchbruch der Informationstechnologie in Verbindung mit einer konsequenteren Politik der öffentlichen Sicherheit die verschandelten Innenstädte von heute in die gentrifizierte Polis von morgen transformieren?" (1) (Übersetzung D.L.)

Zunächst ist unbestreitbar, dass in der Folge des wirtschaftlichen Strukturwandels und neuer Formen internationaler Arbeitsteilung die Städte ihre Rolle als privilegierte Zentren industrieller Produktion weitgehend verloren haben. Diese tiefgreifende Wandlung der ökonomischen Basis der Städte führte jedoch nicht nur zu einem dramatischen Rückgang industrieller Arbeitsplätze, sondern aus diesem Strukturwandel resultieren auch neue, entscheidende Entwicklungschancen für die Städte. Mit der Transformation der traditionellen Industriesysteme, basierend auf den Massenproduktionsvorteilen der großen Fabrikanlagen und Großraumbü-

factories and open-plan offices, new forms of knowledge economy have emerged. They are based on intellectual work, human creativity, social interaction and networking, and above all they have a great affinity with urban locations.

One essential reason for the upgrading of urban contexts derives from the "information paradox" of the information and knowledge society. The more information is available on the internet, the more important the evaluation of information and the distinction between information and knowledge become, or more precisely, between standardised information and context-dependent information.

Information, like for example share prices, turnover, raw material prices or freight rates, is unambiguous and can thus be found, interpreted and understood regardless of context from any net source. Given that information is ubiquitously available through the internet, context-bound knowledge , so-called "tacit knowledge" or "sticky knowledge", becomes very much more significant. This implicit, non-codified knowledge is stuck in people's heads and it is strongly dependent on a shared cognitive, cultural and social context if it is to be communicated and mediated. The most important ways of conveying non-codified knowledge are frequently personal ("face-to-face") contacts and workforce mobility between businesses. So local proximity, linked with social interaction and networking ("social connectivity"), acquires a new meaning for knowledge transfer - particularly in this world of e-mail, fax machines and cyberspace. In other words: "Geography (…) matters for innovation". (2)

These processes of change did not only lead to considerable growth in service work in cities, but also to new forms of work and of everyday organisation. There are significant reasons for assuming that urban metropolises, especially the core cities of urban metropolises, will be a privileged innovation field for producing culture and knowledge as well as incubators for new post-industrial ways of working and living. This does not just make the city considerably more attractive as a location for work, but also as a place to have a home and context to spend one's life in.

The new forms for producing culture and knowledge with their "de-limited" organisation devices and complex, project-related co-operative connections are very heavily concentrated in inner-city quarters with a wide range of urban milieus. The less companies focus on the organisation model of a "standard business" and the "standard working relationship", the more important the specific qualities of the urban milieu become for them. Since they have to rely on a large number of co-operation possibilities for their business existence and have to be constantly on the lookout for new developments, urban areas, with their high levels of economic, social and cultural diversity and wide range of buildings and spaces, represent a gain in terms of available potential.

As new urban organisational forms develop for producing culture and knowledge, the traditional "standard work relationship" is transformed into a cheerful "medley" of working relationships moving within the field of tension created by precarious and autonomous working conditions. In this new urban working society the traditional division of work, home life and leisure blur. One of the key features of the work- and life-style of this new employment type is functional penetration and close integration of professional, social and personal life. Given the time and space conditions of their work

ros, haben sich inzwischen neue Formen einer Wissensökonomie herausgebildet. Sie stützen sich auf intellektuelle Arbeit, menschliche Kreativität, soziale Interaktion und Vernetzung, und sie haben vor allem eine große Affinität zu städtischen Standorten.

Eine wesentliche Ursache für die Aufwertung städtischer Kontexte resultiert aus dem „Informations-Paradoxon" der Informations- und Wissensgesellschaft. Je mehr Informationen über das Internet verfügbar sind, desto wichtiger wird die Bewertung von Informationen sowie die Unterscheidung von Informationen und Wissen, genauer: zwischen standardisierten Informationen und kontextabhängigem Wissen.

Informationen, wie zum Beispiel Aktienkurse, Umsätze, Rohstoffpreise oder Frachtraten, haben eine eindeutige Bedeutung und lassen sich demnach auch kontextunabhängig von jedem Netzzugang aus suchen, interpretieren und verstehen. Mit der ubiquitären Verfügbarkeit von Informationen durch das Internet gewinnt kontextgebundenes Wissen, das so genannte „tacit knowledge" oder „sticky knowledge" außerordentlich an Bedeutung. Dieses implizite, nicht kodifizierte Wissen steckt in den Köpfen von Menschen, und dessen Kommunikation und Vermittlung ist stark abhängig von einem gemeinsamen kognitiven, kulturellen und sozialen Kontext. Die wichtigsten Formen der Übermittlung von nicht kodifiziertem Wissen sind häufige persönliche („face-to-face") Kontakte sowie die zwischenbetriebliche Mobilität von Arbeitskräften. Für den Transfer von Wissen bekommt somit – gerade in einer Welt von E-Mail, Fax-Maschinen und Cyberspace – räumliche Nähe („local proximity") verbunden mit sozialer Interaktion und Vernetzung („social connectivity") eine neue Bedeutung. Mit anderen Worten: „Geography (…) matters for innovation". (2)

Diese Wandlungsprozesse führten nicht nur zu einem starken Wachstum der Dienstleistungsbeschäftigung in den Städten, sondern auch zu neuen Arbeitsformen und neuen Formen der Alltagsorganisation. Es gibt signifikante Gründe für die Annahme, dass Stadtmetropolen, insbesondere die Kernstädte von Stadtmetropolen ein privilegiertes Innovationsfeld der Wissens- und Kulturproduktion sowie Inkubatoren neuer, postindustrieller Arbeits- und Lebensformen sein werden. Dadurch aber gewinnt die Stadt nicht nur als Arbeitsort, sondern auch als Wohnort und Lebensraum wesentlich an Attraktivität.

Die neuen Formen der Kultur- und Wissensproduktion mit ihren „entgrenzten" Organisationsformen und ihren komplexen, projektbezogenen Kooperationsbeziehungen, konzentrieren sich sehr stark auf innerstädtische Quartiere mit vielfältigen urbanen Milieus . Je weniger die Unternehmen auf das Organisationsmodell eines „Normalbetriebes" und das „Normalarbeitsverhältnis" ausgerichtet sind, desto wichtiger werden für sie die spezifischen Qualitäten des urbanen Milieus. Da sie in ihrer betrieblichen Existenz auf eine Vielzahl von Kooperationsmöglichkeiten angewiesen sind und ständig wachsam sein müssen für neue Entwicklungen, bieten ihnen urbane Räume mit einer hohen ökonomischen, sozialen und kulturellen Diversität und einer baulich-räumlichen Vielfalt einen Zugewinn an Möglichkeiten.

Mit der Entwicklung neuer urbaner Organisationsformen der Wissens- und Kulturproduktion wird das tradierte „Normalarbeitsverhältnis" transformiert in vielfältige „bunte" Arbeitsbeziehungen, die sich im Spannungsfeld von prekären und autonomen Arbeitsbedingungen bewegen. In dieser neuen urbanen Arbeitsgesellschaft verflüssigt sich die traditionelle Trennung von Arbeiten, Wohnen und Freizeit. Eine funktionale Durchdringung und enge Integration von beruflichem, sozialem und persönlichem Leben ist eines der wesentlichen Merkmale der Arbeits- und Lebensweise dieses neuen Beschäftigungstypus. Aufgrund der zeitlichen und räumlichen Bedingungen ihrer Arbeit sowie ihrer Wertorientierung bildet sich bei den – in der Regel gutverdienenden – Kreativen und Wissensproduzenten ein arbeitsintensiver Konsumstil heraus, der auf ein dichtes, stadträumlich konzentriertes Netzwerk von Dienstleistern angewiesen ist.

and their value orientation, a work-intensive consumer style tends to be the norm for these - usually high-earning - creative people and knowledge producers, a style that relies on a dense network of service providers, concentrated within a particular urban space.

But the new urban labour market is not shaped by those who gain from structural change alone, in other words the highly qualified professionals who have found professional prospects in knowledge- and culture-based services. The upheaval in the economic basis of the cities has led through the pluralisation of work forms to a heavy segmentation of the labour market and of urban social structures, and this has created new forms of social inequality.

And what about the dream of our "own home in the country" that has been luring younger, higher wage-earning families into the areas outside cities for decades? Since deciding to choose a suburban home is very heavily dependent on time of life, it is worth looking briefly at the population's age structure. The waves of suburbanisation in the last few decades were shaped essentially by years with very high birth-rates (the so-called 'baby boom'). The 'pill blip' generation (born between 1964 and 1975) is now reaching suburbanisation age. This generation showed a decline in births of about 40%. Thus the mass of potential "suburbanites" is also very much smaller than in previous years. We should therefore assume that for this reason alone the number of families migrating into the surrounding areas will fall sharply in the next few years.

At the same time, the labour market has become less secure. Permanent full-time jobs will soon be the exception, and highly qualified people in particular now work for longer and in irregular time intervals. At the same time the number of women working has increased considerably in recent years. Two people working and the erosion of the social time structure has made everyday family life in suburban locations with long journeys and commuting time more and more complicated. And because jobs and incomes are less secure, markedly fewer people can or want to pin themselves down with high mortgages for their own greenfield home.

Against the background of these new development trends, the "home in the country" has lost a great deal of its allure. The demand for living space will continue to increase in the next few years in Germany - despite a dwindling population. Key reasons for this are an average upward trend in the consumption of living space, and the increasing number of households. But the demand for new living spaces is now articulating itself much more selectively in terms of space, and expresses changing living preferences. This leads among other things to falling property prices in the "urban sprawl" of many large cities, a location that was a sought-after place to live a few years ago. So it is not just constantly rising petrol prices or the discontinuation of the state home-buying subsidy that are making people ask: are we really so well off living in the country? Apart from the consequences of demographic change, it is above all profound changes in the labour market in particular, especially the strong increase in the numbers or working women and the erosion of the housewife-marriage model associated with this that have led to a clear drop in suburbanisation. The capital-intensive life-style with a little house in the country was linked to a steady income, increasing leisure and above all a clear division of labour between men and women. The man was the breadwinner, and the woman looked after the household and the children. This model has been suspended.

Given all this, many people are rediscovering the advantages of the city: the city does not just offer a wide range of employment possibilities, but also a great variety of on-the-spot services, and without these an urban lifestyle is unlikely to seem possible or attractive.

In future, businesses will go where there are well-educated people and qualified employees will look for places where they can find a wide range of employment opportunities and urban living conditions in which it is possible to combine work and life, profession and

Der neue städtische Arbeitsmarkt ist jedoch nicht nur geprägt durch die Gewinner des Strukturwandels, also die hochqualifizierten Professionals, die in den wissens- und kulturbasierten Dienstleistungen eine berufliche Perspektive gefunden haben. Der Umbruch der ökonomischen Basis der Städte hat mit der Pluralisierung der Arbeitsformen zu einer starken Segmentierung des Arbeitsmarktes und der städtischen Sozialstrukturen geführt, woraus sich neue Formen sozialer Ungleichheit ergeben.

Und was ist mit dem Traum vom „Eigenheim im Grünen", der jahrzehntelang die jungen, besserverdienenden Familien ins Umland gelockt hat?

Da die Entscheidung für die Wahl eines suburbanen Wohnorts sehr stark abhängig ist vom Lebenszyklus, lohnt sich ein kurzer Blick auf den Altersaufbau der Bevölkerung. Die Suburbanisierungswellen der letzen Jahrzehnte wurden im Wesentlichen geprägt durch die geburtenstarken Jahrgänge (die sog. „Babyboomer"). Inzwischen kommen die Jahrgänge des „Pillenknicks" (geboren zwischen 1964 und 1975) ins Suburbanisierungsalter. In dieser Generation gab es einen Geburtenrückgang von rund 40%. Damit ist jedoch auch die Masse der potenziellen „Suburbaniten" sehr viel kleiner als in den Jahren zuvor. Es ist davon auszugehen, dass allein aus diesem Grunde die Zahl der Familien, die ins Umland abwandert, in den nächsten Jahren stark abnehmen wird.

Gleichzeitig ist der Arbeitsmarkt unsicherer geworden. Feste Vollzeitstellen werden bald die Ausnahme sein, und vor allem Höherqualifizierte arbeiten heute länger und in unregelmäßigen Zeitrhythmen. Gleichzeitig ist die Frauenerwerbstätigkeit in den letzten Jahren deutlich gestiegen. Durch Doppelerwerbstätigkeit und die Erosion des gesellschaftlichen Zeitgefüges wird das familiäre Alltagslebens an suburbanen Standorten mit langen Wegen und Pendlerzeiten immer komplizierter. Und durch die Unsicherheit von Job und Einkommen werden sich deutlich weniger Menschen mit hohen Hypotheken für ein Eigenheim im Grünen festlegen können oder wollen.

Vor dem Hintergrund dieser neuen Entwicklungstrends hat das „Eigenheim im Grünen" inzwischen stark an Glanz verloren. Zwar wird die Wohnflächennachfrage in Deutschland – trotz rückläufiger Bevölkerung – in den nächsten Jahren weiterhin zunehmen. Wesentliche Ursachen dafür sind ein nach wie vor wachsender durchschnittlicher Wohnflächenverbrauch und die zunehmende Zahl der Haushalte. Die Nachfrage nach neuen Wohnflächen artikuliert sich inzwischen jedoch räumlich sehr viel selektiver und ist Ausdruck veränderter Wohnpräferenzen. Dies führt u. a. zu einem Rückgang der Immobilienpreise in den vor einigen Jahren als Immobilienstandort hochgepriesenen „Speckgürteln" vieler Großstädte.

Es sind also nicht nur die immer teureren Benzinpreise oder die Streichung der Eigenheimzulage, die die Leute fragen lässt: Sind wir auf der grünen Wiese wirklich gut aufgehoben? Neben den Folgen des demografischen Wandels führen vor allem die tiefgreifenden Veränderungen auf dem Arbeitsmarkt, insbesondere die starke Zunahme der Frauenerwerbstätigkeit und die damit verbundene Erosion des Modells der Hausfrauenehe zu einer deutlichen Abschwächung der Suburbanisierung. Der kapitalintensive Lebensstil mit dem Häuschen im Grünen war gebunden an ein kontinuierliches Einkommen, wachsende Freizeit und vor allem auch eine klare Arbeitsteilung zwischen Mann und Frau. Der Mann war der Ernährer der Familie, und die Frau kümmerte sich um Haushalt und Kinder. Dieses Modell steht zur Disposition.

Vor diesem Hintergrund entdecken viele die Vorteile der Stadt wieder: Die Stadt bietet nicht nur ein breites Angebot an Beschäftigungsmöglichkeiten, sondern auch vielfältigste Dienstleistungen vor Ort, die einen urbanen Lebensstil erst möglich und attraktiv machen.

Die Unternehmen werden künftig dorthin gehen, wo sie gut ausgebildete Leute vorfinden, und qualifizierte Beschäftigte werden sich nach Orten umsehen, wo sie eine große Vielfalt an Beschäftigungsmöglichkeiten

family with children in a way that makes life worth living. Given this, strengthening home life, the social infrastructure, education and training, i.e. developing a new urban culture, becomes a key issue for future urban policy.

At present it is possible to formulate a wide range of reasons for the renaissance of the city and weakening suburbanisation:
>> new demands made by the knowledge economy >> the many forms taken by border-breakdown in traditional urban institutions >> the erosion of the male breadwinner model linked with a tendency for both man and wife to work together with a tendency towards egalitarian career patterns >> the erosion of the social time structure by linked with an increasingly difficult "work-life balance" within living communities >> the disintegration of the traditional welfare state arrangements >> the end of the dream of the promotion society >> profound demographic change and >> the foreseeable limits of "fossil-fuelled mobility"

But the effect of these tendencies, some of which overlap and reinforce each other mutually, must not be interpreted to mean that development is going back to the traditional city. There is no longer a way back to the monocentric city of industrialism. The traditional urban structures' tendency to degenerate is certainly being muted by the new development trends, but industrially shaped urban structures will not last in the long run. The enduring renaissance of a city is not the result of a return to, but of a reinvention of the city, a reinvention that is currently taking place in the formation of a complex diversity of space-time configurations in work and life organisation in cities and urban regions. (3)

The concept of the "layered city" offers an interesting handle on such space-time configurations. In their study of how globalisation shapes urban spaces, Marcuse and van Kempen formulated this concept as follows: "Each city is multiple cities, layered over and under each other, separated by both space and time, constituting the living and working environment of different classes and different groups, interacting with each other in a set of dominations and dependencies that reflect increasing distance and inequality". (4)

The new urban structures are no longer determined by specialisation, zoning and standardisation, but by diversity, complex superimposition and difference. Given the structural uncertainty and openness of social developments in a globalised knowledge society, the city, with its high economic, cultural and social diversity serves as a "random generator" for contacts, information and context-bound knowledge, and with its many possibility structures offers added opportunities for social participation and for managing the future in civil society.

und urbanen Lebensverhältnissen finden, in denen man Arbeit und Leben, Beruf und Familie mit Kindern in einer lebenswerten Weise verbinden kann. In diesem Sinne wird die Stärkung des Wohnens, der sozialen Infrastruktur, der Erziehung und Ausbildung, d. h. also die Entwicklung einer neuen urbanen Lebenskultur zu einer Schlüsselfrage zukünftiger Stadtpolitik.

Für eine Renaissance der Stadt und eine Abschwächung der Suburbanisierung lassen sich gegenwärtig vielfältige Gründe formulieren:
>> die neuen Anforderungen der Wissensökonomie, >> die vielfältigen Formen der Entgrenzung tradierter gesellschaftlicher Institutionen, >> die Erosion des männlichen Ernährermodells durch die zunehmende Doppelerwerbstätigkeit von Mann und Frau – verbunden mit einer Tendenz zu egalitären Karrieremustern, >> die Erosion des gesellschaftlichen Zeitgefüges – verbunden mit immer schwierigeren „Work-Life"-Balancen innerhalb von Lebensgemeinschaften, >> die Auflösung der tradierten wohlfahrtstaatlichen Arrangements, >> das Ende des Traums von der Aufstiegsgesellschaft, >> ein tief greifender demografischer Wandel, sowie die absehbaren Grenzen „fossiler Mobilität".

Die Wirkungsweise dieser sich teilweise überlappenden und gegenseitig verstärkenden Tendenzen darf allerdings nicht so interpretiert werden, dass die Entwicklung wieder zurück zur traditionellen Stadt geht. Es gibt keinen Weg mehr zurück zur monozentrischen Stadt des Industrialismus. Die Auflösungstendenzen der tradierten städtischen Strukturen werden durch die neuen Entwicklungstrends zwar gedämpft, aber die industriell geprägten städtischen Strukturen werden auf Dauer keinen Bestand haben. Eine dauerhafte Renaissance der Stadt ist nicht das Resultat einer Rückkehr, sondern einer Neuerfindung der Stadt – eine Neuerfindung, wie sie sich gegenwärtig in der Herausbildung einer komplexen Vielfalt raum-zeitlicher Konfigurationen der Arbeits- und Lebensorganisation in den Städten und Stadtregionen vollzieht. (3)

Einen interessanten Ansatz zur Thematisierung derartiger raum-zeitlicher Konfigurationen, bietet das Konzept der „layered city". Bei ihrer Untersuchung der Überformung städtischer Räume durch die Globalisierung haben Marcuse und van Kempen dieses Konzept wie folgt formuliert: „Each city is multiple cities, layered over and under each other, separated by both space and time, constituting the living and working environment of different classes and different groups, interacting with each other in a set of dominations and dependencies that reflect increasing distance and inequality". (4)

Die neuen urbanen Strukturen sind nicht mehr bestimmt durch Spezialisierung, Zonierung und Vereinheitlichung, sondern durch Diversität, komplexe Überlagerung und Differenz. Angesichts der strukturellen Unbestimmtheit und Offenheit gesellschaftlicher Entwicklungen in einer globalisierten Wissensgesellschaft dient die Stadt mit ihrer hohen ökonomischen, sozialen und kulturellen Diversität als „Zufallsgenerator" für Kontakte, Informationen und kontextgebundenes Wissen und bietet mit ihren vielfältigen Möglichkeitsstrukturen einen Zugewinn an Chancen für gesellschaftliche Teilhabe und zivilgesellschaftliche Zukunftsbewältigung.

1) Edward L. Glaeser (1998): "Are Cities Dying?", in: Journal of Economic Perspectives – Volume 12 (2), pp. 139-160
2) Stefano Breschi / Francesco Lissoni (2001): "Localised Knowledge Spillover vs. Innovative Milieux: Knowledge 'Tacitness' Reconsidered", in: Papers in Regional Science, 80 (3), pp. 255-273
3) Dieter Läpple (2005): "Phönix aus der Asche: Die Neuerfindung der Stadt", in: H. Berking; M. Löw (eds.): Soziale Welt, special volume 16: Die Wirklichkeit der Städte, pp. 397-413
4) Peter Marcuse, Ronald van Kempen (2000): "Conclusion: A Changed Spatial Order", in: Dies. (eds.): Globalizing Cities: a New Spatial Order, Oxford: Blackwell Publishers, S. 246- 275

1) Edward L. Glaeser (1998): „Are Cities Dying?", in: Journal of Economic Perspectives – Volume 12 (2), S. 139-160
2) Stefano Breschi, Francesco Lissoni (2001): „Localised Knowledge Spillover vs. Innovative Milieux: Knowledge ‚Tacitness' Reconsidered", in: Papers in Regional Science, 80 (3), S. 255-273
3) Dieter Läpple (2005): „Phönix aus der Asche. Die Neuerfindung der Stadt", in: H. Berking, M. Löw (Hrsg.), Soziale Welt, Sonderband 16: Die Wirklichkeit der Städte, S. 397-413
4) Peter Marcuse, Ronald van Kempen (2000): „Conclusion: A Changed Spatial Order", in: Dies. (eds.): Globalizing Cities: a New Spatial Order, Oxford: Blackwell Publishers, S. 246- 275

Well-Travelled Hotel

Das Hotel zu Gast

The hotel as guest

Project: Hotel Everland **Location:** Yverdon + Burgdorf, Switzerland; Leipzig, Germany; Paris, France | **Artists:** L/B - Sabina Lang und Daniel Baumann, Burgdorf, Switzerland

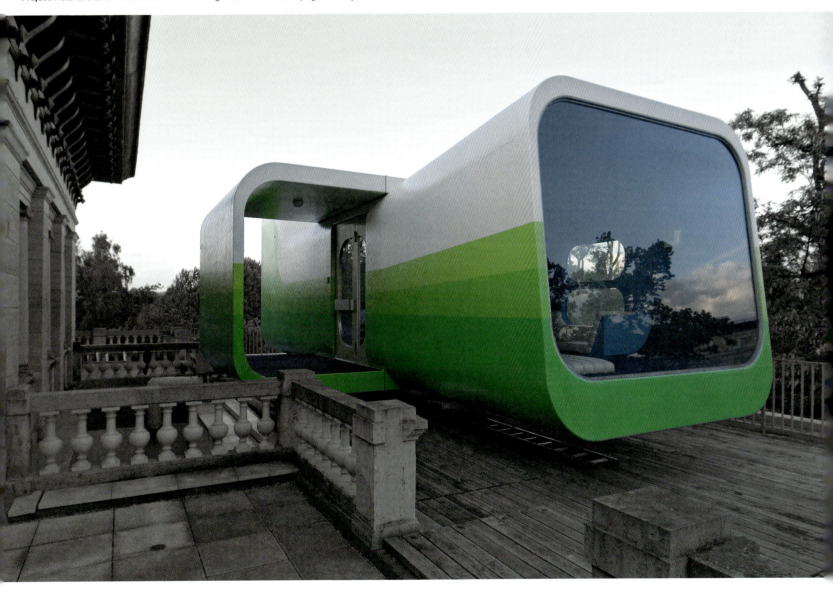

BLESS Wallpaper

Man muss lernen, damit zu leben
You have to learn to live with it

Through one of the windows we can see a building whose greyish brown stucco and dark staring windows illustrates well the city of Berlin's tight financial situation. Through the other, we see the Mehringdamm, climbing gently upwards towards Tempelhof airport; that, now disused, Nazi utopia scheduled to be turned into a huge entertainment venue. The view from this room reveals the leaden weight of history. The room itself is utterly "now".

On the sofa lies a man. He has taken off his shoes and turned his solid back towards the observer. His chihuahua gazes attentively towards the camera. There are champagne bottles on the windowsill and a beautiful rug lies in fornt of the sofa. There are enigmatic objects lying around, such as a cable wrapped in fur. It is a picture of domestic peace and vulnerable intimacy. A distant, ironic or possibly only coincidental reference to Andy Warhol's Sleep or Sam Taylor-Wood's video portrait of David Beckham sleeping. And like those films, this picture also crosses boundaries, invades and disturbs the peace.

Apartment #1C Mehringdamm is a three by four metres work that belongs to a series of large-format photographs of interiors that Bless have had printed on lengths of wallpaper. It is the only picture in the series that has a person in it. Though atypical in this respect, the work conspicuously illustrates the striking effectiveness of Bless wallpapers.

"There is no private space. There are only varying degrees of public space," says Brazilian architect Paulo Mendes da Rocha. BLESS's wallpaper pictures alter not only the public nature of the interiors they have photographed but, even more so, the apartments whose walls are decorated with these works.

They are, of course, a far remove from any ironic reinterpretation of the genre of photomurals. Instead, they aptly illustrate the basic strategy of the two designers by explicitly addressing the potential of large format photograph decoration. While such wallpapers usually tend to bring sunsets, galloping horses or mountain panoramas into the "front room" – in other words, domesticate the sublime and lend domestic constriction a vanishing point, BLESS confront one personal design with another. They provide a twofold perspective: a glimpse inside other people's apartments and the view from those apartments. And they offer insight into their own take on interior decoration, comfortable living and personal style.

In an almost incidental way, BLESS wallpapers also demonstrate how naturally their designs, all too often mistakenly considered extravagant or challenging, fit into everyday life. The fur blanket in #2A Strausberger Platz, or an outfit casually hung in the window lend character to the rooms but do not overpower them.

Adriano Sack

Durch das eine Fenster blickt man auf ein Haus, dessen graubrauner Putz und dunkel starrende Fenster die angespannte Haushaltslage der Stadt Berlin illustrieren. Durch das andere Fenster sieht man den Mehringdamm, der auf dieser Höhe leicht bergan führt, in Richtung des Flughafens Tempfelhof, jener Nazi-Utopie, die nach Stilllegung in eine großflächige Vergnügungsstätte umgebaut werden soll. Der Ausblick aus diesem Zimmer zeigt die Bleischwere der Geschichte. Der Raum selbst spielt ganz im Jetzt.

Auf dem Sofa liegt ein Mann, die Schuhe hat er ausgezogen, der kräftige Rücken dem Betrachter zugewandt. Nur sein Chihuahua blickt aufmerksam in die Kamera. Auf dem Fensterbrett stehen Champagnerflaschen, vor dem Sofa liegt ein schöner Teppich, ringsherum finden sich Objekte, die Rätsel aufgeben, z.B. ein mit Fell umhülltes Ladekabel. Es ist ein Bild häuslichen Friedens und der ungeschützten Intimität. Ein entferntes, ironisches oder vielleicht auch nur zufälliges Zitat von Andy Warhols „Sleep" oder Sam Taylor-Woods Videoporträt des schlafenden David Beckham. Und ebenso wie jene Filme ist auch dieses Bild eins der Grenzüberschreitung, des Eindringens, der Störung des Friedens.

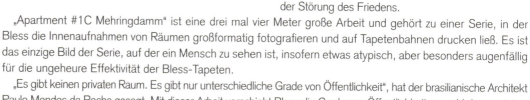

„Apartment #1C Mehringdamm" ist eine drei mal vier Meter große Arbeit und gehört zu einer Serie, in der Bless die Innenaufnahmen von Räumen großformatig fotografieren und auf Tapetenbahnen drucken ließ. Es ist das einzige Bild der Serie, auf der ein Mensch zu sehen ist, insofern etwas atypisch, aber besonders augenfällig für die ungeheure Effektivität der Bless-Tapeten.

„Es gibt keinen privaten Raum. Es gibt nur unterschiedliche Grade von Öffentlichkeit", hat der brasilianische Architekt Paulo Mendes da Rocha gesagt. Mit dieser Arbeit verschiebt Bless die Grade von Öffentlichkeit, sowohl der gezeigten Wohnungen als auch, vielleicht noch mehr, der Wohnungen, in denen ihre Tapeten die Wände schmücken werden.

Natürlich sind sie weit davon entfernt, das Genre der Fototapete ironisch neu zu interpretieren. Stattdessen erkundet Bless, und das macht die Tapeten repräsentativ für die grundsätzliche Strategie der beiden Designerinnen, welches Potential der fotografierte, großflächige Wandschmuck tatsächlich hat. Während jene Sonnenuntergänge, galoppierende Pferde oder Bergpanoramen in die „gute Stube" holten, also das Erhabene domestizierten und der häuslichen Enge einen Fluchtpunkt boten, konfrontieren die Bless-Tapeten einen privaten Entwurf mit einem anderen. Sie sind doppelter Ausblick – in die anderen Wohnungen und aus den Fenstern der anderen Wohnungen. Und sie sind Einblick in die eigenen Vorstellungen von Einrichtungen und Wohnen, Gemütlichkeit und Stil.

Auf beiläufige Art erzählt Bless außerdem auf ihren Tapeten, wie selbstverständlich ihre oft als extravagant oder schwierig missverstandenen Entwürfe sich ins alltägliche Leben einfügen. Die Felldecke auf „#2 Strausberger Platz" oder ein wie zufällig ins Fenster gehängtes Kleid prägen die Räume, aber überwältigen sie nicht.

From Air Raid to Art Shelter

Project: Sammlung Boros – Bunker **Location:** Berlin **Architects:** Realarchitektur, Berlin

Militärisches Bollwerk als Kunstbunker und Sockel für ein Penthouse

A military bastion as art bunker and pedestal for a penthouse

Project: Symbiont | Location: Merzig | Architects: FloSundK architektur+urbanisik, Saarbrücken

Ein Dach für die neue Generation

A roof for the next generation

A Mutually Beneficial Relationship

Urbane Shell Suit

Kultivierung des Städtischen im suburbanen Raum
Cultivating urban quality in suburban space

Project: Wohlfahrt-Laymann House   **Location:** Oberursel, near Frankfurt am Main | **Architects:** Meixner Schlüter Wendt Architekten, Frankfurt am Main

Context

Kontext

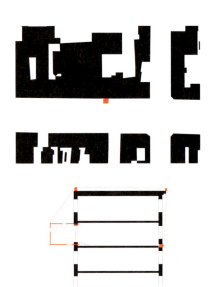

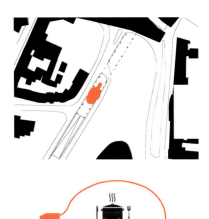

ANDRÉ POITIERS: PANORAMIC CURVE   P a g e / S e i t e >> 2 6

Project: Kemper-Trautmann house | **Location**: Hamburg | **Client**: Norddeutsche Grundvermögen Bau- und Entwicklungsgesellschaft mbH, Hamburg | **Architects**: André Poitiers, Hamburg | **Staff**: Ulrich Engel, Jana Grundmann, Benjamin Holsten, Martin Michel, Alec Müller, Timm Orth, Jörg Rasmussen, Daniela Rohrberg, Catrin Seufert, Ine Spaar, Hartwig Zehm | © **Photos**: Klaus Frahm (artour) | **Completion**: 2006 | **Area**: 1,400 m²

The "Kemper-Trautmann house" is situated in Hamburg's city centre close to the Jungfernstieg promenade and the Binnenalster lake. The nine-storey office and retail building fills what was for years an empty gap in the city's shopping and business district. >> The building's white party walls frame the green glass-fronted building within the narrow site, enabling it to present itself to the street while also expressing the building's relationship to the compact, historic context of existing perimeter building blocks. The facade draws on architectural elements found in neighbouring buildings and, in an abstracted form, reflects their projecting windows and horizontal cornices. A narrow lightwell clad in stone has been created at the rear, which allows the maximum use of office space across the entire depth of the building. With its rounded façade corner, the design also responds to a recessed building adjoining the site, maximising the shop window area on the ground floor and defining the entrance area. On the upper floors, the rounded corner opens up the view towards the Alster river. The building turns itself out of the linear order and offers the visitor not only a view on the opposite building but into the city space.

Das „Kemper-Trautmann Haus" befindet sich in der Innenstadt von Hamburg in unmittelbarer Nähe von Jungfernstieg und Binnenalster. Das neungeschossige Büro- und Geschäftshaus schließt eine jahrelang unbebaute Lücke im Einkaufs- und Geschäftszentrum der Stadt. >> Ein Rahmen aus weißen Brandwänden verleiht dem Gebäude in der schmalen Baulücke eine repräsentative Ausrichtung auf die Straße, während er zugleich den Anschluss zum kompakten, historischen Kontext der vorhandenen Blockrandbebauung herstellt. Die Fassade nimmt die architektonischen Elemente der Nachbarbebauung auf und reflektiert, in abstrakter Form, ihre Erker und horizontalen Gesimse. Zur Rückfront ist ein schmaler, Naturstein verkleideter Lichthof entstanden, der die Nutzung der Büroflächen über die gesamte Gebäudetiefe zulässt. Auf den Rücksprung zum Nachbargebäude in den Großen Bleichen reagiert der Entwurf mit gerundeten Eckfassaden, die im Erdgeschoss die Schaufensterfläche maximiert und die Eingangssituation artikuliert. >> In den Obergeschossen inszeniert die Rundung den Ausblick auf die Alster. Das Gebäude dreht sich aus der linearen Reihung und bietet dem Besucher nicht nur den Blick auf das gegenüberliegende Gebäude, sondern auch in den Stadtraum.

STEFAN EBERSTADT: PARASITE PERSPECTIVE   P a g e / S e i t e >> 2 8

Project: Rucksack house | **Location**: Leipzig, Cologne, Essen | **Client**: Stefan Eberstadt with: Stiftung Federkiel, Leipzig; Dr. Klaus Röckerath, Cologne; Entwicklungsgesellschaft Zollverein mbH, Essen | **Architects**: Stefan Eberstadt, Munich | © **Photos**: Claus Bach, Silke Koch, Hana Schäfer, Octavianne Hornstein | **Statics**: a.k.a. ingenieure, Munich | **Completion**: 2004 | **Area**: 9 m²

Perched between art and architecture, form and function, the Rucksack House is a walk-in sculpture with its own spatial quality. A hovering illuminated space that looks like a cross between temporary scaffolding and minimal sculpture. As mobile as a rucksack, this mini-house is intended to be an additional room that can be suspended from the façade of any residential building. >> The cube is a light and empty space, free from connotations and open to its user's needs. While still being inside a private atmosphere, one has the impression of floating outside of the confines of the actual dwelling above the public space. Folddown furnishings and a multitude of built-in openings on the inside provide extra living space with direct daylight. >> Sections of the walls unfold, with the help of hidden magnets, into a desk, shelves, and a platform for reading or sleeping. The Rucksack box is suspended from steel cables that are anchored to the roof or to the facade of the existing building. The construction is a welded steel cage with a light birch veneered plywood interior cladding. The outside cladding is exterior grade plywood with an absorbent resin surface punctuated by plexiglas inserts. >> The Rucksack house offers a way of improving housing quality on an individual basis. It is a direct visual sign and reactivates the idea of the self-built anarchistic tree house, but one that is more prominently placed and structurally engineered. New space gets slung onto an existing space by a simple, clear, and understandable method.

Angesiedelt zwischen Kunst und Architektur ist das Rucksackhaus eine begehbare Skulptur mit ganz eigener räumlicher Qualität: Ein schwebender, beleuchteter Raum, der wie ein temporäres Baugerüst und eine „Minimalskulptur" zugleich anmutet. >> Universell einsetzbar wie ein Rucksack kann dieses Minihaus als zusätzlicher Raum an die Fassade eines jeden Wohngebäudes angehängt werden. Obwohl man sich darin innerhalb seiner Privatsphäre bewegt, vermittelt sich dennoch der Eindruck, außerhalb der Wohnungsmauern über dem öffentlichen Raum zu schweben. Der Kubus ist mit einer Vielzahl an eingebauten Öffnungen aus Plexiglas durchbrochen und bietet ungewöhnliche Perspektiven auf die Stadt. In seiner Leichtigkeit und assoziationsfreien Neutralität ist die leere Box offen für die Bedürfnisse des jeweiligen Nutzers. Teile der Wände sind als Klappmöbel ausgeführt und können je nach Bedarf mit Hilfe verborgener Magneten in einen Schreibtisch, in Regale, oder auch in eine Schlafgelegenheit umfunktioniert werden. >> Die Konstruktion besteht aus einer geschweißten Stahlkabine, die mittels Stahlkabeln am Dach oder an der Fassade des bestehenden Hauses befestigt wird. Innen ist die Kabine mit Birkenholzfurnier verschalt, während die Außenhaut mit wasserabweisendem Kunstharz beschichtet ist. >> Das Rucksackhaus bietet eine neutrale Raumlösung, die sich jeder ganz individuell aneignen kann. Die Idee des selbstgebauten, anarchistischen Baumhauses lebt wieder auf, allerdings in einer hoch technisierten Version. Mit seiner prominenten Platzierung setzt es ein direktes visuelles Zeichen. Das parasitenartige Gebilde generiert Raum, indem es an einen existierenden Raum angedockt und von dessen Infrastruktur profitiert.

RAUMLABOR: DOLMUSCH X-PRESS / KÜCHENMONUMENT / BERGKRISTALL   P a g e / S e i t e >> 3 2 , 6 5

Project: Dolmusch X-press / Küchenmonument / Volkspalast – der Berg | **Location**: Berlin / Duisburg / Berlin | **Client**: raumlabor_berlin and peanutz architekten in cooperation with HAU / co-production by "PubliCity und Ringlokschuppen, Mülheim/Ruhr" / Sophiensaele, HAU, raumlabor_berlin and Club real | **Architects**: raumlabor_berlin | © **Photos**: David Balzer, Rosa Merk, Rainer Schlautmann, Marco Canevacci | **URL**: www.raumlabor-berlin.de | **Completion**: 2005 / 2006 / 2005 | **Area**: - / 155 m² / -

These are three collaborative projects that explore experimental access to the city. The projects question the social, political and cultural meaning of spatial use by exploring the hidden potential of spaces by temporary interventions. "Experience" is a central issue for these projects. They do not predetermine the experiences of the user but rather set up a framework for individual and collective expression and communication. >> Dolmusch X-press is about alternative public transport: horse-drawn carriages and taxis were driven through the Kreuzberg district of Berlin creating a direct cultural link between Kreuzberg and Istanbul. A dolmusch is a shared taxi, circulating on fixed routes in Turkey. Putting a dolmusch in Berlin is a simple juxtaposition opening a vast space of social interaction and re-appropriation. The Dolmusch X-press on the other hand created something of a cultural muddle in Berlin. Kreuzberg migrants and non-migrants, and also art tourists, experienced the district with enhanced social interaction. >> The Küchenmonument (kitchen monument) travels to urban interstitial spaces. As a stranger it occupies and disturbs habitual relationships and connections. After six days the internal mechanism of the object comes alive and a giant transparent bubble unfolds and inflates. Ordinary people are invited to celebrate a collective banquet together within the new space. >> The Gasthof Bergkristall (rock crystal inn) was a temporary hotel inside a constructed "mountain" in the derelict Palast der Republik in Berlin. The mountain transformed the politically loaded space into a fantastic setting.

Die gemeinschaftlich durchgeführten Aktionen stellen gesellschaftliche Bedeutungen städtischer Raumnutzungen in Frage und erkunden ergänzende Potenziale von Gebäuden und Flächen. Das Raumerlebnis wird zum zentralen Anliegen. Die Projekte schaffen jedoch nur den Rahmen für die individuell initiierte Wahrnehmung und Nutzung der zuvor angeeigneten Orte. Sie bilden damit die Grundlage für subjektive oder kollektive öffentliche Selbstdarstellungen und eine erhöhte soziale Interaktion. >> Provisorisch geschmückte Pferdekutschen, Schiff und Minibus drängelten sich als Dolmusch X-press durch den Kreuzberger Verkehr. Diese Alternativen zu bestehenden öffentlichen Berliner Verkehrsmitteln stellten eine direkte kulturelle Verbindung zum entfernten Istanbul dar. Dort sind Dolmusch ein gängiges Vehikel der täglichen Einwohnermobilität und als Sammeltaxi auf festgelegten Routen unterwegs. Der Dolmusch X-press hingegen erzeugte in Berlin eher ein kulturelles Durcheinander. Kreuzberger Migranten und Nicht-Migranten sowie die Kunsttouristen erlebten den Stadtteil mit erhöhter sozialer Interaktion. >> Das Küchenmonument wurde dagegen in urbanen Zwischenräumen temporär errichtet. Als Fremdling störte es gewohnte räumliche Verbindungen. Nach je sechs Tagen Ruhestellung setzte ein innerer Mechanismus das Objekt in Betrieb, um einen gewaltigen Luftballon hervortreten zu lassen. Dieses fulminante Ereignis wurde mit Passanten bei einem gemeinsamen Essen gefeiert. >> Die Pension Gasthof Bergkristall wurde in einer raumfüllenden Vektorflächen-Konstruktion, genannt „Der Berg", im Berliner Palast der Republik eingerichtet. Der Berg verwandelte den zeitgeschichtlich-politisch aufgeladenen Innenraum des ehemaligen Regierungsgebäudes in eine Fantasiekulisse.

suburbanisation sucks

MESS (MOBILE EINSATZTRUPPE STADT UND STIL): A HOUSE MOVES HOME   Page / Seite >> 33, 93

Project: Lebe-Deine-Stadt.de | **Location**: Germany | **Client**: Self-initiated project | **Architects**: MESS, Kaiserslautern | **URL**: http://www.lebe-deine-stadt.de | **Completion**: active since 2004

"Cities are about change. Instigator and recipient is the human being, whether as an active designer or as a passive follower. We all take part in shaping and changing our environment therefore we should be aware of our actions and consequences as well as possible alternatives and opportunities. This is the only way for us to act in a self-determined and responsible manner. A large proportion of our current and future problems and challenges are affected by the general public's lack of knowledge and awareness regarding the social, ecological and economical effects of our settlement behaviour." >> "MESS", German abbreveation for mobile deployment squad city and style, see themselves as a "transmitter", whose aim it is to generate a public awareness about issues concerning settlement structures and their social implications. They aim to reach as broad a spectrum of society as possible and hence employ a broad range of relevant media from books to pamphlets, postcards, events, installations, lectures, exhibitions, slogans, films and internet platforms. >> "Lebe deine Stadt" (live your city) is a multimedia project that functions as an online magazine. It acts as a pool for articles and discussion about sustainable urban development by linking local projects through a global medium. "Lebe deine Stadt" encourages actions for reclaiming public space such as spontaneous picnic meals in public squares, on traffic islands or other urban spaces. >> The group uses self-produced short films and animations such as "Ein Tag in der Stadt" (A day in the city) and "Ein Haus zieht um" (a house moves home) as optical background music for their events and lectures. They have developed a growing pool of merchandising products such as mugs, pens and t-shirts printed with website addresses that contain further information about their particular projects.

„In Städten geht es um Veränderung. Der Mensch ist dabei zugleich Geber und Nehmer, ob als aktiver Gestalter oder als passiver Nachahmer. Wir alle wirken mit daran, dass unser Lebensumfeld geformt und verändert wird. Deshalb sollten wir uns unser Handeln und dessen Konsequenzen bewusst machen und auch an mögliche Alternativen und Chancen denken." >> Der Name MESS steht für „Mobile Einsatztruppe Stadt und Stil" und das dahinterstehende Team sieht sich als Mittler zwischen Fachwelt und Öffentlichkeit. Das Ziel liegt darin, in der Bevölkerung das Bewusstsein für die sozialen, ökologischen und wirtschaftlichen Auswirkungen des menschlichen Siedlungsverhaltens zu wecken. Nach den Vorstellungen von MESS sollen die Menschen so in die Lage versetzt werden, verantwortlich und selbstbestimmt an der Gestaltung ihres Lebensraums mitzuwirken. >> Das Online-Magazin „Lebe Deine Stadt" dient in diesem Rahmen als Sammelbecken für Presseartikel und Diskussionen und als Schnittstelle für lokale Projekte, die so in einen internationalen Kontext eingebunden werden. Ergänzend werden kleine Lehrfilme als optische Untermalung präsentiert, die wie etwa „Ein Tag in der Stadt" oder „Ein Haus zieht um" spielerisch Themen wie Dichte oder Suburbanisierung aufgreifen. >> Das Projekt „Lebe Deine Stadt" findet aber auch in der Wirklichkeit statt und möchte Menschen dazu anregen, sich den öffentlichen Raum wieder anzueignen. Durch spontane Aktionen strebt die Gruppe eine Neuinterpretation möglicher Raumnutzungsmuster an und möchte so deutlich machen, dass öffentlicher Raum erst aus den bewussten Handlungen der Menschen entsteht. Die Gruppe hat eine wachsende Sammlung von Merchandisingprodukten wie Kaffeetassen, Stifte und T-Shirts konzipiert, die mit der Website-Adresse des Projekts bedruckt sind, wo weiterführende Informationen abgerufen werden können.

133

B+K PLUS: OVER THE TOP   Page / Seite >> 34

Project: Over the top | **Location**: Cologne | **Client**: Dr. Klaus Holtmann | **Architects**: b&k+brandlhuber&co + marc frohn – Arno Brandlhuber, Markus Emde, Martin Kraushaar, Cologne | **Staff**: Jochen Kremer, Chrisoph Salentin, Hagen Urban, Corinna Eger | **Statics**: Ingenieurbüro J. Bernhardt, Cologne | **URL**: www.bukp.de | **Completion**: 2007 | **Area**: 130 m²

The project "over the top" is basically an extension of a postwar building in the city of Cologne achieved by adding a storey. What makes it interesting is the form that this extra storey takes. The volume of the two attic floors derives from the triangulated connection of the existing gable topography of both neighbouring firewalls. The parameters of the shape are drawn from the existing urban context and defined by available materials. The flat repetition of the existing 1950s window format and surface of the tiled façade is continued up into the extension and warped in shape along with it up over the roof and down to the back of the building. >> Despite its unusual and quirky format, the extension is an understandable integration in the existing building situation and the surrounding urban structure. For the architects this project is not about the affirmation of the factual, the recourse to pure form, or the breaking down of the banal through irony, their architecture is defined via an open system which includes terms and circumstances where building norms, regulations and laws are stretched to the limit of their efficacy, where literal meaning ceases to exist and difference begins.

Beim Projekt „Over the Top" handelt es sich um die Aufstockung eines Kölner Nachkriegsgebäudes. Interessant ist dabei die Dreiecksform des aus dem alten und dem aufgestockten Dachgeschoss bestehenden Verbindungsteils zwischen den Brandmauern der Nachbarhäuser. Die Parameter dieser Form leiteten sich aus den Strukturen des städtischen Umfelds ab oder ergaben sich aus den gewählten Baumaterialien. Für das neue Geschoss wurden die Fensterformate aus den 1950er Jahren und die Fassadenverkleidung mit Fliesen übernommen, die sich aber noch „Over the Top", d.h. über das Dach weiter bis in die rückseitige Fassade fortsetzen und dabei in Anpassung an Dachkanten und -konturen verformt wurden. >> Trotz dieser ungewöhnlichen, extravaganten Form fügt sich die Aufstockung auf einleuchtende Weise in den Bestand und den Stadtkontext ein. Für die Architekten ging es bei diesem Projekt nicht um die Bestätigung von faktisch Vorhandenem, um den Rückgriff auf die reine Form oder die Auflockerung des Banalen durch Ironie. Sie definieren Architektur vielmehr als offenes System, das Bedingungen und Umstände einbezieht. Baunormen, -auflagen und -gesetze werden bis an die Grenze ihrer Wirksamkeit gedehnt – auch in diesem Sinne „Over the Top". Und die Grenze ist da, wo der unmittelbare Sinn aufhört und der Unterschied anfängt.

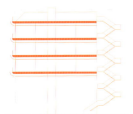

HOYER UND SCHINDELE ARCHITEKTEN + JOACHIM SAUTER (ART+COM): REACTIVE ALLEYWAYS   Page / Seite >> 36

Project: Floating grounds | **Location**: Berlin | **Client**: G+R City-Immobilien GmbH | **Architects**: HSH Hoyer Schindele Hirschmüller with Art+Com AG, Berlin | **Staff**: David Ruic | **Statics**: Hartmut Unterberg, Berlin | **URL**: www.hoyerundschindele.de / www.artcom.de | **Planning**: 2006 | **Area**: 150 m²

This project is designed to fill the gaps in the homogenous block structure that grew out of Berlin's years of rapid 19th century urban expansion. The 3-5 metre wide gaps are not building sites but historical thoroughfares built to connect backyards to the street for fire-fighters. >> Each floating ground module closes the existing development line on the street and leaves the ground-level open. Thus, pedestrians, cars, light and sounds can pass beneath the slabs, leaving the inhabitants to benefit from good views and insulated conditions. Nevertheless their position connects them visually to the urban context and provides direct communication with the surroundings. The backyard is still accessible, the statics are independent from the neighbouring houses and the plot is inexpensive – it is an overbuilding of a passageway. >> The gap is transformed into an activated opening that reveals its special communication with the city by night: Its interactive light slab reacts to passing pedestrians and lights their way underneath it. This creates a direct link between private and public urban worlds and underlines the action of, passing through' the space. >> The apartments will be charged with atmosphere by further interactive light ceilings, which not only illuminate the deep housing unit, but also create illusions, animations or interactions according to the atmosphere desired. By moving the mobile interior space dividers the user can mix, separate and overlay micro-ambiences and affect the impression from outside.

Das Projekt hat zum Ziel, die Aussparungen in der homogenen Wohnblockstruktur zu füllen, die in Berlin im 19. Jahrhundert während des rasanten Wachstums der Stadt entstanden. Als Baugrundstück werden nicht etwa Baulücken genutzt, sondern die drei bis fünf Meter breiten Durchfahrten, die historisch als Feuergasse dienten, um die Hinterhöfe von der Straße aus zu erreichen. >> Jedes schwebende Baumodul schließt die vorhandene Baulinie zur Straße hin zwar ab, lässt jedoch den Durchgang unterhalb des Baukörpers weiterhin offen. Visuell stellt dessen Positionierung trotzdem eine Verbindung zu dem urbanen Kontext her und bietet eine direkte Kommunikation mit dem Umfeld, da der Zugang zu den Hinterhöfen weiterhin möglich ist. Die Vorteile liegen in der statischen Unabhängigkeit von den angrenzenden Häusern und den geringen Kosten für das Baugrundstück. >> Die Lücke verwandelt sich in eine lebendige Öffnung, die ihre spezielle Kommunikation mit der Stadt besonders nachts entfaltet: Der interaktive Lichtkörper reagiert auf die Bewegung vorbeilaufender Fußgänger und beleuchtet deren Weg durch den Durchgang. Die Schwelle zwischen privatem und öffentlichem Raum wird auf besondere Weise artikuliert, indem ihre ursprüngliche Bestimmung – nämlich das Durchschreiten eines Zwischenraumes – hervorgehoben wird. >> Zusätzlich werden die Apartments durch interaktive Lichtdecken, die nicht nur die tiefen Wohneinheiten ausleuchten, sondern je nach Wunsch auch Illusionen, Animationen oder Interaktionen kreieren können, atmosphärisch aufgeladen. Mobile Raumteiler bieten dem Bewohner verschiedenste Möglichkeiten der Kombination, Trennung und Überlagerung von Mikro-Atmosphären und beeinflussen so zugleich die Wirkung des Gebäudes von außen.

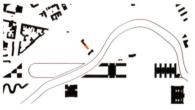

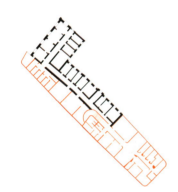

DAVID CHIPPERFIELD ARCHITEKTEN: VERTICAL BUNGALOW   Page/Seite >> 3 7

Project: Town house O – 10 | **Location:** Berlin | **Client:** private | **Architects:** David Chipperfield Architects, Berlin | **Staff:** Alexander Schwarz, Lutz Schütter, Markus Bauer | © **Photos:** David Chipperfield Architects, Senat Berlin | **URL:** www.davidchipperfield.co.uk | **Completion:** 2007 | **Area:** 380 m²

The new quarter of Friedrichswerder near the Museum Island in Mitte is part of the current urban development of central Berlin and an example of the planning concept "critical reconstruction". The paradigm and inspiration for this new quarter stems from the historical city grid and its transformation in rows of high, narrow town houses in limited spaces such as those found in London or Amsterdam. >> Traditional urban elements such as house, courtyard, block, street and square constitute the skeletal structure guidelines defined by the local city planning office. A variety of architects were then individually commissioned by clients who bought the 47 plots to design residences (with a permitted proportion of workspace if desired) within the confines of the guidelines. >> Within the tight typological restrictions of a narrow (6m wide) and deep lot, the 22m high Chipperfield town house achieves generosity through room height. The quality of natural light and space are more important than optimising surface area and flexibility. Unusual for a town house, the location of the staircase on the façade highlights the significance of the vertical aspect of the project concept. While the façade is almost passive from a material aspect, the composition of vertical cuboids with glazed front sides the façade develops profundity and a certain sculptured quality. The house will be used as a high-quality family home of seven levels with an atelier, garden and ground floor garage. It attempts to transcend the atmospheric constriction of the typology by bringing light and space into the vertical.

Das neue Quartier Friedrichswerder in der Nähe der Museumsinsel ist ein Beispiel für die städtische Planungspolitik Berlins, die „kritische Rekonstruktion". Paradigma und Inspiration für die Planung dieses neuen Quartiers entstammen dem historischen Stadtgrundriss und seiner Umgestaltung in Reihen von hohen, schmalen, Stadthäusern auf begrenzter Fläche, wie in London oder Amsterdam. >> Traditionelle städtische Elemente wie Haus, Hof, Block, Straße und Platz bilden die strukturellen Planungsvorgaben des Senats für die Bebauung am Friedrichswerder. Die Bauherren, die eines der 47 Grundstücke gekauft haben, beauftragten verschiedene Architekten, um die Wohnhäuser im Rahmen der städtischen Vorgaben zu entwerfen. >> Innerhalb des typologischen Rahmens einer schmalen (sechs Meter) und tiefen Parzelle gewinnt das 22 Meter hohe Stadthaus von David Chipperfield Großzügigkeit durch die Variation der Raumhöhen. Eine natürliche Belichtung und Raumwirkung haben Priorität gegenüber Flächenoptimierung und Flexibilität. Die für ein Stadthaus ungewöhnliche Anordnung des Treppenhauses in der Fassade unterstreicht die Bedeutung der vertikalen Ausrichtung des Projekts. Während die Fassadenmaterialien eher passiv eingesetzt werden, entwickelt die Fassade selbst durch die Komposition des vertikalen Quaders mit verglasten Vorderfronten Tiefe und eine gewisse skulpturale Qualität. Das Haus wird als hochwertiges Einfamilienhaus genutzt – mit sieben Ebenen, einem Atelier, einem Garten und einer ebenerdigen Garage. Es versucht, die atmosphärische Enge der Typologie zu überwinden, indem Licht und Raum vertikalisiert werden.

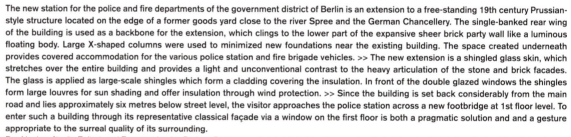

SAUERBRUCH HUTTON: DRESSING UP   Page/Seite >> 3 8

Project: Police and fire station | **Location:** Berlin | **Client:** Senatsverwaltung für Bauen und Wohnen, Berlin | **Architects:** sauerbruch hutton, Berlin | **Staff:** Sven Holzgreve, Jürgen Bartenschlag, Lara Eichwede, Daniela McCarthy, Nicole Winge, Matthias Fuchs, Marcus Hsu, Konrad Opitz, Stefan Bömelburg, Jochen Felten, Benita Hermann, Miriam Ellerbrock, Florian Völker | © **Photos:** Jan Bitter, Landesarchiv Berlin | **Statics:** Arup GmbH, Berlin | **URL:** www.sauerbruchhutton.de | **Completion:** 2004 | **Area:** 6,850 m²

The new station for the police and fire departments of the government district of Berlin is an extension to a free-standing 19th century Prussian-style structure located on the edge of a former goods yard close to the river Spree and the German Chancellery. The single-banked rear wing of the building is used as a backbone for the extension, which clings to the lower part of the expansive sheer brick party wall like a luminous floating body. Large X-shaped columns were used to minimized new foundations near the existing building. The space created underneath provides covered accommodation for the various police station and fire brigade vehicles. >> The new extension is a shingled glass skin, which stretches over the entire building and provides a light and unconventional contrast to the heavy articulation of the stone and brick facades. The glass is applied as large-scale shingles which form a cladding covering the insulation. In front of the double glazed windows the shingles form large louvres for sun shading and offer insulation through wind protection. >> Since the building is set back considerably from the main road and lies approximately six metres below street level, the visitor approaches the police station across a new footbridge at 1st floor level. To enter such a building through its representative classical façade via a window on the first floor is both a pragmatic solution and and a gesture appropriate to the surreal quality of its surrounding.

Der Neubau für die Polizei- und Feuerwache des Berliner Regierungsviertels ist die Erweiterung eines frei stehenden Gebäudes, das im 19. Jahrhundert im preußischen Stil am Rande eines Frachthofs unmittelbar an der Spree erbaut wurde und sich heute in der Nähe des Kanzleramtes befindet. >> Als Rückgrat der baulichen Erweiterung dient der einhüftige rückseitige Flügel des Altbaus, an dessen Brandmauer sich der Neubau wie ein glänzender, schwebender Körper anschmiegt. Durch die Aufständerung auf großen, X-förmigen Pfeilern wurden die Fundamente minimiert und der Raum unterhalb des Anbaus kann als geschützter Stellplatz für die Einsatzfahrzeuge von Polizei und Feuerwehr genutzt werden. >> Die schindelartig vorgehängte Glashaut zieht sich um den gesamten Anbau und bildet einen eleganten und unkonventionellen Kontrast zum steinernen Ausdruck der Altbaufassade. Die aus großen Tafeln bestehenden Glasschindeln verkleiden gewissermaßen die darunter liegende Isolierung und schützen im Bereich der Fenster wie Jalousien vor Sonne und Wind. >> Da das Gebäude in einiger Entfernung von der Straße zurückgesetzt und ca. sechs Meter unterhalb des Straßenniveaus steht, gelangen die Besucher über eine neue Fußgängerbrücke direkt in die Beletage der Polizeistation. Der „Einstieg durchs Fenster" einer repräsentativen, klassizistischen Fassade ist eine pragmatische Lösung und zugleich ein ironischer Kommentar angesichts der Surrealität des Standorts.

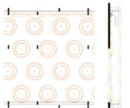

REALITIES:UNITED: SUBCUTANIOUS COMMUNICATION   Page/Seite >> 4 0

Project: SPOTS Light and media façade | **Location:** Berlin | **Client:** HVB Immobilien AG, Munich | **Architects:** realities:united, Berlin | **Staff:** Christoph Wagner, Malte Niedringhaus, Stefan Tietke, Carla Eckhard, Erik Levander, Jan-Philipp Wittrinn | © **Photos:** Bernd Hiepe, Peter Thieme | **URL:** www.realities-united.de | **Completion:** 2005 | **Area:** 1,350 m²

SPOTS is a light- and media installation hardware system comprising a light matrix of 1,800 industrial fluorescent lamps that is integrated into the 11 storey ventilated glass facade of an office building at Potsdamer Platz in Berlin. >> As a result, designs, graphics and animation sequences choreographed by invited artists can be re-created on the façade as moving luminous images. Thus the external shell of the building is transformed into a communicative membrane. The design of the building's multi-layered skin (comprising a conventional solid facade punctuated by windows and a curtain glass façade) is thematically continued by the insertion of new communication layers. >> With its large grid pattern and low resolution, the matrix of fluorescent rings harmonises with the aesthetic "resolution" of the architectural scale of the building and of Potsdamer Platz as a whole. In contrast to the rapid spread of urban media screens, the installation is not a neutral screen made for the perfection of the moving image but a specific extension of the architecture and the urban context. >> SPOTS is simultaneously object, place and medium. A similar parallel is the relationship between the physical light installation and the customized artistic programme being screened on it. The various forms of superimposition that define this project point to a need for researching new ways to adapt or synthesize different realities that define the city's substantial, visual, and mental character.

SPOTS ist eine mediale Installation aus 1.800 Leuchtstoffröhren, die, individuell steuerbar und in einer Matrix angeordnet, die 11-stöckige Glasvorhangfassade eines Bürogebäudes am Potsdamer Platz in ein riesiges Display verwandeln. >> Bespielt werden kann die Fassade mit beliebigen Grafiken, Bildern und Animationen, welche von geladenen Künstlern für den Ort geschaffen werden. Die Außenhaut des Gebäudes wird so zu einer kommunikativen Membran, welche das Gestaltungskonzept der Überlagerung von Loch- und Glasfassade aufgreift und durch eine weitere Mitteilungsebene thematisch fortsetzt. >> Mit seinem groben Raster und der niedrigen Auflösung harmoniert die Bildschirmmatrix der fluoreszierenden Ringe mit der ästhetischen „Auflösung" und dem Detaillierungsmaßstab seiner Umgebung. Auch in der Einfarbigkeit der Neonröhren setzt sich die Installation von den heute sehr weit verbreiteten, extrem hellen und bunten Bildschirmfassaden ab: SPOTS ist nicht auf Perfektion der Darstellung ausgerichtet, sondern stellt eine spezifische Ergänzung der Architektur und des urbanen Kontexts dar. >> Damit ist die Fassade Objekt, Ort und Medium zugleich und es stellt sich eine Parallele zwischen der technischen Realisierung und den speziell entwickelten künstlerischen Bespielungskonzepten ein. Die diversen Formen der Überlagerung sind Ausgangspunkte für die Suche nach neuen Möglichkeiten, welche durch eine Synthese der unterschiedlichen Wirklichkeitsebenen das Wesen der Stadt materiell, bildlich oder ideell definieren.

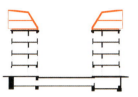

BOLLES + WILSON: CITY HALL SILHOUETTE Page/Seite >> 4 6

Project: City hall extension | **Location**: Frankfurt am Main | **Client**: Bau / Hochbauamt Frankfurt am Main | **Architects**: Bolles + Wilson, Münster | **Staff**: Matthias Anegg, Michael Lin, Philip Neuhaus, André Pannenbäcker, Jim Yohe | **Statics**: ahw Ingenieure, Münster | **URL**: www.bolles-wilson.com | **Competition**: 2001 | **Area**: 3,108 m²

The Frankfurt city hall extension takes the form of a new inverted Mansard roof. The original pre-war roof had a shielding function, whereas the new roof faces outwards, addressing the surrounding city. Frankfurt's original narrow winding alleys now only survive in the form of controversial reconstructions in contrast to the contemporary city, which is one of international finance, high-rise buildings and Europe's central air traffic hub – it is a display window to the sky. >> The proportions of the double-storey rustica and piani nobili of the original building have been rescripted with a new vitrine loggia. The strict modern extension curbs the excesses of early 20th century eclecticism. The straight north façade reinforces the palazzo image whereas the south loggia dramatises the curve of the street. A lightweight wooden construction allows for non-standard moments. A red wall separates the offices from the glazed circulation box and reflects the reddish sandstone rustica below. >> At night the extension transforms into a hovering light box. Data relating to the historical significance of this particular place (the site is opposite the Pauls-kirche where the first German democratic parliament met in 1848) run as an LED strip between the existing façade and extension.

135

Die Aufstockung des Frankfurter Rathauses hat die Form eines nach innen gewendeten Mansarddaches. Das ursprüngliche Dach aus der Vorkriegszeit hatte eine abschirmende Funktion. Das neue Dach hingegen ist nach außen gekehrt und auf die umgebende Stadt ausgerichtet. Die alten, engen und gewundenen Gassen Frankfurts leben nur noch fort in Form kontroverser Rekonstruktionen. Die heutige Stadt ist eines der internationalen Finanzzentren, mit ihren charakteristischen Hochhäusern und dem Luftfahrt-Drehkreuz Europas ist sie ein Schaufenster zum Himmel. >> Die Proportionen der doppelgeschossigen Rustica und der Piani Nobili des ursprünglichen Gebäudes werden mit einer verglasten vitrinenartigen Loggia neu ausgerichtet. Die streng gehaltene moderne Ergänzung zügelt damit die Ausschweifungen des Eklektizismus aus dem frühen 20. Jahrhundert. Die gerade Nordfassade verstärkt den Palazzo-Eindruck, während die südlich gelegene Loggia den geschwungenen Verlauf der Straße dramatisiert. Eine Holzkonstruktion in Leichtbauweise bietet zudem ein weiteres ungewöhnliches Moment. Eine rote Wand trennt die Büros von der zur Straße gelegenen, verglasten Erschließungsbox und reflektiert zugleich den rötlichen Sandstein der Rustica. >> Nachts verwandelt sich die Aufstockung in eine schwebende Lichtskulptur – zwischen ursprünglicher Fassade und Aufstokkung informiert ein LED-Band über die historischen Daten dieses besonderen Ortes gegenüber der Paulskirche, wo 1848 das erste deutsche Parlament zusammentrat.

BARKOW LEIBINGER ARCHITEKTEN: CRYSTALLINE COCOON Page/Seite >> 4 7

Project: Shopping centre refurbishment | **Location**: Bremen | **Client**: BRILLissimo Grundstücksgesellschaft mbH, Bremen | **Architects**: Barkow Leibinger Architekten, Berlin | **Staff**: Kent Wu, Hiroki Nakamura, Jason Sandy, Modell: Jens Wessel | **URL**: www.barkowleibinger.com | **Competition**: 2005, 2nd Prize | **Area**: 1,877 m²

An unspectacular shopping centre dating from the 1960s was modernised and extended by adding a half level to the west building component and two full levels above the office floors to the east. These dissimilar volumes were then connected by creating a wrapping surface that joins them as a sculptural crystalline form. The layer comprises criss-crossing stainless steel cables, like twined around a package, attached to a series of catwalks at each floor level. The new wrapping defines a large terrace and restaurant above the old shopping levels as a dynamic public space with generous views. It provides an animated public gesture to the city. At night the unifying enveloping skin can be artificially lit so that the department store glows like a lantern. >> Rather than hiding the building, the strategy was to react to it. Reacting means doing something, therefore tools were used that relate to a particular action such as selecting, tidying, stacking, connecting and wrapping. The work then becomes suddenly objective, free from intuition and infinite choices. In a performance sense, all of these activities begin to have a status. They unify the building, create a new urban space, construct a new system for the façade and provide new types and hierarchies of space. >> Strategically resembling a merging of "Pimp My Ride" with the wrappings of Christo what eventually emerges is a condition that can be familiar and strange, homogeneous and heterogeneous, sublime and awkward.

Für die Modernisierung und Erweiterung eines unspektakulären Einkaufszentrums aus den 1960er Jahren schlägt der Wettbewerbsentwurf vor, den Gebäudekomplex unregelmäßig aufzustocken. Das so entstehende Volumen wird durch eine allseitige neue Hülle aus Stahl und Glas zusammengefasst, sodass das Einkaufszentrum wie eine kristalline Skulptur erscheint. Der Eindruck einer neuen Verpackung wird metaphorisch durch die Konstruktion evoziert, die aus kreuz und quer über das Volumen verlaufenden Edelstahlseilen besteht, die auf einer Stahlunterkonstruktion befestigt sind und scheinbar die neue Glashaut festzurren. >> Durch die neue Umhüllung über den Verkaufsflächen werden eine große Terrasse und ein Restaurant als dynamische öffentliche Räume innerhalb des Gebäudes geschaffen, die großzügige Aus- und Einsichten eröffnen und den umgebenden Stadtraum mit einbeziehen. Nachts kehrt sich das Verhältnis um: durch ein integriertes Beleuchtungskonzept wird das Gebäude zu einem geheimnisvollen, kristallinen Leuchtkörper, der auf die Umgebung ausstrahlt. >> Mit Hilfe bestimmter „Werkzeuge" wie etwa „Freilegen", „Aufräumen", „Stapeln" und „Verpacken" wurde versucht, den Entwurfsprozess zu objektivieren. In einem performativen Sinne beginnen diese Eingriffe einen Status zu erhalten, indem sie den Stadtraum modifizieren und neben einem neuen Fassadensystem und neuen Raumtypen auch neue räumliche Hierarchien hervorbringen. >> Durch eine Strategie, die sich an einer ausgewogenen Position zwischen „pimp my ride" und Christo's Wrappings verorten lässt, entsteht am Ende etwas, dass vertraut und fremd zugleich ist, ebenso homogen wie heterogen, im einen Moment ein wenig schrill, im nächsten Moment erhaben.

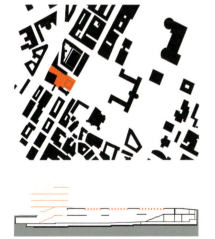

HASCHER + JEHLE ARCHITEKTUR: READJUSTED TRAFFIC STRUCTURE Page/Seite >> 4 8

Project: Museum of Fine Arts | **Location**: Stuttgart | **Client**: Landeshauptstadt Stuttgart | **Architects**: Hascher + Jehle Architektur, Berlin | **Staff**: Frank Jödicke, Michael Mainka, Johannes Raible Andreas Dalhoff, Silvia Keller, Ralf Mittmann, Philipp Nocke, Ausberto Oduardo, Jens-Peter Riepen, Ulrike von Schenck, Juliane Schröder, Thomas Weber, Daniel Wendler | © **Photos**: Roland Halbe | **Statics**: Werner Sobek Ingenieure in cooperation with Fichtner Bauconsulting, Stuttgart | **URL**: www.hascherjehle.de | **Completion**: 2004 | **Area**: 10,700 m²

The Königsplatz is the biggest and most important square in Stuttgart's city centre. The 19th century Kronprinzenpalais used to occupy one of the borders of the square until it was destroyed during the War. In 1968, traffic planners replaced it with a huge traffic node with a concrete lid. Since four lanes of automobiles and streetcars now raced across the square, pedestrians were banished to the upper level of the concrete lid, which had been decorated with tiny retail pavilions. >> Doubts were raised as early as the1970s about this oversized traffic intersection that had destroyed the most beautiful square in downtown Stuttgart. The square was finally reestablished in 2005 with a new building for the local Art Museum which once again closed its northwest corner. The city has regained an urban and public space from the desolation of transportation. >> The entrance to the new museum is invitingly located on the Königstraße. From here the path leads deep into the extended subterranean area of the permanent exhibition (reclaimed from the old underground traffic tunnels). A large staircase leads upwards to the three levels available for temporary exhibitions in the glass cube. >> Without disturbing the character of the quiet, introverted exhibition rooms, the roof of the cube is publicly accessible. It is a restaurant, event and meeting place in a glass-encased space and offers spectacular and panoramic views towards the green hills in which Stuttgart is embedded. >> The building is flanked by two new broad flights of stone steps, which transform the whole square into an open air stage and provide an inviting vantage point from which to enjoy the heart of the city.

Der Königsplatz ist Stuttgarts größter und wichtigster Platz im Zentrum der Stadt. Das Kronprinzenpalais aus dem 19. Jahrhundert begrenzte ursprünglich den Platz, bis dieser während des Kriegs zerstört wurde. Im Jahr 1968 errichteten Verkehrsplaner an dessen Stelle einen riesigen Verkehrsknoten mit Betonüberdachung. Während Autos und Straßenbahnen in vier Spuren über den überdeckelten Platz fuhren, wurden die Fußgänger auf die obere Ebene einer Betonüberdeckung verbannt, die mit kleinen Verkaufspavillons dekoriert war. >> Bereits in den frühen 1970er Jahren wurden Zweifel am überdimensionierten Verkehrsknoten laut, der den schönsten Platz des Stuttgarter Zentrums zerstört hatte. Der Platz wurde schließlich 2005 mit dem Bau des Kunstmuseums Stuttgart neu angelegt. Nach der Zerstörung durch den Verkehr hat die Stadt einen städtischen und öffentlichen Raum wieder gewonnen. >> Der Eingang zum neuen Museum befindet sich – einladend – an der Königstraße. Von dort führt der Weg direkt in den lang gestreckten, unterirdischen Bereich der Dauerausstellung, der in den ehemaligen U-Bahn-Tunneln untergebracht ist. Eine großzügige Treppenanlage führt zu den oberen drei Ebenen, die für Wechselausstellungen im „Glas-Cube" vorgesehen sind. >> Das Dach des „Glas-Cube" ist öffentlich zugänglich. Es gibt ein Restaurant und einen Veranstaltungssaal, der völlig verglast ist und einen spektakulären Panoramablick auf die grünen Hügel bietet, in die Stuttgart eingebettet ist. >> Das Gebäude wird von zwei breiten neuen Treppenfluchten aus Stein begrenzt, die den gesamten Platz in eine Open-Air-Bühne und einen zum Verweilen einladenden Aussichtspunkt verwandeln, von dem man das Zentrum der Stadt erleben kann.

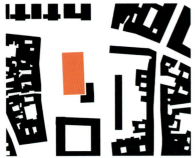

HUFNAGEL PÜTZ RAFAELIAN ARCHITEKTEN: VISUAL SPACE JUNCTION   **P a g e** / S e i t e >>   **4 9**

Project: Museum of Fine Arts | **Location:** Leipzig | **Client:** Stadt Leipzig, Kulturamt | **Architects:** Hufnagel Pütz Rafaelian Architekten, Berlin | **Staff:** Anne Kirsch, Jule Lienemeyer, Christian A. Müller, Jürgen Reisch, Monika Jagielska | © **Photos:** Werner Huthmacher | **Statics:** Leonhardt, Andrä und Partner GmbH, Dresden | **URL:** www.hufnagelpuetzrafaelian.de | **Completion:** 2004 | **Area:** 8,350 m²

As a key project in a bid to reclaim the former density of the northern part of Leipzig's historical city centre, the new Museum of Fine Art arose right in the middle of an unusual city block structure. For over four decades the location was a large GDR square – the Sachsenplatz – which itself was built as a consequence of Second World War destruction and neglect of the homogeneous pre-war city structure. >> The main challenge for the architects was to integrate the large volume needed for the museum into the limited space and yet maintain the sense of inner city variety. The building was placed at the centre of the block to be surrounded later by apartments and businesses facing the enclosing streets. The current building finds itself in an interim phase: At the moment it is a solitary building, an exposed object taking up position on the former square in the heart of a traditional city. >> The nature of the construction, however, with large voids cut out of the volume, viewing terraces and picture windows integrates the building into the city fabric. Grand views and reflections of the city are everywhere, both inside and outside the building, and the interior floors are like theatre stages with Leipzig in the starring role.

Das neue Leipziger Museum der bildenden Künste, ein Schlüsselprojekt im Bemühen um die Wiederherstellung der ehemaligen Dichte des historischen Kerns der Leipziger Innenstadt, wurde an einem unerwarteten Ort in der Mitte des Sachsenplatzes errichtet. Dieser Platz bestand dort zwar bereits seit vier Jahrzehnten, war jedoch vor allem eine Konsequenz aus den Zerstörungen des Zweiten Weltkriegs und der Ablehnung der historischen Stadtstruktur in den Jahren danach. >> Im Sinne der Wiederherstellung war es eine Herausforderung für die Architekten, das für die Unterbringung des umfangreichen Programms benötigte große Volumen in den begrenzten vorhandenen Raum zu integrieren und zugleich den Eindruck von urbaner Vielfalt zu bewahren. Dieses Problem der urbanen Dichte soll in Zukunft durch einen Ring von Wohn- und Geschäftsgebäuden, welche das Museum in das städtische Gewebe integriert, gelöst werden. Bis dahin befindet sich das Gebäude als nahezu monumentaler Solitär an exponierter Stelle gewissermaßen in einer Art Interimsphase. >> Dennoch gelingt es dem Gebäude durch seine räumliche Struktur mit großen Aushöhlungen, Aussichtsterrassen und Sichtfenstern, sich in überraschender Weise in die Umgebung einzufügen. So werden die inneren Räume des Museums zu Theaterbühnen, während umgekehrt in den spektakulären Ausblicken die Stadt selbst die Hauptrolle spielt.

WIEL ARETS ARCHITECTS: HOVERING HABITATS   **P a g e** / S e i t e >>   **5 8**

Project: Urban studio | **Location:** Cologne | **Client:** Urban Investments BV, Maastricht | **Architects:** Wiel Arets Architects, Maastricht, The Netherlands | **Staff:** Wiel Arets, Bettina Kraus, Aynav Ziv, Thomas Tiltag | **URL:** www.wielarets.nl | **Planning:** 2005 | **Area:** 900 m²

This in-fill of a parking block can be described as a pilot project in response to a demand for compact, high standard apartments located within a highly urban context. Its spatial and programmatic layout is intended to be easily transferable and adjustable to similar roofscape conditions. >> The studio apartments form a horizontal perforated volume that is accessed by individual outdoor stairs from below to minimize additional circulation through the entire complex. This means that existing infrastructure can be shared or extended. The layout of the respective units is composed along the lines of organization and room standards found in hotel chains. A system of multiple combinable bath-units, kitchens and furniture were developed to fulfil diverse individual needs, but still encourage mass production. Leading designer furniture manufacturers were involved in the product development. Assembling and placing the flats differently can generate all kind of volumetric and void configurations responsive to the respective site. >> Taking full advantage of the slab's hovering, one-layered and elevated status, all studios not only have spectacular long distance views and skylights, but also visual contact with the public layer below, via the outer voids. Besides parking facilities, this outdoor space contains individual and shared gardens, play and lounge zones. Light and rain passing through the voids form various light and colour nuances, as well as allow natural vegetation, this creates a pleasant atmosphere on the semi-covered layer.

Das Projekt für die Erweiterung eines bestehenden Parkhauses kann als unmittelbare Reaktion auf eine gestiegene Nachfrage nach hochwertigem innerstädtischen Wohnraum gedeutet werden. In diesem Sinne ist der Entwurf auch auf eine Anpassungsfähigkeit an ähnliche räumliche Gegebenheiten hin optimiert worden. >> Die einzelnen Studioapartments bilden zusammen einen flächigen und kompakten, jedoch vertikal perforierten Baukörper und werden über jeweils eigene Außentreppen individuell erschlossen. Die Grundrisse folgen in ihren Konfigurationen den von Hotelketten bekannten flexiblen Raumorganisationen und Ausstattungsstandards. Ein System aus vielseitig kombinierbaren Einheiten für Badezimmer, Küchen oder Mobiliar soll sowohl individuellen Bedürfnissen gerecht werden wie auch den Bedingungen einer späteren industriellen Produktion entsprechen. Diese Flexibilität ermöglicht zugleich auch die räumliche Anpassung der Grundkonfiguration an die jeweilige spezifische Umgebung. >> Durch die erhöhte Lage und die Eingeschossigkeit der Scheibe verfügen alle Apartments nicht nur über Oberlichter und Fernblick, sondern durch die vertikalen Perforierungen auch über einen direkten visuellen Kontakt zu der darunterliegenden öffentlich zugänglichen Ebene. Neben Parkmöglichkeiten bietet dieser Außenraum auch Platz für individuelle oder gemeinsame Gärten und Spielzonen. Zugleich sorgt die vertikale Durchlässigkeit der Scheibe auch für die Belichtung der öffentlichen Zone und soll eine natürliche Vegetation ermöglichen.

ARNO LEDERER + JÓRUNN RAGNARSDÓTTIR + MARC OEI: FEET OVER WHEELS   **P a g e** / S e i t e >>   **6 4**

Project: Hessisches Staatstheater – Provisional theatre in an underground parking | **Location:** Darmstadt | **Client:** Hessisches Baumanagement, Regionalniederlassung Süd, Darmstadt | **Architects:** Arno Lederer + Jórunn Ragnarsdóttir + Marc Oei, Stuttgart | **Staff:** Thilo Holzer, Björn Barkemeyer, Ulrike Hautau, Markus Schwarzbach, Tania Ost, Matthias Schneider, Michael Müller, Wolfram Sponer, Andrea Stahl, Katrin Merk | © **Photos:** Roland Halbe | **Statics:** Professor Pfeifer und Partner, Ingenieurbüro für Tragwerksplanung, Darmstadt | **URL:** www.lederer-ragnarsdottir-oei.de | **Completion:** 2005 | **Area:** 39,783 m²

The original 1972 theatre was designed by Rudolf Prange as part of a modernist car-centric planning of Darmstadt's inner city. It is a large building that, although perfect for the routing of future traffic, stands helplessly among its surroundings without any spatial relationship: a completely oversized box with multi-lane drive-in access but no inviting entrance at street level for pedestrians. >> As part of the building's modernisation, the architects transformed the theatre into a building that is both present and lends character as part of the urban space. They opened up the façade in a new pedestrian entrance onto the square above that permits uninhibited access to the foyer and parking areas. A huge podium above this new entrance brings added drama as a potential stage for summer outdoor performances and open-air events. >> As a temporary housing solution for the main performance area during reconstruction, the architects suggested using the garage space as a provisory theatre which was then later to become an additional studio theatre. The opulent driveway that spreads out in multiple lanes under the building was dispensed with and a new structure inserted into the space, which comfortably accommodates all of the organisational functions needed to run a theatre. Where cars once entered the building is now a studio theatre, a canteen and all of the storage rooms as well as access to the new two storey high foyer in the main building above. >> Thus an outdated functionalist, car-friendly building is transformed into a more flexible, city-friendly theatre.

Das ursprüngliche Theater wurde 1972 von Rudolf Prange als Teil einer modernistischen, autozentrierten Planung für die Innenstadt von Darmstadt entworfen. Es ist ein großes Gebäude, das zwar perfekt positioniert ist zur Führung des zukünftigen Verkehrs, jedoch hilflos wirkt in seiner Umgebung, da es keinen Bezug zu ihr hat: ein überdimensionierter Kasten mit mehrspurigen Zufahrtswegen, aber ohne einen einladenden Haupteingang auf Straßenebene für die Fußgänger. >> Als Teil der Gebäudemodernisierung verwandelten die Architekten das Theater in ein Gebäude, das sowohl seine Präsenz als auch seinen Charakter als Teil des urbanen Raumes behauptet. Sie öffneten die Fassade für einen neuen Fußgängereingang zum Platz, sodass ein uneingeschränkter Zugang zum Foyer und auch zu den Tiefgaragenplätzen möglich ist. >> Ein großes Podium oberhalb des neuen Eingangs erzeugt als mögliche Bühne für im Freien stattfindende Aufführungen oder Open-Air-Events zusätzliche Dramatik. >> Als vorübergehende Lösung für die Hauptveranstaltungen während der Umbauarbeiten schlugen die Architekten vor, die Tiefgarage als provisorisches Theater zu nutzen, welches später als zusätzliche Studiobühne verwendet werden kann. >> Die opulente Einfahrt, die mehrspurig unter das Gebäude führte, wurde entfernt und eine neue Struktur in den gewonnenen Raum eingesetzt. Sie beherbergt sämtliche organisatorischen Funktionen, die benötigt werden, um ein Theater zu bespielen. Dort, wo einst Autos in die Tiefgarage hineinfuhren, gibt es jetzt ein Studiotheater, eine Kantine und Lagerräume sowie den Zugang zum neuen zweistöckigen Foyer des Hauptgebäudes. >> Dadurch wurde ein überholtes, funktionalistisches, autofreundliches Gebäude in ein flexibles, stadtfreundliches Theater verwandelt.

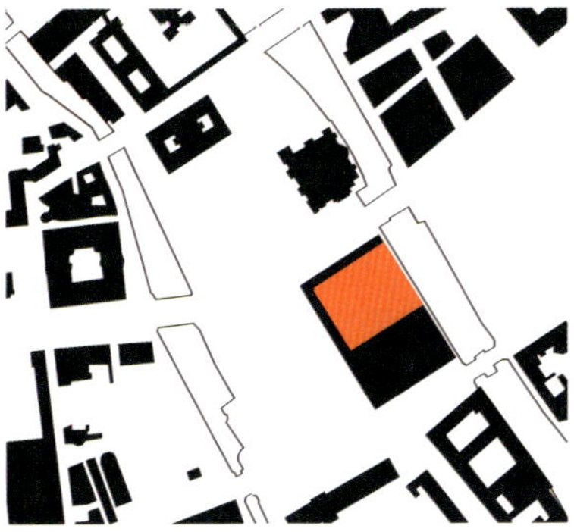

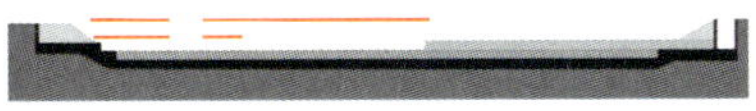

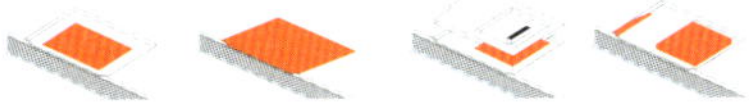

URBAN CATALYST: ACTIVATING THE VOID Page / Seite >> 70

Project: 20,000 sqm x 5 years | **Location**: Berlin | **Client**: self-initiated project | **Architects**: Urban Catalyst: Philipp Oswalt mit Florian Kessel, Matthäus Wirth, Berlin | **Staff**: Philipp Oswalt, Florian Kessel, Matthäus Wirth | **© Photos**: Urban Catalyst, David Baltzer | **URL**: www.urbancatalyst.de | **Planning**: 2005 | **Area**: 11,000 m²

The demolition of the Palace of the Republic in Berlin is scheduled to be completed by April 2007, but redevelopment of the area will not commence until 2012 at the earliest. The current plan is to completely fill the palace's basement floors with 205,000 tonnes of sand, create a temporary garden after the demolition of the upper floors and install an info box about the planned redevelopment of the site. The cost is estimated at 7.5 million. >> These finances could be put to more intelligent use argue Urban Catalyst.They propose using the basement floors of the Palace of the Republic as an experimental setting to realise, test and develop programmes for a public cultural use in the period preceding its redevelopment as the new Humboldtforum. Their proposed interim building relies 100% on the existing construction and is based on the selective removal of building components rather than building new. The only new parts that will have to be provided are the finishing elements. >> The proposal includes an 10,000m² hall for exhibitions, performances and events; an 8,500m² sheltered inner courtyard for open-air events and an area housing a library, exhibitions, offices and café under the access ramp. The site can be accessed from the existing path on the embankment of the river Spree as well as an existing truck ramp. The rooms and the courtyard offer views of the Spree. The location of the floor some 1.5 metres below the water level creates an intimate and sheltered urban space. >> It is a radically pragmatic solution proposing maximum use of the existing structures with an economy of means, adding only that which is absolutely essential. At the same time, the partial deconstruction is a chance to rethink and reinvent what exists, thus integrating the past into the future in a way that creates new possibilities for what was once a major Berlin landmark.

In dem jahrelangen Streit „Palast versus Schloss" ging es allzu oft nur um Bild und Symbol, zu selten aber um Nutzung und Inhalt. Es ist an der Zeit, den Ort von der Nutzung her zu denken. Die Untergeschosse des Palastes der Republik bieten die Möglichkeit, die öffentliche kulturelle Nutzung des zukünftigen Humboldtforums in den nächsten Jahren experimentell zu realisieren, zu testen und weiterzuentwickeln und einen lebendigen urbanen Ort von einzigartiger Qualität zu schaffen, anstatt die nach dem von Walter Ulbricht veranlassten Schlossabriss entstandene öde Leere als Farce zu wiederholen. >> Der Vorschlag von Urban Catalyst sieht vor, den finanziellen Rahmen der derzeit für den Schlossplatz geplanten, siebeneinhalb Millionen teuren Zwischenlösung aus dem „Garten auf Zeit" und der Infobox für ein Experimentierfeld in den Tiefgeschossen des Palastes zu nutzen. Der vorgeschlagene Umbau besteht fast vollständig aus Altbauteilen und erfordert nur einen geringen Rückbau. Als einzige neue Elemente sind Oberflächenverkleidungen vorgesehen. >> Der Entwurf umfasst eine 10.000 m² große Halle für Ausstellungen, Theateraufführungen und Events, einen 8.500 m² großen Innenhof für Freilichtveranstaltungen und einen Bereich mit Bibliothek, Galerien, Büros und Café unter der Zufahrtsrampe. Die Erschließung des Geländes erfolgt über den bestehenden Spreeuferweg und die alte Rampe für den Lastverkehr. Die Innenräume und der Innenhof bieten einen Ausblick über die Spree und bilden, da die Bodenplatte rund anderthalb Meter unter dem Flussniveau liegt, einen geschützten städtischen Ort. >> Diese pragmatische Lösung ermöglicht die maximale Nutzung der bestehenden Räumlichkeiten mit sparsamsten Mitteln. Gleichzeitig bietet der partielle Rückbau die Chance, das Bestehende zu hinterfragen, bis zu einem gewissen Grad umzugestalten und die Vergangenheit in die Zukunft des Ortes so zu integrieren, dass neue Aktivitäten ermöglicht und neue Ideen freigesetzt werden.

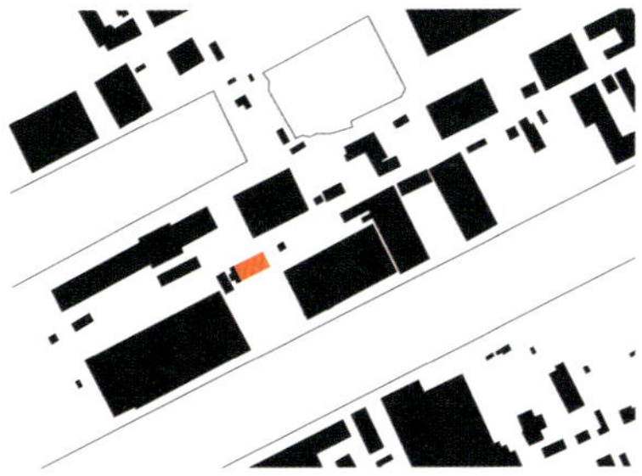

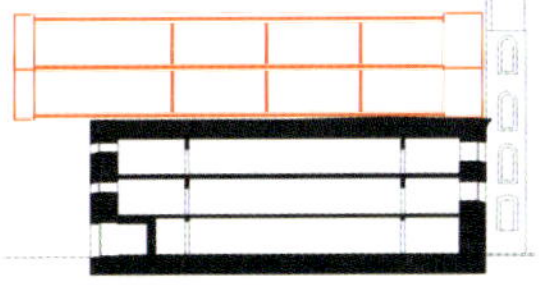

INDEX ARCHITEKTEN: CULTURAL CARGO DOCK Page / Seite >> 73

Project: Culture bunker | **Location**: Frankfurt/Main | **Client**: Amt für Wissenschaft und Kunst, Frankfurt/Main | **Architects**: INDEX Architekten, Frankfurt /Main | **Staff**: Gebhard Jeuring, Rolf Hölzl | **© Photos**: Wolfgang Günzel, Christof Lison | **URL**: www.index-architekten.de | **Completion**: 2005 | **Area**: 595 m²

Redeveloping Frankfurt's 1912 east harbour is a large planning project for the city. The zone around the market hall is already being affected by structural change, but the area behind it is still a no-man's-land of gravel heaps, recycling dumps and container depots. Here too stands an old Second World War bunker on a dead straight, dusty street. Since art projects often act as a magnet for further development in rundown urban areas, the idea was to convert this bunker into a cultural place and to define it as a motor for municipal transformation. >> The cost of repairing the leaking hip-roof was prohibitive – as was demolition – so a large wooden box was built on top of the bunker instead, housing artists' studios and the Institute for New Media. Rehearsal studios for musicians were installed inside the heavy concrete core. The lightweight wooden box is open around its circumference, which turns the communal zone inside outwards in a dialogue with the city. At the same time, this opening up serves as an escape route to the outside. >> The vertical extension of this bunker could be seen as a metaphorical lighthouse for structural change in Frankfurt's east harbour. In the context of the warehouses, cranes, containers and truck-drivers' bars, the new "culture bunker" is a good antipole to the European Central Bank building across the city with its established hotels and residential quarters.

Der Umbau des Osthafenbezirks von 1912 ist ein Großprojekt der Frankfurter Stadtentwicklung. Die Umgebung der Großmarkthalle ist bereits neu gestaltet worden, das Gelände dahinter ist allerdings immer noch ein Niemandsland aus Kieshaufen, Recyclinghöfen und Containerlagern. Hier steht an einer schnurgeraden staubigen Straße auch ein Bunker aus dem Zweiten Weltkrieg. Im Wissen darum, dass Kunstprojekte häufig wie Katalysatoren für die Sanierung und Neubelebung heruntergekommener Stadtquartiere wirken, entstand die Idee, den Bunker als Kulturzentrum umzunutzen und ihn so als Motor für den weiteren Stadtumbau zu instrumentalisieren. >> Die Sanierung des undichten Walmdachs oder der Komplettabriss hätten jeweils den Kostenrahmen gesprengt, sodass der Bunker stattdessen mit einer großen hölzernen Box aufgestockt wurde, in dem die Künstlerateliers und das Institut für neue Medien untergebracht sind. Proberäume für Musiker entstanden im Innern des Bunkers mit seinem schweren Betonkern. Die Holzbox, ausgeführt in einer Leichtbaukonstruktion, ist nach außen rundum geöffnet, so dass der Gemeinschaftsraum im Innern in Dialog mit der Stadt treten kann. Gleichzeitig dienen diese Öffnungen als Fluchtwege. >> Die vertikale Erweiterung des Bunkers könnte im übertragenen Sinne auch als Leuchtturm für den Umbau des Frankfurter Osthafens insgesamt interpretiert werden. Inmitten der Speicherhäuser, Verladekräne, Container und Brummifahrer-Kneipen bildet der „Kulturbunker" ein gutes Gegengewicht zur Europäischen Zentralbank auf der anderen Seite der Stadt mit ihren Hotels und Wohnvierteln.

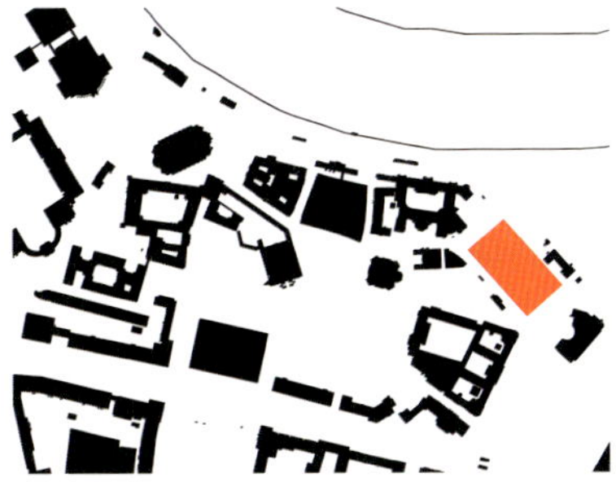

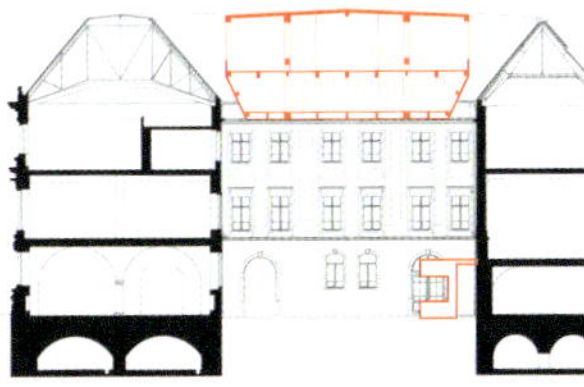

STAAB ARCHITEKTEN: ARK FOR ART Page / Seite >> 76

Project: Albertinum – Central depot for the "Staatliche Kunstsammlungen" | **Location**: Dresden | **Client**: Freistaat Sachsen, Staatsbetrieb Sächsisches Immobilien- und Baumanagement | **Architects**: Staab Architekten, Berlin | **Staff**: Planung: Juergen Rustler, Patric Eckstein, Ulf Theenhausen, Michael Zeeh Birgit Knicker, Gerd Eder | **Statics**: ARGE Erfurth + Partner, Dresden; Ingenieurbüro Kless Mueller GmbH, Dresden | **URL**: www.staab-architekten.com | **Completion**: 2008/09 | **Area**: 7,000 m²

Every alteration is an act of destruction, but in the best cases it is also a significant gain. >> In the planning process for the new central art depot for the Albertinum museum in Dresden, the need for new rooms was closely linked to the primary aim of protecting the hermetical old building and creating a new urban space inside it. The new depot building is designed as an enclosing and protective roof, a sort of Noah's Ark on stilts that holds its contents well out of reach of the floods which occasionally threaten the city. >> The building is inserted into the centre of the courtyard with two joints to let the light pass through. It is mounted on a new lift shaft and two supports behind the existing courtyard facade, leaving the central hall untouched and well lit. Seen from beneath, the structure is like an illuminated ceiling above a fully lit inner courtyard. The light spaces at the sides of the depot reflect the natural fluctuations of daylight and the alternation of cloud and sunlight. The real volume of the roof, and thus the dimensions of the new structure are only apparent at closer inspection. >> A new visitor entrance is also being created in addition to the original. The two entrances will have direct access to the covered inner courtyard, which will underline its role as the central room in the museum and the place where all public infrastructure facilities are situated. >> Hanging a whole extra building above a historical building complex whilst giving the illusion that it is nothing more than a transluscent membrane is a novel form of non-invasive space extension in a sensitive heritage situation.

Jeder Eingriff ist ein Akt der Zerstörung, doch im besten Fall auch ein wesentlicher Gewinn. >> Im Planungsprozess für das neue Zentraldepot des Albertinums in Dresden waren der Schutz der ursprünglichen Bausubstanz und die Schaffung eines neuen urbanen Raums innerhalb dieses alten hermetischen Gebäudes die Hauptziele. Um die kostbaren Inhalte vor den Fluten, die die Stadt gelegentlich heimsuchen, zu bewahren, wird das neue Depotgebäude über dem zentralen Innenhof des Altbaus in sicherer Höhe untergebracht. Das Depot ist somit schützende Überdachung der neu entstehenden zentralen Ausstellungshalle und zugleich eine Art Arche Noah der Kunst. >> Da die gesamte Stützkonstruktion hinter der existierenden Innenhoffassade untergebracht ist, wirkt die Struktur von unten betrachtet wie eine Kunstlichtdecke über einem voll ausgeleuchteten Innenhof. Ferner erhält die Ausstellungshalle Tageslicht über seitliche Fugen, die das Depotgebäude zur Innenhoffassade als Oberlichtband belässt. Der natürliche Wechsel von Sonnenschein und Bewölkung werden in diesen Lichtfugen reflektiert, sodass der neue Baukörper zu schweben scheint. Das tatsächliche Volumen des Dachs und die eigentliche Dimension des neuen Baukörpers werden erst bei näherer Betrachtung offensichtlich. >> Zusätzlich zum ursprünglichen Besuchereingang erschließt ein zweiter neuer Eingang direkt die Ausstellungshalle im Innenhof. Dadurch wird dessen Rolle als zentraler Raum des Museums, in dem sämtliche öffentliche Infrastruktureinrichtungen untergebracht sind, unterstrichen. >> Die Aufhängung eines Neubaus in einem historischen Gebäudekomplex und die dabei erzeugte Wirkung einer leichten, schwebenden und lichtdurchlässigen Membran ist eine neuartige Form der nicht-invasiven architektonischen Erweiterung einer historisch sensiblen Bausubstanz.

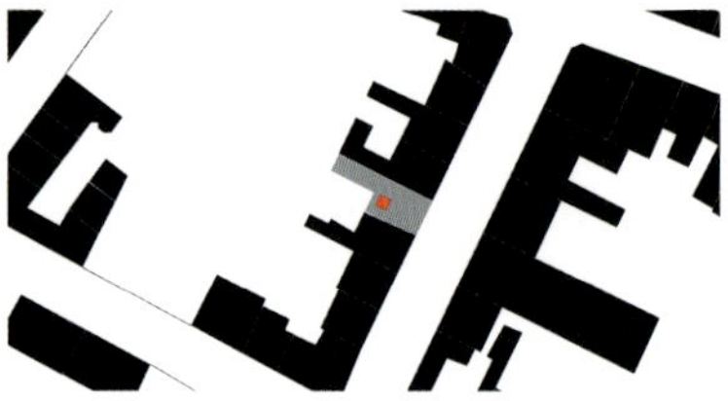

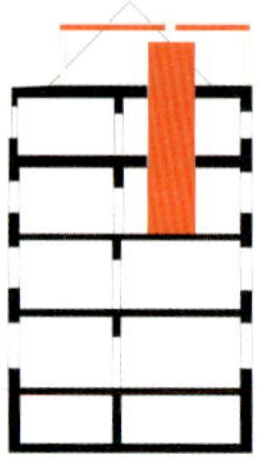

LÜDERWALDT VERHOFF ARCHITEKTEN-HEART OF THE HOUSE Page / Seite >> 77

Project: Neo Leo – Vertical living | **Location**: Cologne | **Client**: Marlies & Michael Schmitz-Kneuper | **Architects**: lüderwaldt verhoff architekten, Cologne | **Staff**: Caroline Wend | **© Photos**: Lukas Roth | **Statics**: Naumann & Partner Ing. GmbH, Cologne | **URL**: www.luederwaldt-verhoff.de | **Completion**: 2005 | **Area**: 210 m²

An additional multifunctional living area created by inserting a prefabricated "wooden box" by crane into a roof extension of a Wilhelminian style family house in the Ehrenfeld district of Cologne. >> The precise slot-in construction comprising large format 56mm plywood sheets functions on three levels as stairs, railings, room-divider, cupboards and shelving. It structures the entire apartment as a bright orange sculptural element. The interplay between these newly defined core functional areas generates an interrelated vertical structure that opens out into a generous glassed studio on the top floor. >> In construction terms the box hangs freely in space. It rests on cams screwed onto the sides attached to newly inserted steel beams within the original building so that no additional load is placed on the wooden-beamed floors below. >> The surface treatment for the wood all took place in the workshop before installation. All visible surfaces are treated with colourless oil and the stairwell cavity is lacquered in bright orange. >> The vertical insertion of space and function effectively connects three floors of the house together into a family home. An affordable architectural solution in a residential area with a vital and mixed society.

Eine maßgeschneiderte Holzbox, die per Kran durch das ausgebaute Dachgeschoss in das Haus eingesetzt wurde, schuf in einem Mehrfamilienhaus aus der Gründerzeit in Köln-Ehrenfeld einen neuen multifunktionalen Wohnbereich. >> Die vorgefertigte Konstruktion, bestehend aus 56 mm-starken, großflächigen Holztafeln, erstreckt sich über drei Etagen und fungiert gleichzeitig als Treppe, Geländer, Raumteiler, Schrank und Regal. Als eine leuchtend orangefarbene Skulptur gliedert sie zudem visuell die Wohnung. Das Zusammenspiel zwischen diesen neu definierten Servicefunktionen, die das Herz des Hauses ausmachen, schafft eine zusammenhängende vertikale Struktur, die sich nach oben in ein geräumiges Glasstudio im Dachgeschoss fortsetzt. >> Konstruktionstechnisch schwebt die Holzbox frei im Raum. Sie ist über seitlich aufgeschraubte Knaggen auf neu in die bestehende Konstruktion eingezogene Stahlträger aufgelagert, sodass keine zusätzliche Belastung für die darunterliegenden Holzbalkendecken entsteht. >> Vor dem Einsetzen in das Haus wurden in der Werkstatt sämtliche sichtbare Oberflächen mit farblosem Öl behandelt und der Hohlraum im Treppenauge orange lasiert. >> Durch die vertikale Einfügung von Raum und Funktion werden drei Etagen des Hauses effektiv miteinander zu einem Haus für eine Familie verbunden. Eine preiswerte architektonische Lösung in einer lebendigen, sozial gemischten Wohngegend.

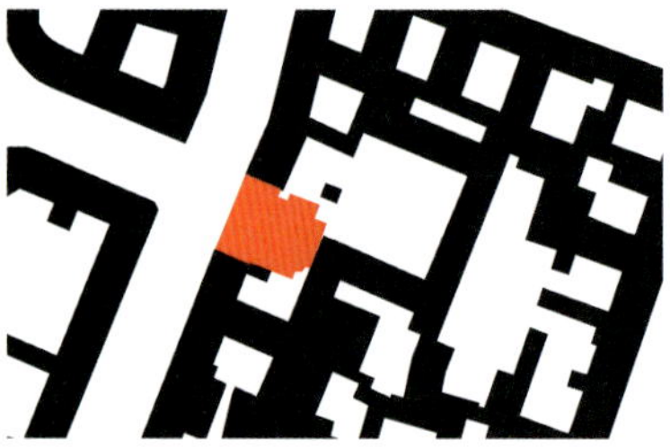

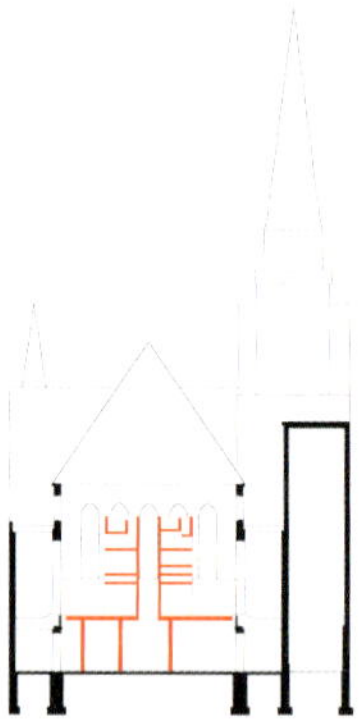

KLAUS BLOCK: MACHMIT! VERTICAL LABYRINTH Page / Seite >> 80

Project: MACHmit! Museum for children | **Location**: Berlin | **Client**: Kinder & Jugend Museum Prenzlauer Berg GmbH, Berlin | **Architects**: Klaus Block, Berlin | **Staff**: Bianka Papke, Jan Hennigsen, Anna Jacobsen, Janek Pfeifer, Chantal Cornu, Nico Zachara, Estela Fernandes Rocafull, Rosario Cegara, Mathias Rösner, Michal Zierau | **© Photos**: Ullrich Schwarz | **Statics**: Dierks, Babilon & Voigt | **URL**: www.klausblock.de | **Completion**: 2003 | **Area**: 1,225 m²

The protestant church of St. Elias, a listed brick building from 1910 shared the fate of other big city churches: it was deserted because the congregation had shrunk and could no longer finance reconstruction and running costs. A new user was found in the form of a local children's museum, which needed bigger premises. They leased the building for 75 years and the conversion was achieved with the help of public funds. Part of this went towards repairs, heating and fire precautions, the rest funded a new independent and detached component inserted into the nave. >> The opportunity to experience the existing rooms in their original condition and the use and the maintenance of the old building substance are an integral part of the didactic concept of the children museum. >> The labyrinthine insertion in the nave reaches the height of the gallery balustrade and consists of a steel construction with pine planks covering the interior and fibre concrete boards attached to the outside. The ground floor area can be used for exhibitions, the former organ gallery contains the café, the organ and further exhibition space. >> The installation consists of two labyrinthine units separated by a ravine which permits a view along the church axis. Located in their base zone are three workspace bunks equipped with extendable workbenches, toolboxes, washbasins and stoves. Beyond these work zones, the open structure offers remarkable rooms for resting, climbing and playing on various levels. The two units are connected by four bridges, which make it possible to move continuously from the north to the south side and vice versa. >> The museum is a temporary installation for a child-friendly city. The special aura of the church is retained and community life is strengthened.

Die im Jahr 1910 errichtete und heute denkmalgeschützte, protestantische Eliaskirche in Berlin teilt das Schicksal vieler großstädtischer Kirchen: Ihre Nutzung wurde eingestellt, da die Zahl der Gemeindemitglieder stark zurückgegangen ist und die Kosten für Instandhaltung und Reparaturen nicht mehr zu finanzieren waren. Ein Museum für Kinder aus der näheren Umgebung, das auf der Suche nach größeren Räumlichkeiten war, konnte als neuer Nutzer gewonnen werden. Der Umbau wurde mit öffentlichen Mitteln gefördert - ein Teil der Gelder floss in umfassende Sanierungsarbeiten, mit der restlichen Fördersumme wurde der Bau eines unabhängigen, frei stehenden Einbaus im Hauptschiff der Kirche finanziert. >> Die vorhandenen Räume in ihrer ursprünglichen Substanz und Beschaffenheit zu belassen und zu nutzen, ist integraler Bestandteil des didaktischen Konzepts des Museums für Kinder. >> Das Erdgeschoss wird für Ausstellungen genutzt. Auf der ehemaligen Orgelgalerie befinden sich nun ein Café, die Orgel und ein weiterer Ausstellungsraum. Der Einbau selbst besteht aus zwei ineinander verschlungenen Einheiten, die durch einen engen, wie eine Schlucht anmutenden Gang voneinander getrennt sind. Dieser Mäander belässt einen freien Blick entlang der Kirchenachse. >> Im unteren Bereich sind drei Arbeitskojen untergebracht, die mit ausziehbaren Werkbänken, Werkzeugkästen, Waschbecken und Öfen ausgestattet sind. Neben diesen Arbeitszonen bietet die offene Struktur bemerkenswert viele Ausweichmöglichkeiten zum Ausruhen, Klettern oder Spielen. Die beiden Einheiten sind über vier Brücken miteinander verbunden, sodass trotz des Einbaus die Durchlässigkeit zwischen Süd- und Nordseite gewährleistet ist. So wirkt das Museum wie eine temporäre Installation für eine kinderfreundliche Stadt. >> Die besondere Aura der Kirche wird bewahrt und das Gemeinwesen gestärkt.

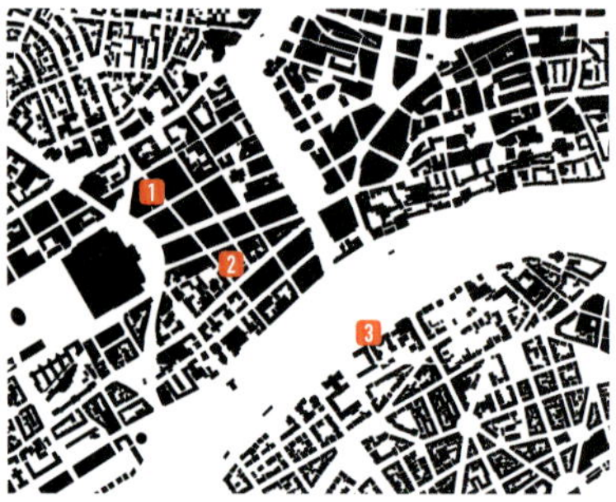

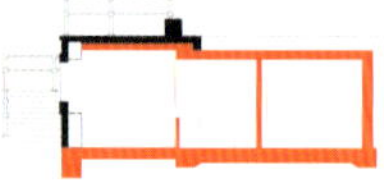

BB22 ARCHITEKTEN + STADTPLANER: IDEENLABOR CENTRAL STATION AREA / MAINCAFÉ / ROOF FOOTBALL Page/Seite >> 82

Project: Idea laboratory Central Station area; Maincafé; Roof football | **Location**: Frankfurt/Main | **Client**: Stadtplanungsamt Frankfurt; Straßenbauamt Frankfurt, bb22 architekten + stadtplaner | **Architects**: bb22 architekten + stadtplaner, Frankfurt am Main | **Staff**: Yvonne Fritsch, Ute Knippenberger, Petra Lenschow, Martin Rössler, Christian Weyell, Christiana Hetzel, Michael Schoner | **URL**: www.bb22.net | **Completion**: since 2004; 2003; - | **Area**: 60 Hectare; 75 m²; 100 m²

With over 40 different projects, bb22 has developed an action based form of planning relating to the strategy and theory of urban intervention. They change the urban space for a little while, bring different players together and offer opportunities for new encounters and possibilities. The urban action in itself does not define nor judge content, idea or intention – it is open. >> Ideenlabor: The quarter surrounding Frankfurt's Central Station is in dire need of change. An extraordinary approach is required to initiate a masterplan, commissioned by the City of Frankfurt, capable of developing the qualities of the neighbourhood while addressing resident attrition and vacancies. bb22's plan was not a plan at all, but a collection of larger and smaller ideas that were exhibited together with a provocative model for the district in a specially rented shop. At a series of events and daily lunchtime meetings, these hypotheses were discussed and improved upon with around 600 residents, commuters, owners and city representatives, activist groups and specialists. >> Maincafé: This is an intervention to bring life back to the bank of the Main River. In a ruined niche, built originally as a public toilet, bb22 developed a concept, which included the planning, operating and financing of a new café. The building itself is lodged in the retaining wall of the River Main, so all expansion had to remain behind the historically preserved embankment. The transformed use of the riverbank, generated through the maincafé, created a new dynamic in the city and its development of the river front promenade. >> Roof Football: The game of football is used to bring a new context and a new quality of life to the epicenter of the Central Station quarter milieu. Football allows a form of communication to occur in which anonymity and public roles are checked at the door. Here on the top level of a parking garage, interested sport enthusiasts have an opportunity for exchange. The location includes changing rooms, the playing field, the audience bench and the sports bar.

Bei mehr als vierzig verschiedenen Projekten haben bb22 einen aktionsorientierten Planungsansatz praktiziert, der interventionistisch in bestehende städtische Strukturen eingreift. Dieser Aktionismus soll mit nur wenig Vordefiniertem auskommen – sein Charakter ist offen. >> Ideenlabor: Das Frankfurter Bahnhofsviertel hat dringenden Entwicklungsbedarf. bb22 erhielt den Auftrag zur Entwicklung eines Masterplans, der Qualitäten des Viertels erkennt und stärkt, um weiteren Einwohnerschwund verhindern und ungewollten Leerstand verringern zu können. Statt eines „Plans" lieferte bb22 eine unsortierte Ideensammlung kleiner und großer Eingriffsmöglichkeiten. Dieses Ideenkonglomerat wurde in einem angemieteten Ladenlokal ausgestellt. In einer Serie von Veranstaltungen zur Mittagszeit wurden die Thesen mit etwa 600 Anwohnern, Berufspendlern, Hauseigentümern, Vertretern der Stadt und Bürgerinitiativen verfeinert. >> Maincafé: Mit dieser Intervention wurde ein Abschnitt des Mainufers wieder belebt. In der Ruine eines ehemaligen Toilettenhäuschens errichtete und betreibt bb22 das Maincafé. Das Objekt befindet sich in einer Nische der Kaimauer. Da die vorgelagerte Promenade unter Denkmalsschutz steht, mussten alle baulichen Transformationen hinter der Kaimauer erfolgen. >> Dachfußball: Fußball wird als Medium eingesetzt, um dem Bahnhofsmilieu eine erweiterte Lebensqualität zu ermöglichen. Das gemeinschaftliche Ballspiel soll die Kommunikation unter Anwohnern intensivieren. Die Anonymität unter den Nachbarn und die gängige soziale Rollenverteilung können beim Betreten des Spielfeldes kurzzeitig abgelegt werden. Auf der obersten Etage eines Parkhauses können Fußballbegeisterte unter freiem Himmel bolzen und ins schnelle Gespräch kommen. Orte des Geschehens sind die Umkleideräume, das Spielfeld, die Zuschauerränge und eine Theke.

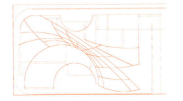

TOPOTEK 1: A NEW SET OF RULES   Page/Seite >> 83

Project: Playground Niebuhrstraße | **Location**: Berlin | **Client**: DB Projektbau GmbH, Berlin | **Landscape Architects**: TOPOTEK 1, Berlin | **Staff**: Georg Mahnke, Björn Krack | © **Photos**: Hanns Joosten | **URL**: www.topotek1.de | **Completion**: 2002 | **Area**: 1,300 m²

In the heart of Berlin's inner city Charlottenburg district, the landscape architects Topotek have created a new venue to encourage off-the-wall and unconventional ways of playing and urban sports. Recessed 1.5 metres below ground level and surrounded with a variety of colourful walls, boundaries and fences, the area resembles more of a toy box than a conventional playground. >> Too small for a standard playing field, the site demanded a different set of rules for a different set of games. A wall comprising curved sections of pre-cast concrete defines the vertical play space. The pitch material covers both floor and walls of the playground. The dynamic layering and distortion of the line markings, which include numbers and text elements as well, offers players an unconventional grid within which to develop their own playful discourse with the space. >> The double weave of the surrounding chain-link fencing creates an optical moiré effect: It is no longer fence, but wall, yet it remains transparent. The entrance ramp is sandwiched between two of these fence walls and acts as an appetiser to the creative game-playing area beyond.

Im Berliner Bezirk Charlottenburg haben die Landschaftsplaner Topotek den Anwohnern einen unkonventionellen Austragungsort für sportliche Aktivitäten zur Verfügung gestellt. Das anderthalb Meter tief in den Boden eingelassene Spielfeld ist rundherum von unterschiedlich farbig gefassten Mauern, Abgrenzungen und Zäunen als Käfig gefasst und gleicht in seiner Vielgestaltigkeit eher einer Spielzeugkiste als einem gewöhnlichen Bolz- und Sportplatz. >> Da das vorgegebene Grundstück für eine reguläre Sportartennutzung zu klein dimensioniert war, wurden neue Regeln und Markierungen für die Fläche konzipiert. Eine Mauer aus unterschiedlich gekrümmten Betonfertigteilen definiert den vertikal orientierten Spielraum. Farbiger Tartan bedeckt sowohl Boden- als auch Wandflächen des Spielplatzes. Dynamisch überlagerte und in sich verzerrte Spielfeldmarkierungen, ergänzt durch Ziffern und schriftliche Erklärungen, bieten ein unkonventionelles Nutzungslayout. Innerhalb dessen haben die Kinder und Jugendlichen die Möglichkeit, ihren eigenen spielerischen Diskurs zu entwickeln. >> Der mit zwei Gewebelagen beschichtete Maschendrahtzaun, der den Spiel- und Sportplatz umgibt, erzeugt einen Moiré-Effekt. Der Zaun ist im Grunde eine Mauer – und als solche dennoch visuell durchlässig. Die Eingangsrampe wird von zwei dieser Zaunmauern eingefasst und soll zum kreativen Spiel auf dem dahinter befindlichen Gelände anregen.

Chemistry
Berlin Mitte

002.0_Maritima 010.0_Linalol 005.0_Farnesol 400.0_Hedione 001.0_CoffeeAroma 100.0_BenzyleSalicylate 010.0_ArgumexVerdox 100.0_Iso e Super 005.0_FucusAbsolute 025.0_CuirVitessence 005.0_StyraxOilPyrogenee 010.0_Muscenone 010.0_MuskKetone 050.0_MuscT-93 010.0_Sandalore 002.5 _TonkaFeves 199.5_DiPropyleneGlycol

SISSEL TOLAAS: SMELL MATTERS   Page/Seite >> 84

Project: City ordours | **Location**: Germany | **Client**: Self-initiated project | **Artist**: Sissel Tolaas, Berlin | © **Photos**: Matti Hillig; Peter Nils Dorén (Stadtimpressionen) | **Project partner**: IFF Inc. New York; Escentric Molecules; Scent Communication | **Completion**: active since 1990

The air surrounding our reality is never neutral, it contains important information in the form of odours – which can be used as terminologies in the language used to communicate the same reality. The different smell spaces of the modern city are largely a product of zoning laws, which regulate the kinds of constructions and sort of activity that may go on in different areas. The smell spaces are also affected by the different cultural and social background of the city's inhabitants. >> There are three main kinds of urban smell domains: The industrial domain includes industrial parks, garbage dumps, sewage treatments plants etc. Unpleasant smells are usually considered legitimate in such spaces – an unavoidable by-product of the industrial process. >> In public spaces, the regime is usually one of a smell neutral. There are exceptions, smells of food and spices often waft from restaurants and bakeries, but offensive smells are usually banned from such areas by municipal sanitary by-laws. >> Smells of all sorts become legitimate again in private space, the space of the home. Any offensive smell that escaped the boundaries of one's home, however, would soon bring complaints from the neighbours, just as would a radio turned up too loud. Thus specific smells, which seems natural in one setting, become intolerable in another.

Die uns umgebende Luft ist niemals neutral, sondern enthält in Form von Gerüchen stets wichtige Informationen über die Orte, an denen wir uns befinden. Zugleich sind die Begriffe, mit denen wir diese Gerüche beschreiben auch Teil jener Terminologie, mit der wir die Wirklichkeit definieren. Dabei sind verschiedene Geruchsräume der modernen Stadt weitgehend das Ergebnis von Planungen, die festlegen, welche Nutzungen wo erwünscht sind. Zugleich werden Geruchsräume aber auch von den jeweiligen kulturellen und gesellschaftlichen Zugehörigkeiten der Bewohner und Nutzer eines Ortes beeinflusst. >> Leicht lassen sich drei Grundtypen von städtischen Geruchsräumen unterscheiden. So gelten in industriell geprägten Gebieten wie Gewerbeparks, Mülldeponien, Kläranlagen auch unangenehme Gerüche als annehmbar, während im Allgemeinen in öffentlichen Räumen, bis auf Ausnahmen wie Restaurants, Neutralität erwartet wird. Dagegen sind im privaten Bereich, solange niemand gestört wird, alle Gerüche erlaubt. Abschließend kann man also sagen, dass über die Annehmbarkeit eines Geruchs vor allem der Ort entscheidet, an dem wir ihm begegnen. >> In ihren Arbeiten versucht Sissel Tolaas, diese unsichtbaren Eigenschaften der Stadt wahrnehmbar zu machen. Sie sammelt Proben von verschiedenen, für bestimmte Stadtteile markante Gerüche und analysiert deren Zusammensetzung. Aus diesen Informationen entstehen olfaktorische Stadtkonzentrate, die uns daran erinnern, wie wichtig unser Geruchssinn für die Entstehung unserer Wirklichkeit ist.

KÜHN MALVEZZI: RED CARPET TREATMENT   Page/Seite >> 90

Project: Festival centre Theaterformen | **Location**: Braunschweig | **Client**: Staatstheater Niedersachsen GmbH, Hannover | **Architects**: Kühn Malvezzi, Berlin | **Staff**: Jan Ulmer | © **Photos**: Ulrich Schwarz, Timm Ringewaldt (Autocolor), Archiv Staatstheater Braunschweig, Kühn Malvezzi | **URL**: www.kuehnmalvezzi.com | **Completion**: 2002 | **Area**: 680 m²

For ten days Braunschweig's city theatre became the venue for Theaterformen, an international biennial theatre festival. The task of creating a festival centre plus a meeting place, programme information, ticket sales, library and a small café was re-interpreted by the architects Kühn Malvezzi and the first floor theatre ballroom, normally reserved for the audience during intermissions, was temporarily converted into a festival centre. For the duration of the festival, this introverted interior space, unfamiliar to many local people, became a freely accessible public place which, independent from the theatre performances, played host to a varied and lively crowd of visitors. >> The structural intervention consisted of erecting a broad staircase on a scaffolding framework that could be assembled or dismantled within two days. It connected the square in front of the theatre directly to the balcony of the ballroom. Taller steps for seating at the centre of the south-facing staircase made it a grandstand during the daytime from which the view followed the prominent street axis between the historical setting of the theatre and Braunschweig's old town. During the festival, audiences entered and left the theatre directly via the steps. The red carpet used for the staircase and in the ballroom became both an invitation and an emblem for the festival, visible from afar.

Zehn Tage lang war das Braunschweiger Stadttheater der Veranstaltungsort von Theaterformen, einer internationalen Biennale. Die Aufgabe, ein Festivalzentrum mit Treffpunkt, Informationszentrum, einem Ort für den Ticketverkauf und einer Bibliothek inklusive kleinem Café zu entwerfen, wurde von den Architekten Kühn Malvezzi neu interpretiert: Der Festsaal im ersten Stock, in dem sich in der Regel das Publikum während der Theatervorführungen aufhält, wurde zum temporären Festivalzentrum umfunktioniert. Für die Dauer des Festivals wurde dieser innenliegende Raum, den viele Bürger der Stadt kaum kennen, zu einem frei zugänglichen öffentlichen Ort, den man auch unabhängig von Theatervorführungen besuchen konnte. Der Saal wurde so zum Anziehungspunkt für ein bunt gemischtes, lebhaftes Publikum. >> Der strukturelle Eingriff bestand im Aufbau einer, von einem Gerüst gestützten, breiten Treppe, die innerhalb von zwei Tagen montiert und demontiert werden konnte. Der Theatervorplatz wurde über die Treppe direkt mit dem Balkon des Festsaals verbunden. Große Stufen in der Mitte der nach Süden ausgerichteten Treppe ließen diese am Tage zu einer Tribüne werden, wodurch ein Blick auf die markante Straßenachse zwischen dem historischen Standort des Theaters und der Altstadt Braunschweigs geboten wurde. Während des Festivals betrat und verließ das Publikum das Theater direkt über diese Treppe. Der aus weiter Ferne sichtbare, für Treppe und Festsaal verwendete rote Teppich wirkte wie eine Einladung und wurde zugleich zum Emblem des Festivals.

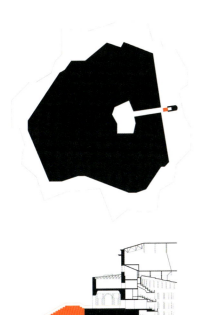

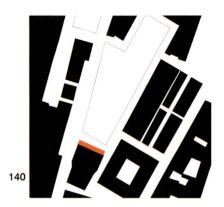

Project: Stage window | Location: Munich | Client: Palos Immobilien- und Projektentwicklung Sarl Objekt München KG, Munich | Artist: Olafur Eliasson, Berlin | Staff: Sebastian Behmann | URL: www.olafureliasson.net | Completion: 2005

This project is part of a larger urban reconstruction project which transformed a huge post-war parking lot into a new urban quarter with offices, shops and cultural buildings designed by GKK architects in cooperation with the landscape architects st raum a, Berlin. >> In his concept for the façade of the new rehearsal studio building for the Bavarian State Opera in Munich, the artist Olafur Eliasson has redefined the front of the building as a form of theatre stage facing onto the Marstallplatz, one of the city's main squares. Through his work, the square becomes both auditorium and stage. >> The central perspective stage layout of the theatre defined by the mirror and glass creates, when seen from the square, a reflected image in red and green, which echoes the green copper rooftops in the area and the red backdrop on the façade (and in the theatre). >> The reflected images in the mirrors have two separate components: The large lower mirror reflects the social activity and life on the Marstallplatz and the upper mirror reflects the sky above the square. Eliasson thus uses both the public area next to the building and the sky above it in his installation: "I have focused on giving a stronger experience of a public space through viewing and engaging in the Marstallplatz using the realtime/space 'theatre play' on the façade. It is a way of reflecting upon yourself and the space in which you happen to be – the definition of society outside the theatre building".

Das Projekt ist Teil einer größeren städtebaulichen Transformation, durch die sich nach einem Entwurf von GKK Architekten in Kooperation mit den Landschaftsarchitekten st raum a in ein riesiger Parkplatz aus der Nachkriegszeit in ein modernes Stadtquartier mit Büros, Läden und Kultureinrichtungen verwandelt hat. >> In dieser neuen Umgebung verwandelt der Künstler Olafur Eliasson mit seinem Projekt für den Marstallplatz, die Fassade des neuen Probengebäudes der Bayerischen Staatsoper in eine Art Theaterbühne aus Glas und Spiegeln. Die Ausrichtung der einzelnen Elemente und ihre changierende Farbigkeit zwischen Rot und Grün wecken dabei Assoziationen an eine zentralperspektivische Bühnenanordnung, greifen zugleich aber auch die Kupferdächer der Umgebung und den roten Innenraum des Theaters auf. >> Anders als zu erwarten, ist der Passant auf dem Platz nicht nur Zuschauer, sondern auch Akteur. Denn das in den Spiegeln reflektierte Bild besteht aus zwei Komponenten: Während der obere Spiegel den Himmel über dem Platz reflektiert, zeigt der untere das Menschen und das Leben auf dem Marstallplatz. Der Platz verwandelt sich mit diesem Eingriff gleichermaßen in ein Auditorium und in eine Bühne. >> Gerade in der Umgebung des neuen Stadtquartiers interpretiert die Installation auf subtile Weise das Werdende. Denn die Wahrnehmung der eigenen Bewegungen auf der großen Bühne erinnert daran, dass Öffentlichkeit erst dort entsteht, wo Menschen den öffentlichen Raum ganz bewusst für sich entdecken und entsprechend frei nutzen: „Ich habe versucht, einen öffentlichen Raum intensiver erlebbar zu machen, indem ich den Echtzeit-Raum eines ,Theaterstücks' auf die Fassade am Marstallplatz projizierte. Dadurch wird man angeregt, über sich selbst und den Raum nachzudenken, in dem man sich gerade aufhält. Dadurch definiert sich die Gesellschaft außerhalb des Theatergebäudes."

Project: Hotel Q! | Location: Berlin | Client: Wanzl & Co Bauträgergesellschaft | Architects: GRAFT Berlin - Los Angeles - Beijing | Staff: Wolfgang Grenz, Johannes Jakubeit, Michael Rapp, Sascha Ganske, Stephanie Bünau, Leo Kocan, Lennart Wiechell, Sven Fuchs, Nikolas Krause, Helge Lezius | © Photos: Hiepler Brunier Architekturfotografie | URL: www.graftlab.com | Completion: 2004 | Area: 3,200 m²

A new type of urban hotel has emerged over the last decade: the "design" or "boutique" hotel. They offer a form of temporary accommodation that is intended to afford unmistakably unique experiences of architectonic spaces and cosmopolitan hubs for the design-conscious traveller. >> On a corner of Berlin's famous shopping mile, the Kurfürstendamm, GRAFT has created a small hotel from an existing building that comprises lobby, lounge, spa, 72 rooms, 4 studios and a penthouse. The Q! is laid out in a hotel landscape that challenges the classic spatial canon through the topographical folding of the programme. The tectonic logic of the construction elements is distorted, blending into hybrid zones with double-function occupancies. The inclined areas are both dividing walls and furniture. The lifted floor is both circulation surface and space emerging from the skin of the house. >> The flow of this "landscape" creates generous connections where an otherwise typical dissection into singular spaces would prevail. The topographical treatment of the design maximises programme utilization and creates a continuous flow of form and space throughout the hotel. The visitor finds a narrative that departs from conventional perceptual experiences and allows ambiguous readings of the space.

Design- oder Boutiquehotels haben sich als neue Art von Stadthotel seit über zehn Jahren etabliert. Neben den üblichen Funktionen eines Hotels bieten sie dem design-bewussten Reisenden ein einzigartiges und unverwechselbares architektonisches Raumerlebnis und dienen ihm als kosmopolitische Anlaufstelle. >> An einer Ecke des Kurfürstendamms, Berlins berühmter Einkaufsstraße, hat GRAFT ein vorhandenes Gebäude in ein kleines Hotel umgebaut, mit Lobby, Lounge, Spa- und Wellnessbereich, 72 Zimmern, vier Studios und einem Penthouse. Das Q! ist als Hotellandschaft konzipiert, die den klassischen Kanon der Raumanordnung durch ihre „topografische Faltung" in Frage stellt. Die tektonische Logik der Bauelemente, die zu hybriden, doppelfunktionalen Zonen verschmelzen, wirkt verzerrt, da Schrägen als Trennwände und Möbel zugleich fungieren. Der aufgeständerte Fußboden, der sich aus der Wand herausfaltet, ist Bewegungsfläche und Raum in einem. >> Der fließende Eindruck der landschaftsartigen Gestaltung lässt großzügige Verbindungen entstehen, wo sonst typische Unterteilungen in einfache Raumsegmente zu finden sind. Die topografische Auslegung der Raumorganisation vervielfacht die Nutzungsmöglichkeiten und lässt durch das gesamte Hotel hindurch Form und Raum fließend ineinander übergehen. Der Gast erlebt eine räumliche Situation, die von konventionellen Wahrnehmungsmustern abweicht und vieldeutige Interpretationen zulässt.

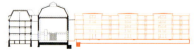

Project: Headquarter Stadtwerke | Location: Düsseldorf | Client: Stadtwerke Düsseldorf AG, Düsseldorf | Architects: Christoph Ingenhoven in Ingenhoven Overdiek und Partner, Düsseldorf | Staff: Jürgen Overdiek, Ben Dieckmann, Klaus Frankenheim, Ralf Dorsch-Rüter, Dieter Henze, Stefan Höher, Hinrich Schumacher, Herbert Voss, Christel Bauscher, Marc Böhnke, Sylvia Domke, Holger Gravius, Thomas Höxtermann, Christof Janoschka, Peter Pistorius, Regina Wuff | © Photos: H. G. Esch | Statics: Werner Sobek Ingenieure mit SPI Schüßler Plan Ingenieurgesellschaft | URL: www.ingenhovenarchitekten.de | Completion: 2003 | Area: 23,500 m²

Düsseldorf's public utilities company decided to establish its new headquarters on a vast derelict power plant site dominated by late 19th century industrial architecture. Ingenhoven architects were asked to design an office building that would gather the previously scattered company departments under one roof. They chose a concept composed of slabs positioned parallel to the two main historic buildings and linked by courtyards. Glazed corridors connect the preserved buildings and link them to the new structure. >> The turbine hall and the former administration building were originally built by Erasmus Kittler in 1889, the converted hall now has a client centre on the ground floor and an auditorium on the first floor, yet the character of the great machine hall is still very much present. The main entrance to the complex is located in a glazed passageway accessible from the street and the neighbouring park. The four new slabs are connected by footbridges, which cross the atria between the buildings. All levels are connected with open vertical circulation. >> A sectioned coal-bearing paternoster lift, the chute, one of the original turbines and a cut-away boiler have also been preserved in the complex – like dinosaurs in a natural history museum – both documenting and highlighting of the building's history.

Die Düsseldorfer Stadtwerke verlegten ihre Hauptverwaltung auf das Gelände eines ehemaligen Kraftwerks. Der neu errichtete Bürokomplex umfasst vier große Baukörper, die parallel zu den zwei historischen Industriegebäuden angeordnet und über Höfe verbunden sind. Die Altbauten sind über gläserne Korridore an die Neubaustruktur angeschlossen. Untereinander sind die neuen Baukörper jeweils durch Fußgängerbrücken verbunden. >> Die Turbinenhalle von Erasmus Kittler aus dem Jahr 1889 und das ehemalige Verwaltungsgebäude verfügen nach dem Umbau über ein Kundenzentrum im Erd- und einen Veranstaltungssaal im Obergeschoss; der Charakter einer Maschinenhalle ist noch immer spürbar. Der Haupteingang zum Bürokomplex befindet sich an einem der verglasten Korridore, welcher von der Anfahrtsstraße und dem angrenzenden Park aus zugänglich ist. >> Je ein ausgedienter Kohle-Paternoster, ein Transportschacht, eine Turbine und ein Kessel sind in räumlicher Nähe zu den Büroarbeitsplätzen ausgestellt – wie Dinosaurier in einem Naturkundemuseum. Sie führen so die industrielle Geschichte des Standorts deutlich vor Augen.

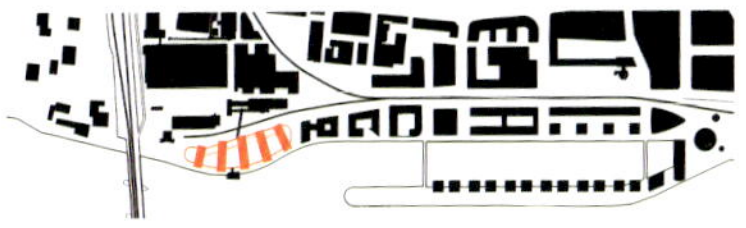

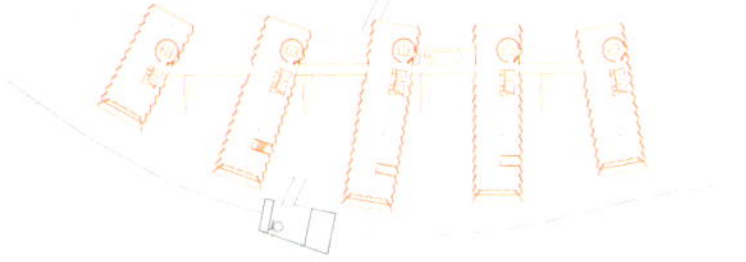

SCHNEIDER + SCHUMACHER: ON THE EDGE

Page/Seite >> 107

Project: Westhafen pier | **Location**: Frankfurt am Main | **Client**: SEB Immobilien Investment GmbH, Frankfurt am Main | **Architects**: schneider+schumacher, Frankfurt am Main | **Staff**: Michaela Artus-Kraft, Miriam Baake, Susanne Burchardt, Andreas Fuchs, Matthias Hohl, Martin Koschlig, Bernward Krone, Kai Otto, Miriam Schneider, Michael Schumacher, Karoline Sievers, Wolfram Welding, Daniel Widrig, Heiko Wüstefeld, Anke Wollbrink | **© Photos**: Waltraud Krase, Jörg Hempel | **Statics**: Schwarzbart + Partner Ingenieurbüro; Kannemacher u. Sturm Ingenieure, Frankfurt am Main | **Building services**: Schindler Ingenieurgesellschaft mbH Dietzenbach; IBK Ingenieure Klöffel GmbH, Bruchköbel | **URL**: www.schneider-schumacher.de | **Completion**: 2004 | **Area**: 31,945 m²

The Westhafen Pier is a new type of synthesis of office buildings with an above-ground parking structure and is located directly in front of the existing coal power station. The design was strongly influenced by the site's industrial surroundings. On its eastern side – the site of the former Westhafen – lies the newly built Westhafen quarter with offices and housing. On its western side lies the Main-Neckar Bridge with heavy train traffic. >> The river Main forms the quarter's southern perimeter, it provides supply infrastructure for the power station to the north of the site. The coal supply line from the river drives straight through the building, and determines the height of the building's "plinth"; a base formed by a three-storey unit with garage showrooms and restaurants. On top of this plinth are five four-storey buildings arranged like an open hand, fanning out towards the river. The supply line acts as a bridge thrown out from the heavy industrial function and aesthetic to the shining elegance of the new buildings moored to it. >> The zig-zag shape of the facades achieves an optimal river view for the inhabitants. Between the building fingers, generous terraces offer great views of the river. The façades are made of anodised aluminium which creates a vivid play of light. Far from denying its "ugly" industrial environment, the smooth, shiny surfaces and technical aesthetic of the pier buildings seem to enhance and highlight the functional beauty of its location. The big panorama windows at the tips of the fingers tie in the industrial past of the location with a view of Frankfurt's contemporary urban landscape.

Der Pier ist Teil eines neuen Stadtquartiers am Westhafen in Frankfurt am Main, welches mit seiner angestrebten Mischnutzung auch zur Stärkung der Innenstadt beitragen soll. In diesem Sinne kann auch das zu integrierende bestehende Kohlekraftwerk als funktionale Erweiterung gesehen werden. Entwurfsbestimmend für die Kombination aus Bürohäusern und Parkgarage war daher das industriell geprägte Umfeld. >> Der Main bildet die südliche Begrenzung des Piers und sein Ufer wird vor allem von der Bedarfsinfrastruktur des nördlich gelegenen Kraftwerks eingenommen. Deshalb verläuft auch das Förderband für die Belieferung mit Kohle mitten durch das Gebäude und bestimmt die Höhe des Sockels, der auf drei Geschossen Parkflächen, Läden und Gastronomie beherbergt. Die eigentliche Büronutzung findet in fünf einzelnen Baukörpern ihren Platz, welche auf diesem Sockel aufliegen und sich zum Fluss hin öffnen. Die gefaltete Fassade und die Terrassen zwischen den Baukörpern geben immer wieder durch große Panoramafenster spektakuläre Ausblicke auf die Flusslandschaft frei. >> Auch in der Materialität folgt die Fassade aus eloxiertem Aluminium dem industriellen Umfeld, zugleich wird aber auch ein lebendiges Lichtspiel erzeugt, welches auf die neue Nutzung des Areals verweist. Durch die technische Ästhetik wird die vermeintlich „hässliche" Umgebung also nicht verleugnet, sondern die funktionale Schönheit des Ortes betont. So erscheint auch die ihrer ursprünglichen Funktion nur scheinbar enthobene Versorgungsleitung wie eine Brücke vom Industrie- ins Kommunikationszeitalter.

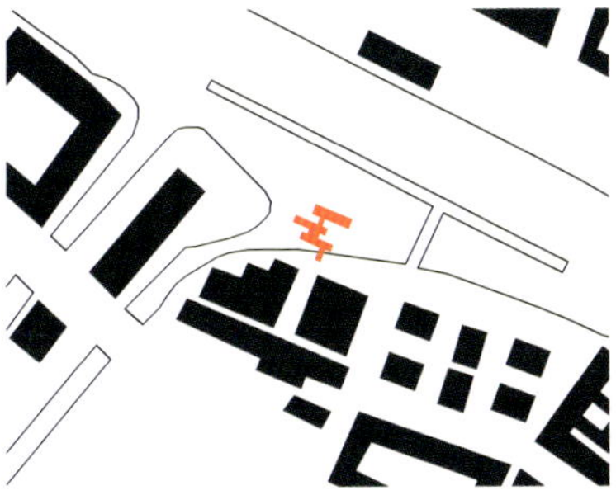

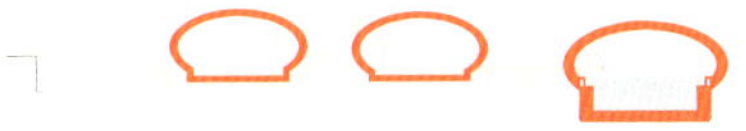

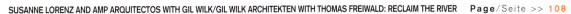

SUSANNE LORENZ AND AMP ARQUITECTOS WITH GIL WILK/GIL WILK ARCHITEKTEN WITH THOMAS FREIWALD: RECLAIM THE RIVER

Page/Seite >> 108

Project: Badeschiff / Winterbadeschiff | **Location**: Berlin | **Client**: Kulturarena Veranstaltungs GmbH, Berlin | **Architects**: Susanne Lorenz and AMP arquitectos with Gil Wilk / Gil Wilk Architekten with Thomas Freiwald, Berlin/Spain | **Staff**: Catharine von Eitzen, Thomas Freiwald, Ann-Kristin Hase, Fabian Lippert, Nora Müller, Ana Salinas, Gilbert Wilk | **© Photos**: Torsten Seidel, Kulturarena Veranstaltungs GmbH, Gil Wilk Architekten | **URL**: www.arena-berlin.de | **Completion**: 2004 / 2005 | **Area**: 500 m² Pontoon, 240 m² Swimming Pool

In 2002, various international architects and artists were invited to deal with bridges in the context of connecting elements in cities. Instead of creating a bridge over the Spree, the Badeschiff team proposed a bridge to the Spree. Following a tradition of public bathing in the river at the turn of the century, the project encouraged a closer connection between the city and its river by floating a pool on it. >> A 30 year old barge was modified in a nearby dockyard. It was reduced to its shell and filled with preheated and chlorinated water to form a 32m long pool complemented with a wooden bridge and a sun terrace. All technical installations are concealed in the edge profile and yet allow an unobstructed view across the river when swimming. >> During the winter, a three-part membrane structure divides the Badeschiff (bathing ship) and its jetty into three separate areas: a lounge, sauna and the pool ship itself. These areas are connected via additional boxes containing technical and service functions. A two-layered membrane is spanned over elliptical wooden trusses maintaining a combination of translucent and transparent surfaces. The space between the membranes is filled with air to optimise insulation and guarantee a comfortable interior temperature of 25°C even when it is extremely cold outside. >> Simple joints, standard materials and easy manual assembly allow for the membrane structure to be dismantled and reerected without the use of a crane. These elements can then be stored during the summer or alternatively used as a pavilion on the shore.

Im Rahmen eines Wettbewerbs 2002 wurden internationale Architekten und Künstler eingeladen, Brücken als verbindende Elemente einer Stadt zu untersuchen. Doch statt eines Brückenbauwerks über die Spree hinweg schlug das Badeschiff-Team eine „Brücke zur Spree" vor. Anknüpfend an die Tradition des öffentlichen Badens im vorletzten Jahrhundert, versucht das Projekt anhand eines schwimmenden Pools wieder eine intensivere Verbindung von Stadt und Fluss herzustellen. >> Eine 30 Jahre alte Schute wurde in einer nahe gelegenen Werft zu einem 32 Meter langen Pool umgebaut, indem die Innenaufbauten bis auf die äußere Schiffshaut entkernt wurden. Das Schwimmbecken wurde anschließend als Schwimmkörper in die Spree gelassen und mit vorgewärmtem, gechlortem Wasser befüllt und durch eine Pontonkonstruktion mit der Sonnenterrasse am Ufer verbunden. Sämtliche technische Installationen sind im Randprofil der ehemaligen Schute verborgen, sodass die Schwimmenden einen ungehinderten Blick auf den Fluss genießen können. >> Im Winter werden das Badeschiff und der Brückensteg durch eine Membranstruktur in eine Lounge, eine Sauna und ein Poolschiff verwandelt. Ein Wechselspiel transparenter Oberflächen wird durch eine zweischichtige Membran erzeugt, welche über elliptisch geformte Holzpaneele gespannt ist. Der Luftraum zwischen den Membranen übernimmt eine isolierende Funktion, was selbst bei extremer Außenkälte für eine komfortable Innenraumtemperatur sorgt. >> Einfache Verbindungsdetails und die Verwendung von standardisierten Baumaterialien erlauben einen Auf- und Abbau der Zusatzkonstruktionen von Hand. Diese Elemente können über den Sommer eingelagert oder als Pavillons entlang der Uferkante genutzt werden.

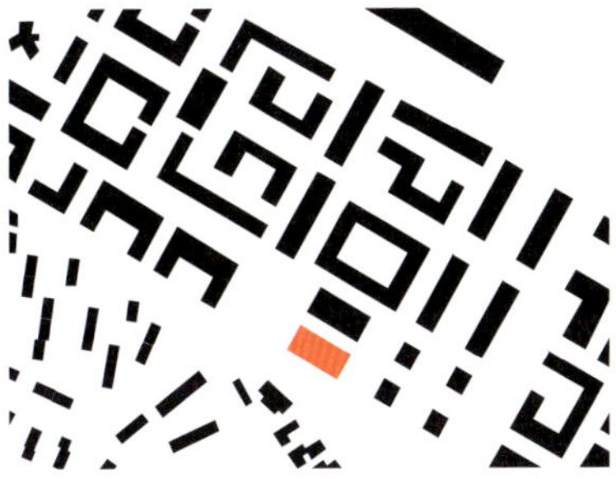

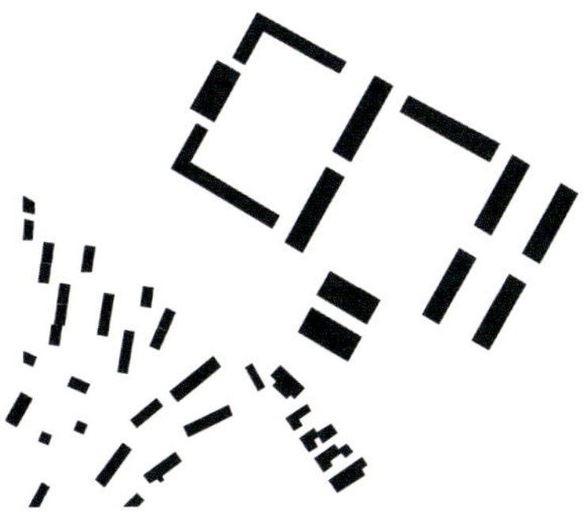

STADTSANIERUNGSAMT, TÜBINGEN: FROM "PANZERHALLE" TO COMMUNITY HOTSPOT

Page/Seite >> 116

Project: Panzerhalle – Barracks conversion | **Location**: Tübingen | **Client**: Universitätsstadt Tübingen | **Architects**: Stadtsanierungsamt, Tübingen | **Staff**: Andreas Feldtkeller, Andreas Pätz, Cord Soehlke, Christa Nerz, Renate Klingenstein, Ingrid Meckseper | **Landscape architecture**: Werkbüro für Freiraum und Landschaft mit Bürgerbeteiligung | **URL**: www.tuebingen.de | **Completion**: 1999-2005 | **Area**: 940 m²

The original Panzerhalle (tank hall) belonging to a former French garrison was built in 1934/35. After World War II the French army used the hall as a garage for large vehicles and tanks. The French then left after German reunification and the city of Tübingen bought the whole area for development. >> As part of the planning for the new "French Quarter", the local department for urban renewal proposed removing the walls, renewing the structure and transforming the tank hall into a large pavilion. This idea was part of the city administration's development concept planned by the local department for urban renewal and LEHEN drei architects and urbanists from Stuttgart under which the former garrison area was transformed into diverse urban neighbourhoods. In the resulting "town of short distances", offices, shops and workshops are plentiful and most of the buildings have been developed by private building ventures on their own parcels. This has encouraged a wide variety of people, functions and architectural concepts to characterise the vitality of the neighbourhoods. >> Integrated into this urban atmosphere and density, the Panzerhalle has become a roofed public square with many functions: in the mornings the police practice traffic exercises here with school classes; in the afternoons kids play basketball or football; in the evening it changes into a meeting point for adults. At the weekends there are flea markets, concerts and exhibitions – all protected from both rain and hot sun. The new Panzerhalle is now a community hotspot which connects the new housing developments with the existing social housing in the neighbourhood.

Die ursprüngliche Panzerhalle wurde in den Jahren 1934/1935 errichtet. Nach dem Zweiten Weltkrieg übernahm die französische Armee die Halle und nutzte sie als Reparaturwerkstatt für Großfahrzeuge und Panzer. Als die Franzosen nach der Wiedervereinigung Deutschland verließen, erwarb die Stadt Tübingen die militärischen Liegenschaften. >> Im Rahmen der Planung für das neue „Französische Viertel" schlug das Stadtsanierungsamt vor, die Wände zu entfernen, die Struktur zu sanieren und die Halle in einen überdimensionalen „Pavillon" zu verwandeln. Die Idee, die ehemalige Kaserne in vielfältige urbane Stadtquartiere umzubauen, basiert auf dem städtebaulichen Entwicklungskonzept des Stadtsanierungsamts Tübingen und dem Stuttgarter Architekten- und Stadtplanerbüro LEHEN drei. In der „Stadt der kurzen Wege" finden sich in nahezu jedem Erdgeschoss Büros, Läden und Werkstätten. Die Gebäude wurden überwiegend von privaten Baugemeinschaften auf eigenen Parzellen errichtet. Eine große Vielfalt von Menschen, Nutzungen und architektonischen Konzepten prägt die Quartiere und sorgt für eine ungewöhnliche Lebendigkeit. >> In dieser atmosphärischen urbanen Dichte entstand mit der Panzerhalle ein überdachter öffentlicher Platz für unterschiedliche Nutzungen: morgens übt die örtliche Polizei mit Schulklassen Verkehrsregeln, nachmittags spielen Kinder Basketball oder Fußball, am Abend wird die Halle zum Treffpunkt für Ältere. An Wochenenden finden Flohmärkte, Feste, Konzerte und Ausstellungen statt – jede Nutzung ist geschützt vor Regen oder starker Sonne. Die umgewidmete Panzerhalle ist zu einem gesellschaftlichen Kulminationspunkt geworden, welcher die neuen Stadtquartiere mit den benachbarten Sozialwohnungsbauten verbindet.

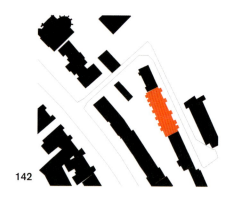

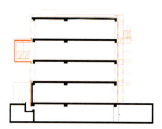

BLAURAUM ARCHITEKTEN: RESIDENTIAL RECHANGE   Page/Seite >> 118

Project: Living+ Bogenallee | **Location**: Hamburg | **Client**: COGITON Projekt Harvestehude GmbH, Hamburg | **Architects**: blauraum architekten, Hamburg | **Staff**: Carsten Venus, Claudia Große-Hartlage, Dirk Fischer-Appelt, Hanna Haerdter, Michael Maurer | © **Photos**: Giovanni Castell, Christian Schaulin, blauraum architekten | **Statics**: WTM / Windels.Timm.Morgen, Hamburg | **Building services**: PlanerWerft GmbH, Hamburg | **URL**: www.blauraum.de | **Completion**: 2005 | **Area**: 7,100 m²

This former office building and parking house from 1974, located in the court of a large urban block, was converted into a residential house with 15 apartments. The building was cored to its shell construction and the housing technology, façade and morphology were rebuilt. Twenty-three parking places were created in the basement accessed by a vehicle lift. >> The underlying idea was to develop a homogeneous building that simultaneously enables and displays the diversity of the individual apartments. From this approach the open ground plans were individually modified by adding extra living spaces, so-called "flex-boxes", at different points. By turning the inner rooms "inside out" these special elements function as spatial extensions accommodating kitchen, bedroom or bathroom, providing space for a sauna, the bath or the dining table. >> Due to the east-west alignment of the building a varying façade concept was chosen with a perforated façade facing the street (Bogenallee) and a completely glazed façade towards the court-yard. Despite the closed street-facing façade, the building interacts intensively with its immediate environment. Through the lateral vitrification of the staggered boxes, the room alignment is rotated by 90 degrees and, in an unusual manner, one is located in an interspace between protected privacy and urban space. >> The Living+ conversion serves as a model for upgrading tired office buildings from the '60s and '70s into desirable and comfortable urban apartments.

Die Aufgabe bestand im Umbau eines gewerblich genutzten Bestandgebäudes in ein Wohnhaus. Das im Jahr 1974 erbaute, im Hof eines großen innerstädtischen Blocks gelegene Gebäude wurde bis auf den Rohbau entkernt, die Bereiche Haustechnik, Fassade und Ausbau neu aufgebaut. Es entstanden 15 neue Wohnungen sowie im Keller 23 Parkplätze, die mit einem Fahrzeuglift zu erreichen sind. >> Der Grundgedanke war, ein homogenes Gebäude zu entwickeln, welches gleichzeitig einzelne variantenreiche Wohnlösungen ermöglicht und diese Vielfalt auch nach außen hin sichtbar macht. Ausgehend von diesem Ansatz veränderte man an verschiedenen Stellen individuell die offenen Grundrisse durch Hinzufügen von Sonderräumen (Boxen). So konnten durch das „Herausstülpen" des Innenraumes spezielle Elemente als räumliche Erweiterungen für Küche, Schlafzimmer oder Badezimmer genutzt werden, um eine Sauna, eine Badewanne oder den Esstisch unterzubringen. >> Durch die Ost-West-Ausrichtung des Gebäudes wurde ein nach beiden Seiten unterschiedliches Fassadenkonzept gewählt: Lochfassade zur Straße (Bogenallee) und vollständige raumhohe Verglasung zum Hof. Trotz der geschlossenen Fassade auf der Straßenseite interagiert das Gebäude intensiv mit seiner näheren Umgebung. Über die seitliche Verglasung der versetzt eingelassenen Boxen wird die Raumausrichtung von innen um 90 Grad umgelenkt. Man befindet sich so auf ungewöhnliche Art zwischen geschützter Privatsphäre und öffentlichem Raum. >> Der Living+-Umbau steht modellhaft für die Modernisierung und Verwandlung alter unansehnlicher Bürogebäude aus den 1960er und 1970er Jahren in begehrte und komfortable, urbane Apartments.

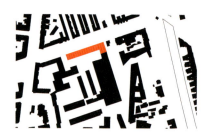

BRT ARCHITEKTEN: WRAP-ON AND OVER   Page/Seite >> 120

Project: Falkenried lofts | **Location**: Hamburg | **Client**: J + O Falkenried apartments GmbH + Co. KG | **Architects**: BRT Architekten, Hamburg | **Staff**: Brigitte Queck, Anja Grannemann, Eike Holst, Anja Kleinschmidt, Tobias Kogelnig | © **Photos**: Klaus Frahm | **URL**: www.brt.de | **Completion**: 2003 | **Area**: 7,300 m²

A walk through the former "building D" of the vehicle workshops in Falkenried is like a journey through time from 1928 to the year 2000. The combination of protected industrial buildings and modern residential units gives the development it's particular charm. The architects have designed 39 units with balconies, terraces or rooftop gardens, together with a ground floor restaurant. >> The design sought to retain the industrial charm of the existing buildings as far as possible, and to highlight the contrast between old and new. The former entrance building to the workshop site kept its original façade on three sides but the south-west facade has been replaced by a large steel and glass construction. With the addition of balconies and loggias, the building is now three metres wider. >> A "skydeck" was created above the existing building, with generous penthouse apartments. The dynamic form of the rooftop extension with its metal roof is in direct contrast to the existing brick building. Loft-like apartments were planned as maisonettes on the third and fourth floors, and as apartments on the ground, first, and second floors. Although all of the different apartment types are designed around an open living room, spatial separation is ensured by the location of kitchens and bathrooms. >> The project combines the charm of an old 19th century red building with the comfort of a new construction contributing to the upgrade process of a desirable residential area.

Ein Gang durch das „Gebäude D" der ehemaligen Fahrzeugwerkstätten in Falkenried ist wie eine Zeitreise von 1928 ins Jahr 2000. Die Überlagerung von denkmalgeschütztem Industriebau und neuen Loft-Wohneinheiten mit Balkonen, Terrassen, Dachgärten und einem Restaurant im Erdgeschoss machen den besonderen Flair des Komplexes aus. >> Die Planung sah vor, den Bestand in seinem industriellen Charakter möglichst zu erhalten und den visuellen Kontrast zwischen alter und neuer Substanz zu schärfen. Das ehemalige Eingangsgebäude des Werkstättenbereiches behielt seine Originalfassade an drei Seiten, während die Südwestfassade durch eine großflächige vorgesetzte Stahl-Glas-Konstruktion erweitert worden ist. In dem dadurch entstandenen drei Meter breiten Zwischenraum sind Balkone, Loggien und Lufträume eingeschnitten. >> Auf dem vorhandenen Gebäude wurde ein „Skydeck" errichtet, dessen geschwungene und metallene Oberfläche einen deutlichen Kontrast zum alten Klinkerbau darunter bildet. Großzügige Penthouse-Apartments sind im dritten und vierten Obergeschoss als Maisonette und im Erdgeschoss, im ersten und zweiten Obergeschoss als normale Wohnungen angelegt. Obwohl sich alle unterschiedlichen Wohnungstypen um einen zentralen offenen Wohnraum herum entwickeln, bleibt durch die besondere Positionierung von Küche und Bad eine nachträgliche, differenzierte räumliche Unterteilung gewahrt. >> Das Projekt kombiniert den Charme eines alten Backsteingebäudes mit dem Komfort einer aufgewerteten zeitgenössischen Wohnlage.

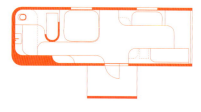

L/B - SABINA LANG UND DANIEL BAUMANN: WELL TRAVELLED HOTEL   Page/Seite >> 125

Project: Hotel Everland | **Location**: Yverdon + Burgdorf/Switzerland; Leipzig/Germany, Paris/France | **Client**: Diréction Artistique Expo.02, Switzerland | **Architects**: L/B - Sabina Lang and Daniel Baumann, Burgdorf, Switzerland | **Staff**: Fabian Stücheli, Jörg Bosshard, Valérie Jomini, Stanislas Zimmermann | **Statics**: Stöcklin/Graf, Bern | **URL**: www.langbaumann.com | **Completion**: 2002 | **Area**: 32 m²

Hotel Everland is a mobile hotel capable of touring and taking up new locations in different rooftop situations in different cities. It was originally created for the Yverdon Expo in Switzerland, where it sat on a jetty looking across the Neuenburger lake, but has now started a city tour testing different urban environments. It currently resides on the roof of the GfzK (Gallery for Contemporary Art) in Leipzig where it affords distinctively novel views of the city. The open room plan of the pod-like module encompasses a lounge with picture window that frames the city context, focusing the view for the inhabitants like a periscope. >> Everland is to be read as a metaphor reflecting the situation of the guest or stranger. It appears welcoming, because it is accessible to the general public for a few hours every day, as well as being an exclusive, isolated space for the lucky few who managed to reserve a room. There are also irrational aspects: a one-room hotel doesn't make financial sense, the operating costs and the revenues are blatantly disproportionate and the desire for exclusivity contradicts the fact that the hotel is also an art exhibit in a gallery with public access. >> It is a form of social sculpture: As a private enclave it underlines the very public nature of urban space and repeatedly challenges visitors and hotel guests to renegotiate the border between private and public interests in ever changing urban situations.

Das Hotel Everland ist als mobiler Einraum an beliebige Standorte versetzbar. Ursprünglich wurde es als einmaliges Kunstprojekt für die Yverdon Expo in der Schweiz konzipiert und auf einem Bootssteg mit Blick auf den Neuenburger See platziert. Dann trat es seine Städtetour an und testet seitdem den urbanen Kontext. Für einen Sommer residiert Hotel Everland in zehn Metern Höhe auf dem Dach der gfzk (Galerie für Zeitgenössische Kunst) in Leipzig und ermöglicht gänzlich neue Blickbeziehungen zur Umgebung. Der offene Raumplan der Wohnkapsel erzeugt eine kleinflächige Lounge mit Panoramafenster, welches den Blick auf die Stadt einrahmt und die Perspektive der Eintagesbewohner wie durch ein Periskop fokussiert. >> Hotel Everland kann tagsüber vom Publikum für einige Stunden als Teil des Museums besichtigt werden, während es bei Nacht exklusiv all jenen wenigen Gästen zur Verfügung steht, die das Zimmer gebucht haben. Das Konzept birgt jedoch auch irrationale Aspekte: Ein Ein-Zimmer-Hotel macht wirtschaftlich nur geringfügig Sinn, denn die anfallenden Betriebskosten liegen weit über den erwarteten Vermietungseinnahmen. Auch dem Wunsch nach Exklusivität widerspricht das Hotel, da es gleichzeitig Teil einer Kunstausstellung mit öffentlichem Zugang ist. >> Bei Everland handelt es sich um eine soziale Skulptur: Als private Enklave betont das Objekt den öffentlichen Charakter des umgebenden Außenraums und fordert wiederholt Besucher und Hotelgäste dazu auf, die Grenze zwischen privaten und öffentlichen Interessen in sich ständig verändernden urbanen Situationen neu zu verhandeln.

REALARCHITEKTUR: FROM AIR RAID TO ART SHELTER   P a g e / S e i t e >> 1 2 8

Project: Boros collection – Art bunker I **Location**: Berlin I **Client**: Christian Boros und Karen Lohmann, Wuppertal I **Architects**: Realarchitektur, Berlin I **Staff**: Jens Casper, Petra Petersson, Andrew Strickland, Wolfgang List, Bernadette Krejs, Karin Maria Derix I © **Photos**: Hanns Joosten I **Statics**: Ingenieurbüro Herbert Fink I **URL**: www.realarchitektur.de I **Completion**: 2006/07 I **Area**: 2,700 m²

This concrete air-raid bunker was built in 1942 on the corner of a city block in the Mitte district of Berlin. Five repetitive storeys contain 80 rooms whose neutrality forms a suitable showcase for the client's contemporary art collection. >> The low ceiling heights made modifications necessary. Selected ceilings and walls were cut out with a diamondtoothed saw and removed. The resulting overlapping spaces now join the floors vertically throughout. Post-war additions were removed, the four façades were cleaned, renovated where required, and the plinth was restored. >> To connect up to the newly created dwelling on top of the building, around 150 cubic metres of reinforced concrete were cut out of the bunker's three metre thick roof. The apartment is reached through this opening by way of a staircase of meshed steel and an internal open lift, which is partly clad in the same material. >> The living spaces in the apartment are characterised by simple reinforced concrete walls, oak woodwork, floors of lacustrine limestone and the reinforced concrete roof, square in form like the Bunker below. The roof is supported almost entirely without columns, resting on the walls and the self-supporting glass façade which, in contrast to the thick walls of the bunker, allows views across the surrounding cityscape. On the south and west, the line of the glass is set back from the edge of the roof. Movable bronze mesh screens along the perimeter of the roof give privacy to the outdoor living spaces, the roof garden with its terraces and flowerbeds, and the pool. >> Thus the forbidding mass of a military bastion finds a new life as an art bunker and a pedestal for a penthouse.

143

Der Luftschutzbunker wurde 1942 auf einem Block-Eckgrundstück in Berlin-Mitte errichtet. Auf fünf gleichartigen Geschossen sind etwa 80 Räume angeordnet, die wegen ihrer neutralen Form gut für die Aufnahme der zeitgenössischen Kunstsammlung des Bauherrn geeignet sind. Die geringen Geschosshöhen machten kleinteilige Umbauten notwendig. Mit Diamantsägen wurden gezielt einzelne Deckenteile und Wände herausgeschnitten. Die so entstandenen Räume verbinden die Geschosse nun über die gesamte innere Höhe miteinander. Außen wurden nachträgliche Anbauten entfernt, die Fassade gesäubert und, wo nötig, instand gesetzt sowie der ehemals umlaufende Sockel wiederhergestellt. >> Um die auf dem Gebäudedach neu errichtete Flachdach-Wohnung zu erschließen, wurden zusätzlich 150 Kubikmeter Stahlbeton aus der drei Meter starken obersten Decke herausgeschnitten. Durch diese Öffnung wird der Wohnraum über eine Treppe aus Streckmetall und einen Aufzug zugänglich. Das Stahlbeton-Dach wiederholt die Grundrissform des Bunkers und lastet nahezu stützenfrei auf den Innenwänden. >> Die umlaufende, selbsttragende Glasfassade gibt im Kontrast zu den massiven Bunkerwänden den Blick über die umliegende Stadtlandschaft frei. An der Süd- und Westseite springt die Glasfassade weit hinter die Dachkante zurück. An der Dachkante verlaufende, verschiebbare Elemente aus bronzenen Gittern schützen die unter dem Dach liegenden Außenräume wie die Terrassen, den Pool und den bepflanzten Dachgarten vor Blicken aus der Nachbarschaft. >> Dadurch ist die dräuende Masse eines militärischen Bollwerks als Kunstbunker und Sockel eines Penthauses zu neuem Leben erwacht.

FLOSUNDK ARCHITEKTUR+URBANISTIK: A MUTUALLY BENEFICIAL RELATIONSHIP   P a g e / S e i t e >> 1 2 9

Project: Extension "Symbiont" I **Location**: Merzig I **Client**: Patrick & Sabah Friedrich, Merzig I **Architects**: FloSundK architektur+urbanistik, Saarbrücken I **Staff**: Achour Belhouchat, Martin Prölsz I © **Photos**: G.G. Kirchner I **Statics**: IBL Baustatik, Saarbrücken I **URL**: www.flosundk.de I **Completion**: 2004 I **Area**: 32 m² + 17,5 m² Roof-deck

The client's house was built in the early 1960s and is located in the heart of a small town next to the old town hall and an idyllic little river. The young couple lived in an 80 m² flat on the top floor of their tile-clad building which houses both family and their longstanding hairdressing business. The brief was for more space and for the little north-facing balcony to be supplemented with a big roof garden and winter garden thus providing lots more light. >> Architects FloSundK rebuilt the flat and gave the roof a new add-on extension. The wall between the former living room and kitchen was demolished to create a new spacious room containing a lightweight steel stairway, which also functions as skylight. The roof extension is divided into 2 boxes: the "living-box" and the "winter garden-box". >> Because the limited budget ruled out changing the existing elevation, FloSundK used the house as base and perched the new rooms on top. The boxes are intentionally not in sync with the geometry and materials of the original structure, which is covered in light blue and cream-coloured tiles. To save time, both boxes were built as prefabricated timberframe constructions, whilst the green firewall facing the neighbours' property is a pre-cast concrete element, which was screwed onto the existing concrete-roof. >> Distinct materials reflect the different functions of the roof boxes: the "noble" living-box is covered with dark grey chipboard, whereas the "natural" winter-garden-box is covered in untreated zinc-plates that will take on their own natural patina with age. >> In a symbiosis-like interaction the already existing building and its extension are associated with one another in a mutually beneficial relationship.

Das bestehende Haus wurde in den frühen 1960er Jahren gebaut und befindet sich – idyllisch an einem kleinen Fluss gelegen - im Zentrum einer Kleinstadt direkt neben dem alten Rathaus. Neben den Auftraggebern selbst, einem jungen Paar, ist noch der seit langem bestehende Friseursalon der Familie auf den 80 m² Nutzfläche untergebracht. Aufgabe war es, den Wohnbereich zu erweitern und um einen Dachaufbau und Wintergarten zu ergänzen. >> Dafür wurden zunächst das frühere Wohnzimmer und die Küche zu einem neuen Raum zusammengefasst und durch ein großes Oberlicht zum Himmel geöffnet. Durch eine leichte Stahltreppe erschlossen, dient dieser Luftraum zugleich auch dem Zugang zum Dach. >> Da auf Grund des begrenzten Budgets eine gewöhnliche Aufstockung des Hauses nicht möglich war, wurden die neuen Funktionen in zwei preiswerten, vorgefertigten Boxen untergebracht. Diese bestehen aus einer Holzrahmenkonstruktion und wurden gemeinsam mit der Brandwanderweiterung auf dem Dach montiert. >> Um ihre konstruktive Eigenständigkeit auch äußerlich sichtbar werden zu lassen, unterscheiden sie sich sowohl in der Geometrie als auch in den verwendeten Materialien deutlich vom bestehenden Haus mit seinen hellblauen und cremefarbenen Fassadenkacheln. Ihrer Funktion entsprechend ist die „noble" Wohnbox mit dunkelgrau lackierten, zementgebundenen Spanplatten verkleidet, während der „natürlichere" Wintergarten eine eigene Patina entwickeln darf und darum unbehandeltes Zinkblech Verwendung findet. >> Es kommt zu einer Symbiose zwischen dem Bestands- und Erweiterungsbau – ein Zusammenleben ungleicher Lebewesen zu gegenseitigem Nutzen.

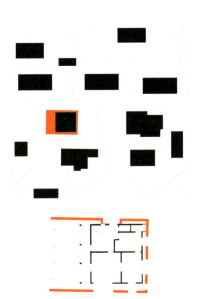

MEIXNER SCHLÜTER WENDT ARCHITEKTEN: URBANE SHELL SUIT   P a g e / S e i t e >> 1 3 0

Project: Wohlfahrt-Laymann house I **Location**: Oberursel near Frankfurt/Main I **Client**: Jürgen Wohlfahrt-Laymann, Oberursel I **Architects**: Meixner Schlüter Wendt Architekten, Frankfurt/Main I **Staff**: Dipl.Ing. Nina Kreiter Dipl.Ing. Moritz Thierfelder I © **Photos**: Christoph Kraneburg, Meixner Schlüter Wendt Architekten I **Statics**: Haus Gruhn, Frankfurt/Main I **URL**: www.meixner-schlueter-wendt.de I **Completion**: 2005 I **Area**: 243 m²

The "Wohlfahrt-Laymann house" is situated in a relatively exclusive residential area in the Taunus outside Frankfurt am Main. The original house, an archetypal wooden "simple country cottage", was built in the 1930s and the initial idea was to replace it with a larger house. However, after a detailed inspection of the site and the quality of this very picturesque, traditional home, it was decided to use the existing building as a starting point for further planning. >> A new shell was built around the house thus creating a new interior and intermediate space. The position of the shell and its distance at different points from the "inner" house is dictated by the functional requirements of the ground plan structure. The inner house is broken open at points where light or space are required for the interior – these light or room extensions are projected onto the outer shell in the form of "light connections" or "space connections" and transferred to it as perforations. The roof of the inner house has been removed and the attic rooms are extended upwards with vertical spacing connections. Inner-, outer-, intermediate- and unrooms of manifold and sometimes curious variations are generated. Complex and seemingly simple rooms alternate with each other. >> Paradoxes occur in the "Wohlfahrt-Laymann house", where an apparently normal reality becomes distorted and a simple, traditional country cottage becomes as a dream of cosmopolitan density in the suburbs.

Das Wohnhaus liegt in einem exklusiven Wohngebiet im Taunus in der Nähe von Frankfurt am Main. Das ursprüngliche Haus, ein archetypisches, einfaches Landhaus aus Holz, wurde in den 1930er Jahren erbaut und sollte eigentlich durch einen Neubau ersetzt werden. Nach einer eingehenden Beschäftigung mit dem Ort wurden jedoch die Qualitäten des malerischen Häuschens offenbar und man beschloss, das bestehende Gebäude als Ausgangspunkt für weitere Planungen zu nehmen. >> Um das Haus herum wird eine Hülle errichtet und so ein neuer Raum zwischen Innen und Außen geschaffen. Die Position der Hülle und ihre Relation zum alten Haus ergeben sich aus den funktionalen Erfordernissen des Grundrisses. Geöffnet wird die bestehende Struktur überall dort, wo es dem Wunsch nach Licht und Raum entsprechend notwendig erscheint. Die Erweiterungen des Innenraums wurden auf die neue Hülle projiziert und so auch im Außenraum ablesbar. Das bestehende Dach wird entfernt und die Dachräume nach oben erweitert. >> Durch diese Manipulationen und Transformationen entstehen vielfältige und manchmal auch merkwürdig anmutende Innen-, Außen-, Zwischen- und Unräume; komplexe Räume wechseln sich mit scheinbar einfachen ab. Durch diese Paradoxien wird die Realität verfremdet und das Landhaus einem urbanen Habitus anverwandelt.

Contributors

AMP arquitectos were originally the architects Felipe Artengo Rufino (*1954), José Maria Rodríguez-Pastrana Malagón (*1952), Fernando Martin Menis (*1951) Office founded in 1981. www.amparquitectos.com, www.plugindc.com/menis
Anderhalten Architekten are Claus Anderhalten (*1962), Petra Vondenhof-Anderhalten (*1965) and Hubertus Schwabe (*1958). Office founded in 1993 in Berlin. www.anderhalten.de
Wiel Arets Architects are Prof. Wiel Arets (*1955) and Bettina Kraus (*1970). Office in Maasstricht and Amsterdam. www.wielarets.nl
atelier le balto are Marc Pouzol (*1966), Veronique Faucheur (*1963), Laurent Dugua (*1967) and Marc Vatinel (*1967). Office in Berlin and Le Harve F. www.lebalto.de
Augustin und Frank Architekten are Georg Augustin (*1951) and Ute Frank (*1952). Office founded 1986 in Berlin. www.augustinundfrank.de
Barkow Leibinger Architekten are Frank Barkow (*1957) and Regine Leibinger (*1963). Office founded in 1993 in Berlin. www.barkowleibinger.com
Baupiloten are Susanne Hofmann (*1963) and a group of students at the faculty of architecture, TU Berlin. www.baupiloten.com
bb22 architekten + stadtplaner are Melanie Bareuther (*1973), Friedemann Benrath (*1974), Aspasia Maheras (*1969), Sonja Müller (*1965), Felix Nowak (*1966), Sabine Sameith (*1967), Wolf Gunter Schlief (*1967), Jan Schulz (*1964), and Martin Wilhelm (*1961). Office founded in Frankfurt a. M. in 2003. www.bb22.net
Stephan Becker (*1978) is editor of archplus magazine. He lives and works in Berlin.
Regina Bittner (*1962) is a researcher, curator and cultural theorist teaching at Bauhaus Dessau.
bhl-architekten is Heiner Limbrock (*1954). Office founded in 1887 in Hamburg. www.bhl-architekten.de
b&k+brandlhuber&co – Arno Brandlhuber (*1964) architctural offices founded in Berlin & Cologne in 2006. www.brandlhuber.com
blauraum architekten are Rüdiger Ebel (*1970), Volker Halbach (*1969), Maurice Paulussen (*1968) and Carsten Venus (*1967). Their office was founded in Hamburg in 2002. www.blauraum.de
BLESS are Ines Kaag (*1970) and Desiree Heise (*1971). They are artists and fashion designers and founded their label in 1997. BLESS is based in Berlin and Paris. www.bless-service.de
Klaus Block (*1952) is an architect and established his office in Berlin in 1988. www.klausblock.de
Bolles + Wilson are the architects Julia B. Bolles-Wilson (*1948) and Peter L. Wilson (*1950). Office was founded in 1980 and is based in Münster. www.bolles-wilson.com
Gernot Böhme (*1937) is a philosopher and writer. He lives and works in Darmstadt.
Johanna Bornkamm (*1977) is an architect, living and working in Berlin.
Thomas Bratzke (*1976) ZAST is an artist based in Berlin
BRT Architekten was founded in 1991 by Jens Bothe (*1959), Kai Richter (*1958) and Hadi Teherani (*1954). They are based in Hamburg. www.brt.de
Burger Landschaftsarchitekten was founded in 2000 by Susanne Burger (*1961) in Munich. www.burgerlandschaftsarchitekten.de
Chaos Computer Club www.ccc.de
Chestnutt_Niess are Rebecca Chestnutt (*1958) and Robert Niess (*1958). Office was founded in 1988 in Berlin. www.chestnutt-niess.de
David Chipperfield Architects David Chipperfield (*1953) founded his office in London in 1984 and also has a base in Berlin. www.davidchipperfield.co.uk
Kees Christiaanse (*1953) is an architect and professor. He is a partner in the offices KCAP in Rotterdam and ASTOC in Cologne. www.kcap.nl
CODE UNIQUE ARCHITEKTEN are Volker Giezek (*1966) and Martin Boden (*1968). Their office was founded in 1998 in Dresden. www.codeunique.de
Complizen Planungsbüro are Andreas Haase and Tore Dobberstein. Their office was founded in 1998 in Halle. www.complizen.de
Frank Daubner member of www.urbanacker.net
DEGELO ARCHITEKTEN was founded in 2005 by the architect Heinrich Degelo (*1957) in Basel CH. www.degelo.net
dinse feest zurl architekten are Peter Dinse (*1945), Prof. Isabell Feest (*1951) and Johann Zurl (*1958). Their office was founded in 1990 in Hamburg. www.dfz-hh.de
Stefan Eberstadt (*1961) is an artist living and working in Munich.
Olafur Eliasson (*1967) is an artist based in Berlin. www.olafureliasson.net
Lukas Feireiss (*1977) is a curator and writer. He lives and works in Berlin.
Andreas Feldtkeller is a analyst of contemporary cities. He was the director of city planning for the old city of Tübingen.
FloSundK architektur+urbanistik are Daniela Flor (*1970), Jens UKFW Stahnke (*1967) and Mario Krämer (*1972). They founded their office in Saarbrücken in 2001. www.flosundk.de
Tita Giese lives and works in Düsseldorf. www.tita-giese.com
Massimiliano Gioni (*1973) is a curator and art critic based in Milan and New York.
GRAFT are Lars Krückeberg, (*1968), Wolfram Putz(*1967), Thomas Willemeit (*1967). Their architecture offices are based in Berlin, Los Angeles and Beijing. www.graftlab.com
Gruentuch Ernst Architekten are Armand Gruentuch (*1963) and Almut Ernst (*1966). They founded their office in Berlin in 1991. www.gruentuchernst.de
Gruppe F Landschaftsarchitektur Freiräume are ThoMi Bauermeister, Nikolai Koehler and Gabriele Pütz. Office in Berlin. www.gruppef.de
Ruth Habermehl (*1969) is an artist, living and working in Leipzig. www.ruth-habermehl.de
Hascher + Jehle Architektur are Prof. Rainer Hascher (*1950) and Prof. Sebastian Jehle (*1965). They founded their office in Berlin in 1992. www.hascherjehle.de
Christian Hasucha (*1955) is an artist, living and working in Berlin. www.hasucha.de
Susanne Hauser (*1957) is an architectural theorist and professor for art history and cultural studies at the University of the Arts, Berlin.
Hild und K Architekten BDA are Andreas Hild (*1961) and Dionys Ottl (*1964). Their office was founded in 1999 in Munich. www.hildundk.de
HSH Hoyer Schindele Hirschmüller are Florian Hoyer (*1961), Harald Schindele (*1966), Markus Hirschmüller (*1967). Office was founded in Berlin in 1997. www.hoyerundschindele.de
Hufnagel Pütz Rafaelian Architekten are Karl Hufnagel (*1958), Peter Pütz (*1957) and Michael Rafaelian (*1955). They founded their office in Berlin in 1992. www.hufnagelpuetzrafaelian.de
INDEX Architekten are Ulrich Exner (*1956) and Sigrun Musa (*1959). Office was founded in Frankfurt a. M.1990. www.index-architekten.de
Ingenhoven Architekten was founded in 1985 by the architect Christoph Ingenhoven (*1960) in Düsseldorf. www.ingenhovenarchitekten.de
Susanne Jaschko (*1967) is a curator and artist and is based in Berlin. www.sujaschko.de
Gert Kähler (*1942) is an architecture critic. He lives and works in Hamburg.
Claus Käpplinger (*1963) is an architecture critic. He lives and works in Berlin.
Kiefer Landschaftsarchitekten was founded in 1989 by Gabriele G. Kiefer (*1960) in Berlin. www.buero-kiefer.de
kister scheithauer gross architekten und stadtplaner are Prof. Johannes Kister (*1956), Reinhard Scheidthauer (*1950) and Prof. Susanne Gross (*1960). www.ksg-architekten.de
knerer und lang architekten are Prof. Thomas Knerer (*1963) and Eva Maria Lang (*1964). Their office was founded in 1993 in Dresden. www.knererlang.de
Peter Kulka (*1937) is an architect and professor. He established his office in Köln in 1979. In 1991 he opened a second office in Dresden. www.peterkulka.de
M.Link Architekt was founded in 1997 by the architect Markus Link (*1964) in Munich.
Kühn Malvezzi are Simona Malvezzi (*1966), Wilfried Kühn (*1967), Johannes Kühn (*1969); They founded their architetcure office in Berlin in 2001. www.kuehnmalvezzi.com
Dieter Läpple (*1942) is an urban expert and professor of City and Regional Economy at the Technical University Hamburg-Harburg since 1986.
L/B comprises the artists Sabina Lang (*1972) and Daniel Baumann (*1967). Their office was founded in Burgdorf in Switzerland in 1990. www.langbaumann.com
Lederer Ragnarsdóttir Oei are Prof. Arno Lederer (*1947), Jórunn Ragnarsdóttir (*1957) and Marc Oei (*1962). They founded their office together in Stuttgart in 1985. www.archlro.de
Susanne Lorenz (*1969) is an artist. She lives and works in Berlin. www.susanne-lorenz.de
luczak architekten was founded in 1997 by Thomas Luczak (*1952) in Cologne. www.luczak-architekten.de
Lüderwaldt Verhoff Architekten are Dirk Lüderwaldt (*1960) and Josef Verhoff (*1959). They founded their office in Köln in 2004. www.luederwaldt-verhoff.de
Jürgen Mayer H. (*1965) is an architect and established his office in Berlin in 1996. www.jmayerh.de
Ramo Mayer (*1975) TCLY lives and works as an artist in Frankfurt am Main.
Meixner Schlüter Wendt Architekten are Claudia Meixner (*1964), Florian Schlüter (*1959) and Martin Wendt (*1955). The office was founded in Frankfurt am Main in 1997. www.meixner-schlueter-wendt.de
Doreen Mende (*1976) is a curator. Since 2006 she teaches at HfG Karlsruhe.
MESS are city planers Timo Amann (*1976), Florian Groß (*1977), Sebastian Hermann (*1977), Thomas Müller (*1973). The group was founded in Kaiserslautern in 2003. www.lebe-deine-stadt.de
Anh-Linh Ngo (*1974) is editor of archplus magazine. He is an architect and founding member of Methode Architektur Berlin/Milan. He lives and works in Berlin. www.archplus.net
Tazro Niscino (*1960) is an artist, living and working Cologne. www.galeriemichaeljanssen.de
Ochs-Architekten was founded by Prof. Stefan Ochs in Darmstadt. www.ochs-architekten.de
VALERIO OLGIATI was founded in 1996 by Valerio Olgiati (*1958) in Zürich. www.olgiati.net
Horst W. Opaschowski (*1941) is professor and founder of the BAT "Institut für Freizeitforschung". He lives and works in Hamburg.
Park Fiction founded by Christoph Schäfer and Margit Czenk in Hamburg. www.parkfiction.org
PLATOON.cultural development are Tom Büschemann (*1965) and Christoph Frank (*1969). Their office was founded in 2000 in Berlin. www.platoon.org
André Poitiers (*1959) is an architect. His office was founded in Hamburg in 1995.
Raderschall Architekten are Ute Bielenberg Raderschall, (*1955) and Wolfgang Raderschall, (*1952). Their office was founded in 1989 in Cologne. www.raderschall-architekten.de
raumlabor_berlin are Francesco Apuzzo (*1972), Axel Timm (*1973), Jan Liesegang (*1968), Andrea Hofmann (*1969), Matthias Rick (*1965), Benjamin Foerster-Baldenius (*1968), Martin Heberle (*1967), Markus Bader (*1968) Christof Mayer (*1967). They founded their office in Berlin in 1998. www.raumlabor-berlin.de
raumtaktik are Friedrich von Borries (*1974) and Matthias Böttger (*1974). Their office was founded in Berlin in 2003. www.raumtaktik.de
raumzeit are Jan Läufer (*1971), Julia Neubauer (*1973), Gunnar Tausch (*1969) and Friedrich Tuczek (*1970). The architcural office was founded in 2002 in Berlin. www.raumzeit.org
Realarchitektur are Jens Casper (*1967) and Petra Petersson (*1966). They founded their office in Berlin in 2003. www.realarchitektur.de
realities:united are Jan (*1970) and Tim Edler (*1965). The office was founded in Berlin in 2000. www.realities-united.de
Helmut Riemann Architekten (*1943) is an architect and established his office in Lübeck in 1977.
Horst J. Rittel (* 1936, †1990) was professor of the Science of Design at the University of California, Berkley and professor and director of the Institute for the Foundations of Planning at the Faculty of Architecture and Urban Planning at the University of Stuttgart.
CARSTEN ROTH ARCHITEKT was founded in 1987 by the architect Carsten Roth (*1958) in Hamburg. www.carstenroth.com
Adriano Sack (*1967) is a journalist. He lives and works in New York City.
Yutta Saftien (*1963) is an artist, living and working in Hamburg. www.yutta-saftien.com
sauerbruch hutton architekten are Louisa Hutton (*1957), Prof. Matthias Sauerbruch (*1955), Juan Lucas Young (*1963) and Jens Ludloff (*1964 Their office was founded in 1993 and is based in Berlin. www.sauerbruchhutton.de
Joachim Sauter (*1959), Art+Com AG, is an artist, designer and professor. His office was founded in Berlin in 1988. www.artcom.de
Schaubühne Lindenfels was founded 1876 in Leipzig. www.schaubuehne.com
SMAQ is a studio for architecture, urbanism and research. Sabine Müller (*1969) and Andreas Quednau (*1967), New York 1998 www.smaq.net
schneider+schumacher are Till Schneider (*1959) and Michael Schumacher (*1957). They founded their office in Frankfurt am Main in 1988. www.schneider-schumacher.de
Thomas Schregenberger (*1950) is an architect and critic and lives and works in Zurich.
Boris Sieverts (*1969) is an artist, living and working in Cologne.
Gerhard Spangenberg Architekt was founded in 1968 by the architect Gerhard Spangenberg (*1940) in Berlin. www.gerhardspangenberg.de
Staab Architekten are Volker Staab (*1957) and Alfred Nieuwenhuizen (*1953). Office in Berlin since 1990. www.staab-architekten.com
Wolfgang Tiefensee (*1955) is the German Federal Minister for Transport, Building and Urban Affairs and in this capacity responsible for the German Pavilion at the Biennale in Venice.
Sissel Tolaas (*1961) is an artist based in Berlin since 1987. www.tolaas.de
TOPOTEK 1, are landscape architects Martin Rein-Cano (*1967) and Lorenz Dexler (*1968). Office founded in Berlin in 1996. www.topotek1.de
Urban Catalyst are architects Philipp Misselwitz (*1974), Philipp Oswalt (*1964), Klaus Overmeyer (*1968). www.urbancatalyst.de
Stadtsanierungsamt Tuebingen Urban Redevelopment Department Tuebingen founded by the City of Tuebingen in 1961. Developed by the urban planners Andreas Feldtkeller, Andreas Pätz and Cord Soehlke. www.tuebingen.de
Sasha Waltz & Guests is a Berlin based dance company lead by Sasha Waltz (*1963) and Jochen Sandig (*1968). Founded in 1993 in Berlin. www.sashawaltz.de
Melvin M. Weber (*1920) is Professor Emeritus of Planning at the University of California, Berkeley. He is the former director of the Institute of Urban and Regional Development and of the University of California Transportation Center.
Wim Wenders (*1945) is a director and photographer and currently lives in Los Angeles and Berlin.
Gil Wilk Architekten were originally Gilbert Wilk (*1966) and Thomas Freiwald (*1969). Since 2006 Wilk-Salinas Architekten. www.gil-wilk.de
Yellow Arrow is a spatial annotation project by Counts Media, New York. www.yellowarrow.net

a worldwide series of conferences
investigating the future of cities

organised by the Cities Programme
at the London School of Economics and
Political Science and the Alfred Herrhausen Society,
the International Forum of Deutsche Bank

The Urban Age Conference Series
Investigating the Future of Cities

Further information: www.urban-age.net

BERLIN
First summit

LONDON
Europeans Global City?

HALLE
German Cities: Success beyond Growth?

NEW YORK CITY
Is almost alright?

SHANGHAI
The Fastest City?

MEXICO CITY
Growth at the Limit?

JOHANNESBURG
Challenges of Inclusion?

www.drapilux.com

Intelligence and Aesthetics

Textiles for Urban Life

drapilux combines intelligence and aesthetics. Collections especially made for hotels, office buildings and healthcare establishments ensure an exceptional quality of design and advanced possibilities of application.

Virtually limitless combinations of intelligent functions', colour and design will compliment the style of every property.

- drapilux flammstop meets the highest standards in fire protection
- drapilux bioaktiv reduces bacteria and germs effectively
- drapilux air uses a catalytic process to break down pollutants and odours
- drapilux akustik features strong sound-absorbing qualities

progressive | aesthetic | safe

„Der Mensch ist das Tier,
das mit den Händen staunen kann."

Peter Sloterdijk für FSB

Mehr dazu finden Sie im Handbuch 04l05. Zu bestellen bei: Franz Schneider Brakel GmbH + Co,
Postfach 1440, 33029 Brakel, Telefon 05272 608-120, Telefax 05272 608-300 oder info@fsb.de

FSB

Carpet Concept entwickelt Bodenbeläge für öffentliche und private Räume. Sie prägen das Interieur und steigern die Wirkung von Architektur. Mit neuen Materialien und ungewohnten Anwendungen finden wir Wege für innovative Produkte: vielfältig, glaubwürdig und authentisch. Davon zeugen Klassiker im Markt und mehr als sechzig internationale Designpreise.

Carpet Concept | Objekt-Teppichboden GmbH | T +49 521 9 24 59 0 | info.carpet-concept@jab.de | www.carpet-concept.de

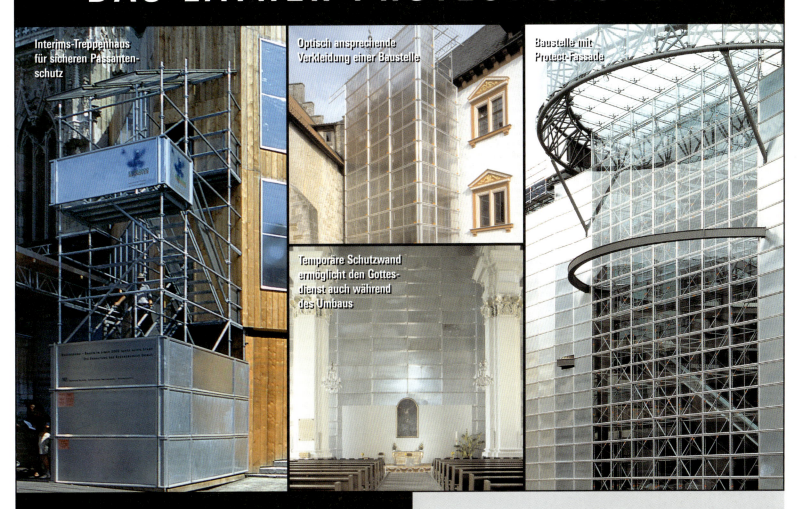

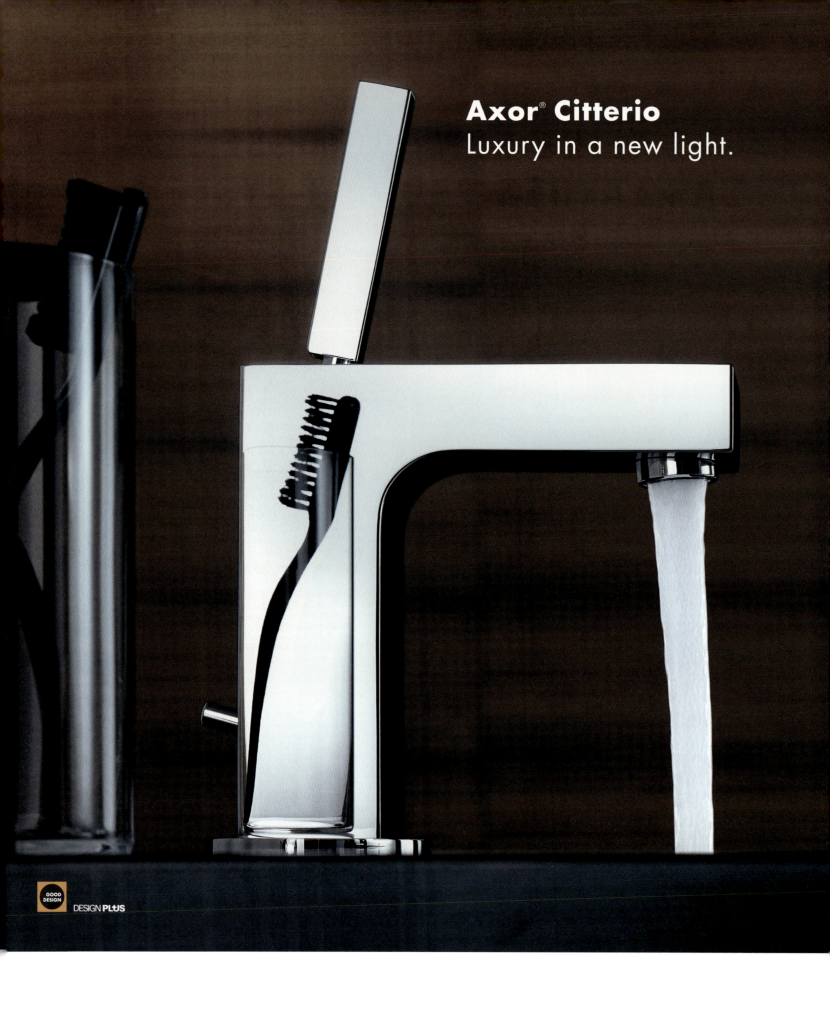

Axor® Citterio
Luxury in a new light.

The new luxury: The Axor Citterio bathroom line, designed by the Italian architect and designer, Antonio Citterio. Mixers, showers and bathtubs - expressed in a new design language which links angle and curve harmoniously. Clear in form, rich in detail, diverse in use. For more information visit our website at **www.axor-citterio.com.**

Lassen Sie Ihrer Fantasie freien Lauf

DuPont™ Corian® ist Schönheit, Farbe und Tiefe. Es ist Stärke, Verlässlichkeit und Leistung. Vor allem aber ist es Inspiration: Es vermag einen Raum zu verwandeln, es verleiht ihm Persönlichkeit, Flair und Ausdruck. Corian® fällt aus dem Rahmen, denn es kann eigentlich alles sein. An jedem Ort. Für jeden Zweck. Es liegt ganz in Ihrer Hand.

Design Nicholas Gwenael

Design Julie Mathias und Michael Cross

Design C. Colucci

Design Claudio Silvestrin

www.corian.de
www.corian.com
Hotline (gebührenfrei): 0800 18 100 18 (D)
Email: info.surfaces@dupont.com

DuPont™
CORIAN®
SOLID SURFACES

The miracles of science™

"Our infrastructure is essentially developed. The easy problems have been solved. Designing systems today is difficult because there is no consensus on what the problems are, let alone how to resolve them."

Horst W. J. Rittel

Picture credits Bildnachweis

Impressum

Convertible City – German Pavilion September 10 – November 18 2006
10th International Architecture Exhibition 2006 – Venice Biennale
Convertible City – Deutscher Pavillon 10. September – 18. November 2006
10. Internationale Architekturausstellung 2006 – Biennale Venedig

Host Veranstalter:
Bundesministerium für Verkehr, Bau und Stadtentwicklung
Commissioners Generalkommissare:
Armand Gruentuch und Almut Ernst

Produced by Realisiert durch: Gruentuch Ernst Architekten
Hackescher Markt 2-3, 10178 Berlin, www.gruentuchernst.de
Production management exhibition Produktionsleitung Ausstellung: Arno Löbbecke
Production assistance and participant coordination
Produktionsassistenz und Koordination Teilnehmer: Julia Wolter
Project management Projektmanagement: Lukas Feireiss
Project assistance Projektassistenz: Anja Fischer, Sandy Lindner, Caroline Steinchen
German PR Nationale Pressearbeit: Beate Engelhorn
International PR Internationale Pressearbeit: Sybille Fanelsa
PR assistance Pressearbeit Assistenz: Eleonora Fasina
Visualisation Visualisierung: Alessio Fossati
Corporate design and graphic design
Grafisches Gesamtkonzept: Peter Dorén (Dorén+Koester)
Lithography Bildbearbeitung: Bildpunkt, LVD
Website: Gruentuch Ernst Architekten mit Stilkonzil
Structural planning Tragwerksplanung: Ingenieurbüro Martin Krone, Berlin
Lighting design Lichtplanung: Licht Kunst Licht
Local partner architect Kontaktarchitekt: cfk Architetti, Venedig
Legal advice Rechtsberatung: Christian Bauschke (Heller&Partner Rechtsanwälte, Berlin)
Media partners Medienpartner: archplus, Baunetz

Catalogue is commissoned by Katalog erscheint im Auftrag von:
Bundesministerium für Verkehr, Bau- und Stadtentwicklung
Editors in chief Herausgeber des Katalogs: Armand Gruentuch und Almut Ernst
Editorial staff Redaktion: Lukas Feireiss, Anh-Linh Ngo
English editor: Sophie Lovell
Editorial advisors Redaktionelle Berater: Stephan Becker, Martin Luce
Editorial and production assistance Redaktions- und Produktionsassistenz:
Julia Wolter, Anja Fischer, Sandy Lindner, Caroline Steinchen
Translation Übersetzung: Daniel Bickermann, Karola Handwerker, Michael Robinson,
Fritz Schneider, Annette Wiethüchter,
Proof reading Lektorat: Sophie Lovell, Anabel Bach, Tina Zürn
Graphic design and Art direction Grafische Gestaltung und Art Direction: Walter Schönauer
Graphic design assistance Grafikdesign Assistenz: Maj Mlakar
Cover design Titelgestaltung: Walter Schönauer, Logodesign: Peter Dorén
Reproductions Reproduktionen: Bildpunkt, LVD
Printed by Gesamtherstellung: Medialis Offsetdruck GmbH, Berlin

© 2006 Gruentuch Ernst Architekten
Publisher: ARCH+ Verlag GmbH, www.archplus.net
ISBN 978-3-931435-09-7, ISBN 3-931435-09-1
ISSN: 0587-3452

We thank all contributors for their support Wir danken allen Teilnehmern für ihre Unterstützung.
Many thanks for advice and support to Ein herzlicher Dank für Rat und Unterstützung geht an:
Beate Barner, Sally Below, Bartholomeus Englmann, Kristin Feireiss, Hilde Léon, Claus Käpplinger,
Nikolaus Kuhnert, Jochen Sandig, Werner Sobek, Barbara von Raffay, Katia Reich, Wolf Reuter
**We would like to thank all the members of the Biennale team for their excellent teamwork and
enormous personal engagement.** Wir danken allen Mitgliedern des Biennaleteams für die sehr gute
Zusammenarbeit und das enorme persönliche Engagement. **A thankyou too to all the staff in our
practice who managed to integrate the Biennale project into the busy everyday schedule of the
office and still managed to keep on track with all the building sites, projects and competitions
during what were often hectic times.** Ein Dankeschön auch an alle Mitarbeiter in unserem Büro, die
das Biennaleprojekt in den Arbeitsalltag des Büros integriert haben und dabei auch noch alle laufenden
Baustellen, Projekte und Wettbewerbe durch diese zeitweise hektische Zeit getragen haben.
**We are also indebted to friends and family whose support give us the space necessary
to complete the task.** Dank geht auch an Freunde und Familie, deren Unterstützung uns den nötigen
Freiraum für diese Aufgabe ermöglicht haben.

archplus

Journal for Architecture and Urbanism
Zeitschrift für Architektur und Städtebau
Volume 39 39. Jahrgang

Publishers Herausgeber
ARCH+ Verlag GmbH, Sabine Kraft,
Nikolaus Kuhnert, Günther Uhlig

ARCH+ Verlag GmbH
Charlottenstr. 14, 52070 Aachen
Internet: www.archplus.net
eMail: verlag@archplus.net

Addresses Redaktionsadressen

archplus Aachen
Fon 0241-50 83 02; Fax 0241-548 31
eMail: aachen@archplus.net

archplus Berlin
Bergengruenstr. 35, 14129 Berlin
Fon 030-802 69 86, 030-80 90 31 34
Fax 030-802 81 20, eMail: berlin@archplus.net

Editors Redakteure
Nikolaus Kuhnert, Sabine Kraft, Julia von Mende,
Anh-Linh Ngo, Stephan Becker, Martin Luce

Art Direction
Walter Schönauer, Berlin
Assistance Assistenz: Maj Mlakar

Permanent Contributors Ständige Mitarbeiter
Florian Böhm, Gregor Harbusch, Joachim Krausse,
Arno Löbbecke, Philipp Misselwitz, Philipp Oswalt,
Susanne Schindler, Angelika Schnell, Werner Sewing,
Schirin Taraz-Breinholt

Distribution Vertrieb
Ute Stauch
Fon 0241-50 83 29; Fax 0241-548 31
eMail: vertrieb@archplus.net

Advertising & Sales Anzeigenverwaltung
Gabriele Lauscher-Dreess
Fon 0241-50 83 03; Fax 0241-548 31
eMail: anzeigen@archplus.net

Subscription service Aboverwaltung
A.B.O. Verlagsservice GmbH, Ickstattstr. 7,
80469 München
Fon 089-20959103; Fax 089-20028116
eMail: silke.gross@csj.de
Konto: Postgiroamt Mü 221560-808
BLZ 700 100 80

Orders & Back issues Einzelbestellungen
ARCH+ Verlag GmbH
Account Konto: Deutsche Bank 2525426
BLZ 390 700 24
IBAN DE80 3907 0024 0252 5426 00
BIC DEUTDEDB390

Prices Preise
Single issue Einzelheft Euro 14
Double issue Doppelheft Euro 19

Subscription Abonnement
Germany Inland Euro 49
Other countries Ausland Euro 57
(Advanced payment only Ausland nur gegen
Vorauszahlung)

Reduced Prices for Students and Graduates
Ermäßigtes Abonnement für Studenten,
Absolventen, Arbeitslose gegen Bescheinigung:
Germany Inland Euro 29
Other countries Ausland Euro 37

Subscription Terms Abonnementbedingungen
4 issues including 1 double issue per year.
For further information please contact the publisher.
Das Abonnement kann mit jedem gewünschten
Heft beginnen. Ein Jahresabonnement umfasst 4
Einzelhefte, inkl. eines Doppelhefts. Das Abonnement
verlängert sich automatisch um ein weiteres Jahr, wenn
es nicht bis 6 Wochen vor Ablauf der Abonnementfrist
gekündigt wird. Bestellungen können innerhalb von
sieben Tagen widerrufen werden.

Change of address Umzug
**Please contact the subscription service or
the publisher immediately.**
Bitte teilen Sie uns unverzüglich eine etwaige
Adressenänderung mit, da Zeitschriften leider vom
Nachsendeantrag ausgeschlossen sind.